OTHELLO
THE MOOR OF VENICE

William Shakespeare

WITH RELATED READINGS

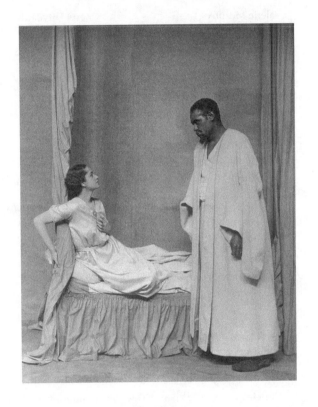

THE EMC MASTERPIECE SERIES

Access Editions

EMC/Paradigm Publishing
St. Paul, Minnesota

Staff Credits

Laurie Skiba
Managing Editor

Brenda Owens
Editor

Jennifer J. Anderson
Associate Editor

Nichola Torbett
Associate Editor

Paul Spencer
Art and Photo Researcher

Valerie Murphy
Editorial Assistant

Shelley Clubb
Production Manager

Lisa Beller
Design and Production Specialist

Petrina Nyhan
Electronic Production Specialist

Leslie Anderson
Cover Designer

Parkwood Composition
Compositor

Cheryl Drivdahl
Proofreader

Cover image: Paul Robeson as Othello and Peggy Ashcroft as Desdemona in a stage production of *Othello,* London, 1930. © Bettmann/Corbis.

[back cover] Engraving of William Shakespeare from the First Folio, courtesy of the Library of Congress.

Library of Congress Cataloging-in-Publication Data

Shakespeare, William, 1564–1616.

Othello : the Moor of Venice / by William Shakespeare ; with related readings.

p. cm. – (The EMC masterpiece series access editions)

ISBN 0-8219-2956-9

1. Othello (Fictitious character)—Drama. 2. Shakespeare, William, 1564-1616. Othello. 3. Othello (Fictitious character) 4. Venice (Italy)—Drama. 5. Jealousy—Drama. 6. Muslims—Drama. 7. Cyprus—Drama. I. Title. II. Series.

PR2829.A1 2004

822.3'3—dc22

2004053207

ISBN 0-8219-2956-9

Published by EMC/Paradigm Publishing
875 Montreal Way
St. Paul, Minnesota 55102
800-328-1452
www.emcp.com
E-mail: educate@emcp.com

Printed in the United States of America.
9 10 xxx 16 15

Table of Contents

THE LIFE AND WORKS OF

William Shakespeare

Engraving of William Shakespeare from the First Folio.
Image courtesy of the Library of Congress.

William Shakespeare (1564–1616) may well be the greatest dramatist the world has ever known. Certainly he is the most famous writer in all of English literature. Today, nearly four hundred years after his death, Shakespeare's plays are still being performed for audiences all over the world. As fellow poet Ben Jonson famously put it, Shakespeare's art is "not of an age, but for all time."

Little is known about Shakespeare's early life. His mother, Mary Arden Shakespeare, was from a well-to-do, well-connected family. His father, John Shakespeare, was a prosperous glove maker and local politician. William's exact birthdate is unknown, but he was baptized in his hometown of Stratford-upon-Avon on April 26, 1564, and tradition has assigned him a birthdate of April 23, which was also the day of his death and the feast day of Saint George, England's patron saint.

Shakespeare's birthplace in Stratford-upon-Avon.
Photo by Melissa Baker.

Shakespeare attended the Stratford grammar school, where he likely studied classical literature in Latin and Greek, as was typical for students of that era. However, he did not go on to a university. At the age of eighteen, he married Anne Hathaway, eight years his senior. At the time of their marriage, Anne was pregnant with their first child, a daughter whom they named Susanna. Several years later, in 1585, the couple had twins, Hamnet and Judith. There is no record of what Shakespeare did in the years after the twins were born. He may have worked for a while as a schoolteacher, as there are many references to teaching in his plays. However, it is clear that by 1592 he had moved to London, leaving his family behind while he pursued a life in the theater. Shakespeare continued to provide for his family and to expand his holdings in Stratford while living in London.

Shakespeare's Professional Career

Once in London, Shakespeare soon made himself known as a successful actor and playwright. His history plays *Henry the Sixth*, Parts 1, 2, and 3 and *The Tragedy of Richard the Third* established him as a significant force in London theater. In 1593, however, all London theaters were forced to close due to an outbreak of the plague. During this time, Shakespeare turned to narrative poetry, producing *Venus and Adonis* and *The Rape of Lucrece,* both dedicated to a wealthy patron, the Earl of Southampton.

When the theaters reopened the following year, Shakespeare became a partner in a theater company known as the Lord Chamberlain's Men. The group soon became the most popular acting troupe in London and performed regularly at the court of Queen Elizabeth I. In 1599, they were wealthy enough to build their own playhouse, which they called "The Globe." When Queen Elizabeth died in 1603, Shakespeare's company found a new patron in her successor King James I, and their name was changed to the King's Men.

While Shakespeare acted in the troupe, writing the material soon became his primary vocation. In the span of twenty years he penned at least thirty-seven plays, including comedies such as *The Taming of the Shrew, A Midsummer Night's Dream, The Merchant of Venice, Twelfth Night,* and *All's Well That Ends Well;* tragedies such as *Romeo and Juliet, Julius Caesar, Hamlet, Othello, Macbeth,* and *King Lear;* romances such as *The Winter's Tale* and *The Tempest;* and histories such as *The Tragedy of King Richard the Second.*

The last play Shakespeare wrote on his own was *The Famous History of the Life of Henry the Eighth,* which was performed in London in 1613. Later that same year, he collaborated with John Fletcher on the romance *The Two Noble Kinsmen.* At that time Shakespeare was probably living again in Stratford, in a large house called New Place that he had bought in 1597. When he died at age 52, survived by his wife and his two daughters, Shakespeare was a wealthy man. He was buried April 25, 1616 in the Holy Trinity Church in Stratford-upon-Avon. The stone over his grave reads:

> Good frend for Jesus sake forbeare,
> To digg the dust encloased heare:
> Blest be the man that spares thes stones
> And curst be he that moves my bones.

The Publication of Shakespeare's Plays

Shakespeare himself never sought to have his plays published; however, many individual plays were published during his lifetime in unauthorized editions known as **quartos**. These quartos are quite unreliable. Although some may have been based on final manuscript versions produced by the author, others were probably put together from actors' memories of the scripts, or reprinted from so-called prompter's copies used in production of the plays.

In 1623, seven years after Shakespeare's death, his friends and fellow actors John Heminge and Henry Condell published a collected edition of thirty-five of Shakespeare's plays. This collection is known to literary historians as the **First Folio.** In the centuries since 1623, and especially during the last century and a half, editors have worked diligently to compare the various early printed versions of Shakespeare's works to determine which version or versions of each play best represent what Shakespeare intended. Editors have also updated Shakespeare's spelling so that the the plays can be more easily understood by a modern audience. If you are interested, you can view the texts of Shakespeare's plays in their original spelling on the Internet.

The Authorship of Shakespeare's Plays

The fact that Shakespeare was a commoner and led, according to the few facts we have, a rather ordinary life, has led many people to doubt that he could have written such great works of literature. Over the years it has been suggested that the true author could have been someone else—such as the Earl of Oxford, Christopher Marlowe, or Ben Jonson. While there is no way to conclusively prove or disprove such theories, there are good reasons to believe that Shakespeare was, indeed, the true author of the plays attributed to him. For one thing, the plays show an understanding of the lives of people in all stations of life, from the lowliest peasants to men and women of the court. We know that Shakespeare came from a common background and later moved in court circles; this fact is consistent with his understanding of people from all walks of life. At the very least, a careful reader must conclude that the plays attributed to Shakespeare are the work of a single author, for they have a distinct voice not to be found in the work of any other dramatist of his day—a voice that has enriched our language as none other has ever done.

Shakespeare's Language

Shakespeare used one of the largest vocabularies ever employed by an author. In fact, according to the *Oxford English Dictionary*, Shakespeare actually introduced an estimated 3,000 new words into the English language, many of which are in common use today, including *bedazzle, silliness, critical, obscene, hurry,* and *lonely.* Numerous well-known phrases came from his plays, such as "wear my heart upon my sleeve" (*Othello*) and "the world is my oyster" (*The Merry Wives of Windsor*).

Shakespeare's language tends to be dense, metaphorical, full of puns and wordplay, and yet natural, so that—to steal a line from *Hamlet*—it comes "trippingly off the tongue" of an actor. A scene of Shakespeare tears across the stage, riveting and dramatic, and yet it bears close rereading, revealing in that rereading astonishing depth and complexity.

Shakespeare's Poetic Technique

Shakespeare used in his plays a combination of prose, rhymed poetry, and blank verse. **Blank verse** is unrhymed, or "blank," poetry with a distinct rhythm known as **iambic pentameter**. Each line of iambic pentameter consists of five **iambs**, rhythmic units made up of a weakly stressed syllable followed by a strongly stressed one as in the word *forget*. A simpler way of describing this type of verse is to say that it contains ten syllables per line, and every other syllable is stressed. The following are some typical lines:

Her fa ther lov'd me, oft in vi ted me

Still ques tion'd me the sto ry of my life

(*Othello*, act I, scene iii, lines 28–29)

In order to maintain the verse, the lines of two or more characters are often combined to create one ten-syllable line. This accounts for the unusual line numbering and formatting in Shakespeare's plays. In the following example, the words spoken by Cassio and Iago are all counted as one line:

CASSIO. I do not understand.

IAGO.   He's married.

CASSIO.   To who?

(*Othello*, act I, scene ii, line 52)

If you scan the dialogue in *Othello*, you will find most of it is written in blank verse, although with some variations in stress and syllable count. Shakespeare and other playwrights of his time favored the use of blank verse in drama because they believed it captured the natural rhythms of English speech, yet had a noble, heroic quality that would not be possible with ordinary prose. (You will notice that when Shakespeare does use prose, it is because the characters are speaking informally or are from the lower class.) Blank iambic pentameter can also be used in poetry, although it is more often rhymed, as in Shakespeare's sonnets.

Reading Shakespeare

Shakespeare wrote his plays about four hundred years ago. Because the English language has changed considerably since then, you will find that reading Shakespeare presents some special challenges. Although the spelling has been modernized in this version of *Othello,* as in virtually all contemporary editions of Shakespeare's plays, there are still differences in style and vocabulary that could not be edited out without changing the flavor of the work. The editors of this text have provided footnotes to help you understand words and phrases that have changed in meaning or spelling since Shakespeare's day. However, try not to get bogged down in the footnotes. Remember that a play is a dramatic action and should move quickly. Try first reading through each scene without looking at the footnotes, so that you can get a general sense of what is happening. Then reread the scene, referring to the footnotes to discern the details. If possible, you may want to listen to an audio version of the play, or better yet, view a production of the play on film or on stage. All drama comes alive when it is performed by actors and is best experienced in that way.

Time Line of Shakespeare's Life

April 23, 1564	William Shakespeare is born in Stratford-upon-Avon, to parents Mary Arden Shakespeare and John Shakespeare.
April 26, 1564	William Shakespeare is baptized.
1582	William Shakespeare marries Anne Hathaway.
1583	Shakespeare's first daughter, Susanna, is born and christened.
1585	Anne Hathaway Shakespeare gives birth to twins: a boy, Hamnet, and a girl, Judith.
1589–1591	Shakespeare's first histories, *Henry the Sixth,* Parts 1 and 2, are produced.
1592–1593	*The Tragedy of Richard the Third* is produced. Not long afterward, the plague afflicts London and the theaters close. Shakespeare writes *Venus and Adonis* and *The Rape of Lucrece.*
1592–1594	Shakespeare's first comedy, *The Comedy of Errors,* is produced.
c. 1593	Shakespeare begins writing a series, or cycle, of sonnets.
1593–1594	*The Taming of the Shrew* is produced.
1594–1595	*Love's Labor's Lost* is produced.
1595	*The Tragedy of King Richard the Second* is produced.
1595–1596	*The Tragedy of Romeo and Juliet* and *A Midsummer Night's Dream* are produced.
1596–1597	*The Merchant of Venice* and *Henry the Fourth,* Part 1, are produced.
1596	Shakespeare's son, Hamnet, dies at age eleven.
1597	Shakespeare acquires a fine home called New Place in Stratford-upon-Avon. He produces *The Merry Wives of Windsor,* possibly at the request of Queen Elizabeth I.
1598	Shakespeare produces *Henry the Fourth,* Part 2.
1598–1599	*Much Ado about Nothing* is produced.
1599	Shakespeare's Globe Theater opens. *The Life of Henry the Fifth, The Tragedy of Julius Cæsar,* and *As You Like It* are produced.
1600–1601	*The Tragedy of Hamlet, Prince of Denmark* is produced.

Twelfth Night, or What You Will and *The History of Troilus and Cressida* are produced.	1601–1602
All's Well That Ends Well is produced.	1602–1603
Queen Elizabeth I dies. Shakespeare's troupe, The Lord Chamberlain's Men, is renamed The King's Men in honor of their new king and sponsor, James I.	1603
Measure for Measure and *The Tragedy of Othello, the Moor of Venice* are produced.	1604
The Tragedy of King Lear is produced.	1605
The Tragedy of Macbeth is produced.	1606
The Tragedy of Antony and Cleopatra is produced.	1607
The Tragedy of Coriolanus and *Pericles, Prince of Tyre* are produced.	1607–1608
Cymbeline is produced.	1609–1610
The Winter's Tale is produced.	1610–1611
The Tempest is produced.	1611
The Famous History of the Life of Henry the Eighth is produced.	1612–1613
Shakespeare collaborates with John Fletcher to write *The Two Noble Kinsmen*. On June 19, the Globe Theater is burned to the ground in a fire caused by a cannon shot during a performance of *Henry the Eighth*. Shakespeare retires to his home in New Place.	1613
The Globe Theater rebuilt.	1614
Shakespeare dies and is buried in Holy Trinity Church in Stratford-upon-Avon.	April 23, 1616

Shakespeare's Plays

The Renaissance in England

The word *renaissance* means "rebirth." Historians use the term to refer to the period between the fifteenth and early seventeenth centuries (1400s–1600s), when Europe was influenced by a rebirth of interest in Greek and Latin learning and experienced a flowering of literature and the arts.

In England, the Renaissance did not truly begin until 1558, when Queen Elizabeth I ascended to the throne. Elizabeth was a great patron of the arts, and during her reign from 1558 to 1603—a period known as the **Elizabethan Age**—English literature reached what many people consider to be its zenith. Shakespeare wrote and produced his plays at the height of the Elizabethan period and throughout much of the **Jacobean period**, the period from 1603 to 1625 when James I ruled England.

Portrait of Queen Elizabeth I.
Courtesy the National Portrait Gallery of London.

Shakespeare's writing is a good example of the spirit of the Renaissance—his plays often focus on memorable and complex characters, his plots often derive from classical sources, and his themes often involve challenges to authority. Although Shakespeare's scholarly contemporary and fellow playwright Ben Jonson wrote of Shakespeare, "thou hadst small Latin, and less Greek," Shakespeare knew far more of these languages than most people do today, and he probably read many of the classical works of Rome in their original Latin. He was inspired by classical works and by the history of Rome to write such plays as *The Tragedy of Julius Cæsar* and *The Tragedy of Antony and Cleopatra,* and all of his works contain allusions to classical subjects.

Renaissance Drama

The two most common types of drama during the English Renaissance were **comedies** and **tragedies.** The key difference between comedies and tragedies is that the former have happy endings and the latter have unhappy ones. (It is only a slight exaggeration to say that comedies end with wedding bells and tragedies with funeral bells.)

A comedy is typically lighthearted, though it may touch on serious themes. Action in a comedy usually progresses from initial order to humorous misunderstanding or confusion and back to order again. Stock elements of comedy include mistaken identities, puns and word play, and coarse or exaggerated characters. Shakespeare's comedies frequently end with one or more marriages.

A tragedy tells the story of the downfall of a person of high status. Often it celebrates the courage and dignity of its hero in the face of inevitable doom. The hero is typically neither completely good nor completely evil but lives and acts between these extremes. The hero's fall may be brought about by some flaw in his or her character, known as a **tragic flaw.** In Macbeth that flaw was ambition; in Hamlet, indecisiveness. As you read this play, try to decide what tragic flaw, if any, you can find in the character of Othello.

Other kinds of plays produced during the period included **histories**—plays about events from the past—and **romances**—plays that contained highly fantastic elements, such as fairies and magic spells. Also popular were short plays called **interludes**, as well as elaborate entertainments, called **masques**, that featured acting, music, and dance.

Theater in Renaissance London

In the late sixteenth century, London was a bustling city of perhaps 150,000 people—the mercantile, political, and artistic center of England. The city proper was ruled by a mayor and alderman who frowned upon theater because it brought together large crowds of people, creating the potential for lawlessness and the spread of controversial ideas and disease. Many times, London city officials or Parliament ordered the theaters closed, once because they objected to the political content of a play called *Isle of Dogs,* and regularly because of outbreaks of plague. Parliament, which was dominated by Puritans, passed laws that made it possible for traveling actors and performers to be arrested as vagabonds and cruelly punished. For protection, actors sought the patronage of members of the nobility. Actors would become, technically, servants of a famous lord, and troupes went by such names as The Lord Worcester's Men.

Fortunately for actors and playwrights, Queen Elizabeth and other members of the nobility loved the theater and protected it. Elizabeth herself maintained two troupes of boy actors, connected to her royal chapels. In addition to such troupes, London boasted several professional troupes made up of men. In those days, women did not act, and women's roles were played by men, a fact that further increased Puritan disapproval of the theaters. When the

Puritans took control of England in 1642, theater was banned altogether.

The Renaissance Playhouse

The first professional theater in England was built in 1576 by James Burbage. Burbage located his playhouse, which he called simply The Theater, just outside the northern boundaries of the City of London, where he could avoid control by city authorities. Another professional theater, the Curtain, was built nearby shortly thereafter. In 1598, Burbage's son Richard and other members of the Lord Chamberlain's Men tore down the Theater and used its materials to build a new playhouse, called the Globe. One of the shareholders in this new venture was William Shakespeare.

The Globe Theater is described in one of Shakespeare's plays as a "wooden O." The theater was nearly circular. It had eight sides and was open in the middle. The stage jutted into the center of this open area. Poorer theatergoers called "groundlings," who paid a penny apiece for admission, stood around three sides of the stage. Wealthier playgoers could pay an additional penny or two to sit in one of the three galleries set in the walls of the theater.

The stage itself was partially covered by a canopy supported by two pillars. Trapdoors in the stage floor made it possible for actors to appear or disappear. Backstage center was an area known as the "tiring house" in which actors could change costumes. This area could be opened for interior scenes. A second-story playing area above the tiring

Illustration by Carol O'Malia.

The Globe Theater.

house could be used to represent a hilltop, a castle turret, or a balcony (perhaps used in the famous balcony scene from *Romeo and Juliet*). On the third level, above this balcony, was an area for musicians and sound-effects technicians. A cannon shot from this area during a performance of Shakespeare's *Henry the Eighth* in 1613 caused a fire that burned the Globe to the ground.

Because the playhouse was open to the air, plays were presented in the daytime, and there was little or no artificial lighting. Scenery in the modern sense was nonexistent, and very few props, or properties, were used. Audiences had to use their imaginations to create the scenes, and playwrights helped them do this by writing descriptions into their characters' speeches.

The Renaissance Audience

Audiences at the Globe and similar theaters were quite heterogeneous, or mixed. They included people from all stations of society: laboring people from the lower classes, middle-class merchants, members of Parliament, and lords and ladies. Pickpockets mingled among the noisy, raucous groundlings crowded around the stage. Noble men and women sat on cushioned seats in the first-tier balcony. The fanfare of trumpets that signaled the beginning of a play was heard by some twenty-five hundred people, a cross-section of the Elizabethan world. As noted in the preface to the First Folio, Shakespeare's plays were written for everyone, from "the most able, to him that can but spell." That may explain why even today, they have such a universal appeal.

Othello, the Moor of Venice

Shakespeare probably wrote *The Tragedy of Othello, the Moor of Venice,* in 1603 or 1604, since we know that it was first performed at court on November 1, 1604. A classic story of love, jealousy, and betrayal, *Othello* is considered one of Shakespeare's greatest tragedies. It tells the story of Othello, a Moorish (North African) general who marries a Venetian lady and then is cruelly tricked into believing that his wife is unfaithful.

The plot itself was taken from a novella by Italian writer Giraldi Cinthio, which was published in 1565. (See page 218 for a translation of this tale.) This should not be considered plagiarism; in Shakespeare's day, it was common for playwrights to borrow subjects and storylines from other works and then adapt them for the stage. Furthermore, although Shakespeare's plot was not original, his gift for dialogue, characterization, and poetic imagery and phrasing transformed the story into something altogether his own.

Venice, Cyprus, and the Ottoman Empire

The setting of *Othello* must have seemed very exotic to Shakespeare's audience in London. The first act of the play is set in Venice, a city-state in northern Italy, and the following four acts in Cyprus, an island in the Mediterranean Sea. (See the map on the facing page.)

Today, Venice is a part of the modern nation of Italy, but in the 1500s, it was a powerful seafaring empire ruled by a Duke, or *doge,* and a council of noblemen. Seated in a lagoon on the Adriatic Sea, Venice was a major trade port with control over strategic points in the Mediterranean such as the islands of Crete and Cyprus.

The Venetians' main rivals were the Turks, or Ottomans, who controlled a vast empire stretching from the Persian Gulf in the East to Hungary in the West, including the territories of Greece and Egypt. The Ottoman Empire and Venice were constantly at war. The objective was power and land, of course, but religion entered into the equation as well. The Venetians were Christian, and the Turks were Muslim. To Venice and indeed to Shakespeare's England, the Turks were the hated enemy whom Christians had fought during the Crusades. This conflict between

Christian and Muslim, European and foreign, "civilized" and "barbarian," is a major theme that runs throughout *Othello*.

In the play, Othello is sent to Cyprus to fend off a Turkish invasion of the island. This incident is probably inspired by an actual battle that took place in 1571. However, in real life the Turks were successful in capturing Cyprus, whereas in the play, they are held off by a storm. Although it has a small part in the plot, the battle at sea serves an important role, as it provides a backdrop and a mirror for the smaller conflict brewing between Iago and Othello. The play asks us to examine which man, the Christian European Iago, or the Muslim-born, "barbarian" foreigner Othello, is the true enemy of civilization.

There is no record of Shakespeare having traveled to Venice, so it is likely that he relied on books to help him create an accurate picture of Venetian life. One source he

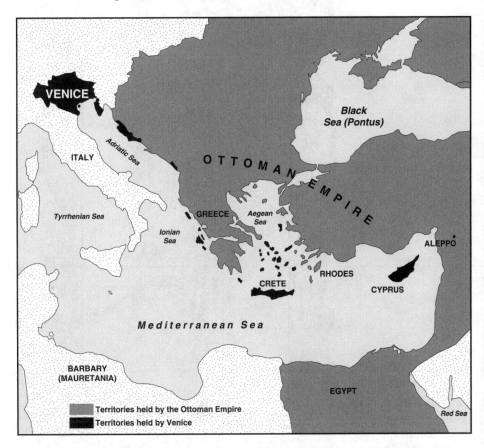

Map showing territories held by Venice and the Ottoman Empire in the 16th century.

almost certainly used was *The Commonwealth and Government of Venice (De magistratibus et republica Venetorum)* by Italian author Gasparo Contarini, written in 1543 and translated into English by Lewis Lewkenor in 1599.

The Moors and Race in *Othello*

The Moors were a Muslim people who lived on the northern coast of Africa, an area the Europeans called Barbary. These people had a mixed heritage: they were descended from the Berbers (a Caucasian people native to north Africa) and the Arabs, who came from the east. In the eighth century, the Moors invaded Spain and brought it under Islamic rule, in the process bringing to Western Europe their vast knowledge of art, architecture, medicine,

MORO DI CONDITIONE.

Illustration of a Moor from Degli habiti antichi et moderni *(1590) by Cesare Vecellio.*

and science, much of which they inherited from the Arabs and ancient Greeks. The Moors ruled over various parts of Spain for several centuries. Today, Moorish architecture and art can be seen all over Spain, especially in the cities of Toledo, Cordoba, and Seville.

When Shakespeare wrote about "the Moor of Venice," therefore, he was envisioning a north African man, well-educated, and raised in the Muslim faith (although baptized Christian as an adult). It is unclear, however, whether Shakespeare meant us to see Othello as a black man, or one more Arab in appearance. The Moors of Barbary were a dark-skinned people compared to Europeans, but they were not black. However, in Shakespeare's day, the term *Moor* was often used broadly, to refer to any person with dark or black skin, including black Africans. Several references in the play seem to describe Othello as a black African. But no matter what the exact color of his skin, the important point is that Othello was an outsider in Venice, an exotic figure who, while being admired and valued for his military prowess, more often provoked curiosity, fear, and even hatred.

These same feelings toward Africans were probably shared by the members of Shakespeare's audience. To the English of Shakespeare's time, Africans were strange and foreign enemies of Christianity, given to heathen practices such as witchcraft and voodoo. In the literature of the time, they were invariably portrayed as villains. The Africans who came to England were viewed with suspicion and hostility. In 1596, Queen Elizabeth I issued an edict against these unlucky foreigners, reading as follows: "Her Majesty under-standing that several blackamoors have lately been brought into this realm, of which kind of people there are already too many here . . . her Majesty's pleasure therefore is that those kind of people should be expelled from the land." Considering this climate, it is rather suprising that Shakespeare should have written a play in which the hero was an African, and a very noble character at that.

To create the character of Othello, a man whose back-ground was so different from his own, Shakespeare again relied upon books. He may have consulted *The History and Description of Africa*, a book written in 1526 by Moorish author Leo Africanus. See page 231 for an excerpt from this work. You may also refer to the critical readings by Samuel Taylor Coleridge (page 245) and A. C. Bradley (page 250) for more discussion on the subject of Othello's race.

The Time Scheme of *Othello*

As many critics have noted, the time scheme in *Othello* is somewhat confusing. The events appear to take place in only a few days, but throughout the play, there are references that suggest much more time has passed. Shakespeare may have been torn between two objectives: on the one hand, increasing the dramatic tension by making the events take place in a short time frame, but on the other, allowing enough time to pass so that the plot would be believable. In using a short time frame, Shakespeare was probably following the model of the Greek dramatist Aristotle who advised playwrights to keep the action of a tragedy "within one revolution of the sun." Shakespeare likely realized that his story could not take place in such a short time, but tried to limit the span of time as much as possible.

If the events actually did take place in only two or three days, there would not have been enough time for Desdemona to have been unfaithful, and the outcome of the play would have been unbelievable. Therefore, Shakespeare creates the *illusion* of more time having passed, even as, when we examine the scenes, the group has only been in Cyprus for two days.

As you read, decide whether Shakespeare's "double time scheme" is effective, or whether it can be considered a flaw in the play.

Characters in *Othello*

The names in Shakespeare's plays are often symbolic, and the names *Othello* and *Desdemona* may be seen as symbolic of the doom that befalls the characters in this tragedy. The name *Desdemona* (or *Disdemona,* as it was spelled by Giraldi Cinthio in the original story) is Greek for "unlucky." Also, it may or may not be coincidental that Othello's name contains the word *hell* and Desdemona's name contains the word *demon.* As you read, look for other ways in which Shakespeare expands on the motif of hell and demons.

Shakespeare probably molded Iago, the villain in *Othello,* after the character of Vice in the medieval morality plays. Vice was a villainous stock character who made his intent known through asides and soliloquies to the audience. In the morality plays, Vice's role was to tempt the protagonist into doing something that would cause his own damnation. He did this purely for his own gratification and for no other purpose. As you read, decide whether Iago, like Vice, does evil for his own gratification or whether he has a real motive for wanting revenge.

Echoes:

Famous Lines from Othello

For when my outward action doth demonstrate
The native act and figure of my heart
In compliment extern, 'tis not long after
But I will wear my heart upon my sleeve
For daws to peck at: I am not what I am.

—Iago, act I, scene i

I saw Othello's visage in his mind,
And to his honour and his valiant parts
Did I my soul and fortunes consecrate.

—Desdemona, act I, scene iii

[N]oble signior,
If virtue no delighted beauty lack,
Your son-in-law is far more fair than black.

—The Duke of Venice, act I, scene iii

Look to her, Moor; have a quick eye to see.
She has deceiv'd her father; may do thee!

—Brabantio, act I, scene iii

Reputation, reputation, reputation! O, I have lost my
reputation! I have lost the immortal part of myself, and what
remains is bestial. My reputation, Iago, my reputation!

—Cassio, act II, scene iii

Excellent wretch! Perdition catch my soul,
But I do love thee! and when I love thee not,
Chaos is come again.

—Othello, act III, scene iii

O, beware, my lord, of jealousy!
It is the green-ey'd monster which doth mock
The meat it feeds on.

—Iago, act III, scene iii

But yet the pity of it, Iago! O Iago, the pity of it, Iago!

—Othello, act IV, scene i

Speak of me as I am; nothing extenuate,
Nor set down aught in malice. Then must you speak
Of one that loved not wisely but too well;
Of one not easily jealous, but being wrought,
Perplexed in the extreme . . .

—Othello, act V, scene ii

Illustrations:
Performances of *Othello*

Since it was first enacted at the court of Queen Elizabeth in 1604, Shakespeare's *Othello, the Moor of Venice* has been performed countless times on stages and in cinemas all over the world. Here are a few glimpses.

Image courtesy of the Library of Congress.

Poster for an 1884 production of Othello *starring American actor Thomas Keene. Keene was a white actor and played the title role in blackface, as was customary in the theater until the late 1900s.*

Photo © Bettmann/Corbis.

American actor Paul Robeson and British actor Peggy Ashcroft in a production of Othello *in London, 1930. The casting of a black actor in the role of Othello generated a great deal of controversy, especially at home in the United States.*

Actor/director Orson Welles stars in the 1952 film adaptation of Othello. *Welles liked to take risks as a director, and his is an edgy film with dramatic closeups and atmospheric imagery.*

The 1995 film Othello, *directed by Oliver Parker, featured excellent performances by Laurence Fishburne (as Othello) and Kenneth Branagh (as Iago).*

Patrick Stewart as Othello and Patrice Johnson as Desdemona in The Shakespeare Theatre's *1997–1998 production of Othello, directed by Jude Kelly. Rather than play the character in blackface as actors had done in the past, Stewart conceived the idea of a "photo-negative Othello"—a white man in a black country.*

OTHELLO

THE MOOR OF VENICE

by WILLIAM SHAKESPEARE

Dramatis Personae

DUKE OF VENICE

BRABANTIO, *a senator*

Other Senators

GRATIANO, *brother to Brabantio*

LODOVICO, *kinsman to Brabantio*

OTHELLO, *a noble Moor in the service of the Venetian state*

CASSIO, *his lieutenant*

IAGO, *his ancient*

RODERIGO, *a Venetian gentleman*

MONTANO, *Othello's predecessor in the government of Cyprus*

CLOWN, *servant to Othello*

DESDEMONA, *daughter to Brabantio and wife to Othello*

EMILIA, *wife to Iago*

BIANCA, *mistress to Cassio*

Sailor, Messenger, Herald, Officers, Gentlemen, Musicians, and Attendants

Scene
Venice; a Sea-port in Cyprus.

<u>ACT I, SCENE i</u>
1. **this.** Othello's marriage to Desdemona
2. **'Sblood.** An oath, or curse, meaning "by God's blood"
3. **Off-capp'd.** Took off their caps, in a gesture of pleading
4. **bombast circumstance.** A bombastic, or overblown, speech meant to avoid the question. *Circumstance* here means *circumlocution*, a type of speech that is unecessarily wordy and has no point to it.
5. **epithets of war.** Terms having to do with war; military jargon
6. **Nonsuits.** Refuses; that is, turns down their suit
7. **Certes.** In truth; certainly
8. **arithmetician.** One who is schooled in military theory, but has no practical experience on the battlefield. Mathematics were an important part of warfare then, as they are today. For instance, they could be used to calculate the trajectory and angle of a cannonball.
9. **Florentine.** From Florence
10. **wife.** Probably a mistake, since later in the play it is apparent Cassio is not married. Shakespeare may have originally intended to have Cassio be a married man, but changed his mind later. Or, it may be a misprint for *life* or *wise.*
11. **spinster.** A housewife; one who spins
12. **theoric.** Theory
13. **toged consuls.** Senators in togas
14. **propose.** Speak
15. **his.** Othello's
16. **At Rhodes, at Cyprus . . . Christian and heathen.** In the 1500s, Venice was a powerful seafaring empire and controlled the islands of Rhodes and Cyprus, both located in the eastern Mediterranean. Their main rivals were the Turks, who, as Muslims, were considered heathens by Christian Europe. *Heathen* here simply means "non-Christian."
17. **be-lee'd and calm'd.** Had the wind taken out of his sails and made calm
18. **counter-caster.** Accountant
19. **ancient.** An ancient, or ensign, was a low-ranking officer several steps below a lieutenant. The ancient was responsible for carrying the flag, or standard, and usually stayed by the commander's side during battle.

words for everyday use

ab • hor (əb hȯ[ə]r´) *vt.,* hate strongly; loathe. *Dessa declared that she <u>abhorred</u> being bored.*

suit (süt´) *n.,* act or instance of seeking by entreaty: an appeal. *Fiona's <u>suit</u> to Dieter's mercy fell on deaf ears.*

prat • tle (prat´ əl) *n.,* idle chatter; chattering noise. *The <u>prattle</u> in the lunchroom sounded like the humming of bees in a hive.*

ACT I

SCENE i: Venice. A street.

Enter RODERIGO *and* IAGO.

RODERIGO. Tush! never tell me; I take it much unkindly
That thou, Iago, who hast had my purse
As if the strings were thine, shouldst know of this.[1]

IAGO. 'Sblood,[2] but you will not hear me:
5   If ever I did dream of such a matter,
Abhor me.

RODERIGO. Thou told'st me thou didst hold him in thy hate.

IAGO. Despise me, if I do not. Three great ones of the city,
In personal suit to make me his lieutenant,
10   Off-capp'd[3] to him: and, by the faith of man,
I know my price, I am worth no worse a place:
But he; as loving his own pride and purposes,
Evades them, with a bombast circumstance[4]
Horribly stuff'd with epithets of war;[5]
15   And, in conclusion,
Nonsuits[6] my mediators; for, "Certes,"[7] says he,
"I have already chose my officer."
And what was he?
Forsooth, a great arithmetician,[8]
20   One Michael Cassio, a Florentine,[9]
A fellow almost damn'd in a fair wife;[10]
That never set a squadron in the field,
Nor the division of a battle knows
More than a spinster;[11] unless the bookish theoric,[12]
25   Wherein the toged consuls[13] can propose[14]
As masterly as he: mere prattle, without practice,
Is all his soldiership. But he, sir, had the election:
And I, of whom his[15] eyes had seen the proof
At Rhodes, at Cyprus and on other grounds
Christian and heathen,[16] must be be-lee'd and calm'd[17]
30   By debitor and creditor: this counter-caster,[18]
He, in good time, must his lieutenant be,
And I—God bless the mark!—his Moorship's ancient.[19]

◄ *What reason does Iago give for hating Othello? Who is Cassio?*

◄ *What position was Iago assigned?*

20. **old gradation.** Seniority
21. **affined.** Obligated
22. **knave.** A servant or man of humble position
23. **doting on . . . bondage.** Loving his own enslaved condition
24. **provender.** Animal feed
25. **cashier'd.** Rejected or dismissed from duty
26. **trimm'd.** Dressed up
27. **lined their coats.** That is, with money
28. **native act and figure of my heart.** My true feelings and intentions
29. **compliment extern.** Outward appearance
30. **daws.** Jackdaws, a type of bird. The entire line can be interpreted as, "If I were to be so foolish as to show my true feelings and intentions to the world, then I might as well wear my heart on my sleeve for daws to peck at."
31. **owe.** Own; possess
32. **carry't thus.** Carry off this marriage
33. **him.** Othello

---

words for everyday use

ob • se • qui • ous (əb sē′ kwē əs) *adj.,* showing an exaggerated desire to help or serve; fawning. *Lew's obsequious behavior led others to call him "teacher's pet."*

vis • age (viz′ əj) *n.,* appearance; face. *The boy's angelic visage concealed his mischievous nature.*

in • cense (in sen[t]s′) *vt.,* cause to become angry. *News of the government scandal incensed the public.*

RODERIGO. By heaven, I rather would have been his
    hangman.

IAGO. Why, there's no remedy; 'tis the curse of
35   service,
Preferment goes by letter and affection,
And not by old gradation,[20] where each second
Stood heir to the first. Now, sir, be judge yourself,
Whether I in any just term am affined[21]
To love the Moor.

40 RODERIGO.   I would not follow him then.

IAGO. O, sir, content you;
I follow him to serve my turn upon him:
We cannot all be masters, nor all masters
Cannot be truly follow'd. You shall mark
45 Many a duteous and knee-crooking knave,[22]
That, doting on his own <u>obsequious</u> bondage,[23]
Wears out his time, much like his master's ass,
For nought but provender,[24] and when he's old,
    cashier'd:[25]
Whip me such honest knaves. Others there are
50 Who, trimm'd[26] in forms and <u>visages</u> of duty,
Keep yet their hearts attending on themselves,
And, throwing but shows of service on their lords,
Do well thrive by them and when they have lined
    their coats[27]
Do themselves homage: these fellows have some
    soul;
55 And such a one do I profess myself. For, sir,
It is as sure as you are Roderigo,
Were I the Moor, I would not be Iago:
In following him, I follow but myself;
Heaven is my judge, not I for love and duty,
60 But seeming so, for my peculiar end:
For when my outward action doth demonstrate
The native act and figure of my heart[28]
In compliment extern,[29] 'tis not long after
But I will wear my heart upon my sleeve
65 For daws[30] to peck at: I am not what I am.

RODERIGO. What a full fortune does the thicklips
    owe[31]
If he can carry't thus![32]

IAGO.   Call up her father,
Rouse him: make after him,[33] poison his delight,
Proclaim him in the streets; <u>incense</u> her kinsmen,

◀ What two types of
men does Iago
describe? Which type
does he profess
himself to be?

◀ How does Iago
plan to "poison
[Othello's] delight"?

34. **timorous accent.** Tone of alarm
35. **'Zounds.** An oath meaning "by God's wounds"
36. **snorting.** Snoring
37. **grandsire.** Grandfather
38. **distempering draughts.** Intoxicating beverages
39. **malicious bravery.** Wicked boldness
40. **start.** Startle, alarm

words for everyday use

vex • a • tion (vek sā´ shən) *n.*, state of being vexed, or irritated. *I thought that the babysitting job would be easy, but the children were naughty and caused me much vexation.*

dire (dī[ə]r´) *adj.*, dreadful. *Dire predictions were made at the end of the millennium, but few of these frightful visions came true.*

70 And, though he in a fertile climate dwell,
Plague him with flies: though that his joy be joy,
Yet throw such changes of <u>vexation</u> on't,
As it may lose some color.

RODERIGO. Here is her father's house; I'll call aloud.

75 IAGO. Do, with like timorous accent[34] and <u>dire</u> yell
As when, by night and negligence, the fire
Is spied in populous cities.

RODERIGO. What, ho, Brabantio! Signior Brabantio, ho!

IAGO. Awake! what, ho, Brabantio! thieves! thieves! thieves!
80 Look to your house, your daughter and your bags!
Thieves! thieves!

BRABANTIO *appears above, at a window.*

BRABANTIO. What is the reason of this terrible summons?
What is the matter there?

RODERIGO. Signior, is all your family within?

IAGO. Are your doors lock'd?

85 BRABANTIO.   Why, wherefore ask you this?

IAGO. 'Zounds,[35] sir, you're robb'd; for shame, put on your gown;
Your heart is burst, you have lost half your soul;
Even now, now, very now, an old black ram
Is topping your white ewe. Arise, arise;
90 Awake the snorting[36] citizens with the bell,
Or else the devil will make a grandsire[37] of you:
Arise, I say.

BRABANTIO. What, have you lost your wits?

RODERIGO. Most reverend signior, do you know my voice?

BRABANTIO. Not I; what are you?

RODERIGO. My name is Roderigo.

95 BRABANTIO.   The worser welcome:
I have charged thee not to haunt about my doors:
In honest plainness thou hast heard me say
My daughter is not for thee; and now, in madness,
Being full of supper and distempering draughts,[38]
100 Upon malicious bravery,[39] dost thou come
To start[40] my quiet.

◄ How does
Brabantio know
Roderigo? What has
he told Roderigo in
the past?

41. **grange.** Farmhouse or granary; i.e., a remote place where burglary would be more likely to occur

42. **Barbary horse.** A type of horse from Barbary, the northern coast of Africa. Iago implies that Othello is no better than a stud horse.

43. **you'll have coursers . . . germans.** You'll have horses for relatives. A *courser* is a spirited horse; a *gennet* (today spelled *jennet*) is a small Spanish horse. *Cousins* and *germans* both meant simply "relatives." The reference to a horse from Spain might refer to the fact that the Moors occupied Spain for several centuries.

44. **This thou shalt answer.** You'll be punished for this.

45. **odd-even and dull watch.** Time between day and night, that is, around midnight, when nobody is around

46. **gondolier.** One who pilots a gondola, a type of boat used to transport people through the canals of Venice

47. **gross clasps.** Vulgar or indecent embraces

48. **from the sense of all civility.** In violation of civility

49. **reverence.** Respect

50. **extravagant and wheeling.** Here, both words mean "wandering; vagabond."

words for everyday use

ruf • fi • an (rəf´ ē ən) *n.*, bully. *The ruffians taunted Okema and blocked his way.*

pro • fane (pro fān´) *adj.*, vulgar. *The movie was rated PG-13 for its profane language.*

las • civ • i • ous (lə siv´ ē əs) *adj.*, lustful; obscene. *The manager was fired for sexual harassment after making lascivious comments to an employee.*

re • buke (ri byük´) *n.*, expression of strong disapproval. *The principal issued a strong rebuke to the students who had been caught vandalizing school property.*

tri • fle (trī´ fəl) *vi.*, treat something or someone as unimportant. *The knave cruelly trifled with the maiden's feelings.*

RODERIGO. Sir, sir, sir,—

BRABANTIO.   But thou must needs be sure
My spirit and my place have in them power
To make this bitter to thee.

RODERIGO.   Patience, good sir.

BRABANTIO. What tell'st thou me of robbing? this is
105   Venice;
My house is not a grange.[41]

RODERIGO.   Most grave Brabantio,
In simple and pure soul I come to you.

IAGO. 'Zounds, sir, you are one of those that will not
serve God, if the devil bid you. Because we come to
110   do you service and you think we are <u>ruffians</u>, you'll
have your daughter covered with a Barbary horse;[42]
you'll have your nephews neigh to you; you'll have
coursers for cousins and gennets for germans.[43]

BRABANTIO. What <u>profane</u> wretch art thou?

115 IAGO. I am one, sir, that comes to tell you your
daughter and the Moor are now making the beast
with two backs.

BRABANTIO. Thou art a villain.

IAGO.   You are—a senator.

BRABANTIO. This thou shalt answer;[44] I know thee,
Roderigo.

RODERIGO. Sir, I will answer any thing. But, I beseech
120   you,
If't be your pleasure and most wise consent,
As partly I find it is, that your fair daughter,
At this odd-even and dull watch[45] o' the night,
Transported, with no worse nor better guard
125 But with a knave of common hire, a gondolier,[46]
To the gross clasps[47] of a <u>lascivious</u> Moor—
If this be known to you and your allowance,
We then have done you bold and saucy wrongs;
But if you know not this, my manners tell me
130 We have your wrong <u>rebuke</u>. Do not believe
That, from the sense of all civility,[48]
I thus would play and <u>trifle</u> with your reverence:[49]
Your daughter, if you have not given her leave,
I say again, hath made a gross revolt;
135 Tying her duty, beauty, wit and fortunes
In an extravagant and wheeling[50] stranger

◄ *What has
Desdemona done?*

51. **Strike on the tinder.** Light a match
52. **taper.** Candle
53. **accident.** Happening
54. **meet.** Appropriate
55. **produced . . . against the Moor.** Shown to be working against Othello
56. **gall him with some cheque.** Irritate him with some small punishment. Eloping with a nobleman's daughter would have been considered a punishable offense.
57. **cast him.** Dismiss him from service
58. **Cyprus wars.** Wars between Venice and Turkey over the island of Cyprus, located south of Turkey in the Mediterranean Sea. At the time of this play, the Venetians controlled Cyprus and were defending it against the Turks.
59. **even now stand in act.** Are happening right now
60. **fathom.** Worth
61. **Sagittary.** An inn where the newlyweds are staying
62. **raised search.** A party of searchers who have been raised, or roused, from their beds

words for everyday use   de • lude (di lüd´) *vt.,* mislead; trick. *The con artist deluded his victims into depositing their money into his bank account.*

Of here and every where. Straight satisfy yourself:
If she be in her chamber or your house,
Let loose on me the justice of the state
For thus <u>deluding</u> you.

140   **BRABANTIO.**   Strike on the tinder,[51] ho!
Give me a taper![52] call up all my people!
This accident[53] is not unlike my dream:
Belief of it oppresses me already.
Light, I say! light!

Exit above.

  IAGO.   Farewell; for I must leave you:
145 It seems not meet,[54] nor wholesome to my place,
To be produced—as, if I stay, I shall—
Against the Moor:[55] for, I do know, the state,
However this may gall him with some cheque,[56]
Cannot with safety cast him,[57] for he's embark'd
150 With such loud reason to the Cyprus wars,[58]
Which even now stand in act,[59] that, for their souls,
Another of his fathom[60] they have none,
To lead their business: in which regard,
Though I do hate him as I do hell-pains,
155 Yet, for necessity of present life,
I must show out a flag and sign of love,
Which is indeed but sign. That you shall surely find
    him,
Lead to the Sagittary[61] the raised search;[62]
And there will I be with him. So, farewell.

Exit.

Enter, below, BRABANTIO, and SERVANTS with torches.

160 **BRABANTIO.** It is too true an evil: gone she is;
And what's to come of my despised time
Is nought but bitterness. Now, Roderigo,
Where didst thou see her? O unhappy girl!
With the Moor, say'st thou? Who would be a father!
165 How didst thou know 'twas she? O she deceives me
Past thought! What said she to you? Get more tapers:
Raise all my kindred. Are they married, think you?

  RODERIGO. Truly, I think they are.

  BRABANTIO. O heaven! How got she out? O treason
    of the blood!
170 Fathers, from hence trust not your daughters' minds
By what you see them act. Is there not charms
By which the property of youth and maidhood

◀ *Why does the Venetian government need Othello?*

◀ *What does Brabantio say of his daughter's possible marriage to Othello?*

63. **deserve.** Reward

ACT I, SCENE ii

1. **contrived.** Premeditated; intentional
2. **yerk'd.** Stabbed
3. **prated.** Chattered
4. **scurvy.** Despicable
5. **I did full hard forbear him.** I found it hard to keep myself from hurting him.
6. **fast.** Securely
7. **magnifico.** Brabantio is a *magnifico,* or person of great standing in Venice
8. **Will give him cable.** Will give him the power, or the means [to punish Othello]
9. **signiory.** Venetian government
10. **I fetch my life . . . royal siege.** I am descended from royalty.

words for everyday use

ap • pre • hend (ap´ ri hənd´) *vt.,* arrest; seize. *The police officer apprehended the burglars at the scene of the crime.*

in • iq • ui • ty (in ik´ wə tē) *n.,* wickedness. *The teens had no motive for attacking the homeless man; they did it out of sheer iniquity.*

pro • vok • ing (prə vō´ kiŋ) *adj.,* causing anger or outrage. *The politician's provoking comments caused outrage in the community.*

pro • mul • gate (präm´ əl gāt´, prō´ məl gāt´) *vt.,* declare openly or make known; also, to spread (knowledge or ideas). *The teachings of Socrates were largely promulgated by his foremost pupil, Plato.*

May be abused? Have you not read, Roderigo,
Of some such thing?

RODERIGO.   Yes, sir, I have indeed.

BRABANTIO. Call up my brother. O, would you had
175   had her!
Some one way, some another. Do you know
Where we may <u>apprehend</u> her and the Moor?

RODERIGO. I think I can discover him, if you please,
To get good guard and go along with me.

180 BRABANTIO. Pray you, lead on. At every house I'll call;
I may command at most. Get weapons, ho!
And raise some special officers of night.
On, good Roderigo: I'll deserve[63] your pains.

Exeunt.

◀ How does
Brabantio feel about
Roderigo now?

SCENE ii: Another street.

Enter OTHELLO, IAGO, *and* ATTENDANTS *with torches.*

IAGO. Though in the trade of war I have slain men,
Yet do I hold it very stuff o' the conscience
To do no contrived[1] murder: I lack <u>iniquity</u>
Sometimes to do me service: nine or ten times
I had thought to have yerk'd[2] him here under the
5   ribs.

OTHELLO. 'Tis better as it is.

◀ What does Iago
claim he wanted to
do to Roderigo?

IAGO.   Nay, but he prated,[3]
And spoke such scurvy[4] and <u>provoking</u> terms
Against your honor
That, with the little godliness I have,
10 I did full hard forbear him.[5] But, I pray you, sir,
Are you fast[6] married? Be assured of this,
That the magnifico[7] is much beloved,
And hath in his effect a voice potential
As double as the duke's: he will divorce you;
15 Or put upon you what restraint and grievance
The law, with all his might to enforce it on,
Will give him cable.[8]

◀ What might
Brabantio have the
power to do?

OTHELLO.   Let him do his spite:
My services which I have done the signiory[9]
Shall out-tongue his complaints. 'Tis yet to know,—
20 Which, when I know that boasting is an honor,
I shall <u>promulgate</u>—I fetch my life and being
From men of royal siege,[10] and my demerits

11. **my demerits . . . reach'd.** My merits, in all modesty, are equal to those of Desdemona's family. By *unbonneted*, he means "with my hat off," a gesture of courtesy and humility. He may doff his hat when speaking this line.

12. **But that I.** If I did not

13. **circumscription.** Restriction; limits

14. **the sea's worth.** All the treasure in the sea

15. **Janus.** The two-faced god of the Romans [see illustration below], an appropriate idol for the "two-faced" Iago

16. **heat.** Urgency

17. **galleys.** Long, low ships used for war and trade in the Mediterranean Sea from the Middle Ages to the 19th century

18. **what makes he here?** What is Othello doing here at the inn?

19. **carack.** Treasure ship

Janustopf (römischer As).

© Bettmann/Corbis

Janus, the Roman god of doorways, was depicted with two faces and thus is an appropriate idol for the "two-faced" Iago.

words for everyday use	man • i • fest (man´ ə fest) *vt.*, show. *Shakespeare's dramatic works* <u>manifest</u> *his extraordinary ear for dialogue.*	di • vine (də vīn´) *vt.*, discover intuitively; infer. *From the bits of conversation I overheard, I was able to* <u>divine</u> *that there was some trouble afoot.*

May speak unbonneted to as proud a fortune
As this that I have reach'd:[11] for know, Iago,
25 But that I[12] love the gentle Desdemona,
I would not my unhoused free condition
Put into circumscription[13] and confine
For the sea's worth.[14] But, look! what lights come
     yond?

IAGO. Those are the raised father and his friends:
You were best go in.

30 OTHELLO.   Not I, I must be found:
My parts, my title and my perfect soul
Shall <u>manifest</u> me rightly. Is it they?

IAGO. By Janus,[15] I think no.

Enter CASSIO, *and certain* OFFICERS *with torches.*

OTHELLO. The servants of the duke, and my
     lieutenant.
35 The goodness of the night upon you, friends!
What is the news?

CASSIO.   The duke does greet you, general,
And he requires your haste-post-haste appearance,
Even on the instant.

OTHELLO.   What is the matter, think you?

CASSIO. Something from Cyprus as I may <u>divine</u>:
40 It is a business of some heat:[16] the galleys[17]
Have sent a dozen sequent messengers
This very night at one another's heels,
And many of the consuls, raised and met,
Are at the duke's already: you have been hotly call'd
     for;
45 When, being not at your lodging to be found,
The senate hath sent about three several guests
To search you out.

OTHELLO.   'Tis well I am found by you.
I will but spend a word here in the house,
And go with you.

                              Exit.

CASSIO.   Ancient, what makes he here?[18]

50 IAGO. 'Faith, he to-night hath boarded a land carack:[19]
If it prove lawful prize, he's made for ever.

CASSIO. I do not understand.

IAGO.   He's married.

◀ Who comes to find Othello at the inn? What news do they have for him?

◀ To what does Iago compare Desdemona?

20. **Marry.** Indeed (originally an oath using the name of the Virgin Mary), with a pun on his previous line.

21. **Have with you.** I'll go with you.

22. **I am for you.** I will fight you.

23. **Keep up.** Keep sheathed

24. **opposite to.** Opposed to

25. **guardage.** Guardianship

26. **sooty.** Black

27. **gross in sense.** Obvious

28. **motion.** The senses or mental powers

29. **disputed on.** Argued in the court of law

30. **attach thee / For an abuser of the world.** Arrest you as a corrupter of the community. *Apprehend* and *attach* both mean "arrest."

31. **inhibited and out of warrant.** Prohibited and unjustifiable

---

words for everyday use   **sub • due** (səb düʹ) *vt.*, bring under control; conquer. *The dictator sent his army to* <u>subdue</u> *rebel forces.*

CASSIO.   To who?

Re-enter OTHELLO.

IAGO. Marry,[20] to—Come, captain, will you go?

OTHELLO.   Have with you.[21]

CASSIO. Here comes another troop to seek for you.

55 **IAGO.** It is Brabantio. General, be advised;
He comes to bad intent.

Enter BRABANTIO, RODERIGO, *and* OFFICERS *with torches
and weapons.*

OTHELLO.   Holla! stand there!

RODERIGO. Signior, it is the Moor.

BRABANTIO.   Down with him, thief!

They draw on both sides.

◀ How does Othello
respond to the threat
of violence?

IAGO. You, Roderigo! Come, sir, I am for you.[22]

OTHELLO. Keep up[23] your bright swords, for the dew
  will rust them.
60 Good signior, you shall more command with years
Than with your weapons.

BRABANTIO. O thou foul thief, where hast thou
  stow'd my daughter?
Damn'd as thou art, thou hast enchanted her;
For I'll refer me to all things of sense,
65 If she in chains of magic were not bound,
Whether a maid so tender, fair and happy,
So opposite to[24] marriage that she shunned
The wealthy curled darlings of our nation,
Would ever have, to incur a general mock,
70 Run from her guardage[25] to the sooty[26] bosom
Of such a thing as thou, to fear, not to delight.
Judge me the world, if 'tis not gross in sense[27]
That thou hast practiced on her with foul charms,
Abused her delicate youth with drugs or minerals
75 That weaken motion:[28] I'll have't disputed on;[29]
'Tis probable and palpable to thinking.
I therefore apprehend and do attach thee
For an abuser of the world,[30] a practicer
Of arts inhibited and out of warrant.[31]
80 Lay hold upon him: if he do resist,
<u>Subdue</u> him at his peril.

◀ Of what does
Brabantio accuse
Othello?

OTHELLO.   Hold your hands,
Both you of my inclining, and the rest:

32. **course of direct session.** Proper channels of justice
33. **idle.** Unworthy, lacking in merit
34. **have passage free.** Be freely allowed

ACT I, SCENE iii

1. **composition.** Consistency
2. **gives them credit.** Makes them believable
3. **disproportion'd.** Contradictory
4. **they jump not on a just account.** They do not agree on an exact number

Were it my cue to fight, I should have known it
Without a prompter. Where will you that I go
To answer this your charge?

85 BRABANTIO.   To prison, till fit time
Of law and course of direct session[32]
Call thee to answer.

OTHELLO.   What if I do obey?
How may the duke be therewith satisfied,
Whose messengers are here about my side,
90 Upon some present business of the state
To bring me to him?

FIRST OFFICER.   'Tis true, most worthy signior;
The duke's in council and your noble self,
I am sure, is sent for.

BRABANTIO.   How! the duke in council!
In this time of the night! Bring him away:
95 Mine's not an idle[33] cause: the duke himself,
Or any of my brothers of the state,
Cannot but feel this wrong as 'twere their own;
For if such actions may have passage free,[34]
Bond-slaves and pagans shall our statesmen be.

Exeunt.

SCENE iii: A council-chamber.

The DUKE *and* SENATORS *sitting at a table;* OFFICERS
attending.

DUKE OF VENICE. There is no composition[1] in these
    news
That gives them credit.[2]

FIRST SENATOR.   Indeed, they are disproportion'd;[3]
My letters say a hundred and seven galleys.

DUKE OF VENICE. And mine, a hundred and forty.

SECOND SENATOR.   And mine,
    two hundred:
5 But though they jump not on a just account,[4]—
As in these cases, where the aim reports,
'Tis oft with difference—yet do they all confirm
A Turkish fleet, and bearing up to Cyprus.

DUKE OF VENICE. Nay, it is possible enough to
    judgment:
10 I do not so secure me in the error,
But the main article I do approve
In fearful sense.

◀ *What do all the
scouts' reports
confirm?*

5. **Turkish preparation . . . Rhodes.** The Turkish fleet is heading for the island of Rhodes, which at the time of the play was controlled by the Venetians.

6. **assay of reason.** Test of reason

7. **'tis a pageant . . . false gaze.** It is a mere show meant to distract us.

8. **as it . . . bear it.** The Turks are more interested in Cyprus than in Rhodes, and have a much better chance of capturing it besides.

9. **warlike brace . . . abilities.** Military readiness; that is, Cyprus does not have the same military defense that Rhodes does. *Brace* literally means "armor."

10. **wake.** Risk

11. **for.** Headed for, or aiming for

12. **Ottomites.** Another name for the Turks. Turkey at that time was at the heart of the great Ottoman Empire, which had control of many regions including Syria, Arabia, Egypt, Greece, Israel, and parts of Russia and Hungary. The phrase "reverend and gracious" does not refer to the Ottomites, but to the senators and Duke whom the messenger is addressing.

13. **injointed . . . after fleet.** Joined up with a second fleet

14. **restem / Their backward course.** Re-steer, or change course

SAILOR. [*Within*]   What, ho! what, ho! what, ho!

FIRST OFFICER. A messenger from the galleys.

Enter a SAILOR.

DUKE OF VENICE.   Now, what's the business?

SAILOR. The Turkish preparation makes for Rhodes;[5]
15 So was I bid report here to the state
By Signior Angelo.

DUKE OF VENICE. How say you by this change?

FIRST SENATOR.   This cannot be,
By no assay of reason:[6] 'tis a pageant,
To keep us in false gaze.[7] When we consider
20 The importancy of Cyprus to the Turk,
And let ourselves again but understand,
That as it more concerns the Turk than Rhodes,
So may he with more facile question bear it,[8]
For that it stands not in such warlike brace,
25 But altogether lacks the abilities[9]
That Rhodes is dress'd in: if we make thought of this,
We must not think the Turk is so unskilful
To leave that latest which concerns him first,
Neglecting an attempt of ease and gain,
30 To wake[10] and wage a danger profitless.

DUKE OF VENICE. Nay, in all confidence, he's not
    for[11] Rhodes.

FIRST OFFICER. Here is more news.

Enter a MESSENGER.

MESSENGER. The Ottomites,[12] reverend and gracious,
Steering with due course towards the isle of Rhodes,
35 Have there injointed them with an after fleet.[13]

FIRST SENATOR. Ay, so I thought. How many, as you
    guess?

MESSENGER. Of thirty sail: and now they do restem
Their backward course,[14] bearing with frank
    appearance
Their purposes toward Cyprus. Signior Montano,
40 Your trusty and most valiant servitor,
With his free duty recommends you thus,
And prays you to believe him.

DUKE OF VENICE. 'Tis certain, then, for Cyprus.
Marcus Luccicos, is not he in town?

45 FIRST SENATOR. He's now in Florence.

Marginal notes:

◄ Why are the Turks heading for Rhodes? Why would they not attack Rhodes, according to the First Senator?

◄ How are the First Senator's suspicions proved correct? What are the Turks doing?

15. **aught.** Anything
16. **engluts.** Swallows
17. **mountebanks.** People who sell quack medicines
18. **the bloody book of law . . . your own sense.** You can read the law to this criminal yourself. The making of love-potions was against the law in Venice.
19. **though our proper son / Stood in your action.** Even if it were my own son who you were accusing [you would get justice].

words for everyday use

sans (sanz´) *adj.,* without. *We found ourselves lost in the jungle, sans map and sans compass.*

be • guile (bə gīl´) *vt.,* lead astray by means of tricks or deception. *The Pied Piper beguiled all the children of Hamelin town, leading them into a mountain and then shutting them inside.*

man • date (man´ dāt´) *n.,* formal order. *Everyone had to obey the queen's mandate.*

DUKE OF VENICE. Write from us to him; post-post-
    haste dispatch.

FIRST SENATOR. Here comes Brabantio and the valiant
    Moor.

Enter BRABANTIO, OTHELLO, IAGO, RODERIGO, *and*
OFFICERS.

DUKE OF VENICE. Valiant Othello, we must straight
    employ you
Against the general enemy Ottoman.

[*To* BRABANTIO.]

50 I did not see you; welcome, gentle signior;
We lack'd your counsel and your help tonight.

BRABANTIO. So did I yours. Good your grace, pardon
    me;
Neither my place nor aught[15] I heard of business
Hath raised me from my bed, nor doth the general
    care
55 Take hold on me, for my particular grief
Is of so flood-gate and o'erbearing nature
That it engluts[16] and swallows other sorrows
And it is still itself.

DUKE OF VENICE.   Why, what's the matter?

BRABANTIO. My daughter! O, my daughter!

DUKE OF VENICE.   Dead?

BRABANTIO.   Ay, to me;
60 She is abused, stol'n from me, and corrupted
By spells and medicines bought of mountebanks;[17]
For nature so preposterously to err,
Being not deficient, blind, or lame of sense,
Sans witchcraft could not.

DUKE OF VENICE. Whoe'er he be that in this foul
65   proceeding
Hath thus beguiled your daughter of herself
And you of her, the bloody book of law
You shall yourself read in the bitter letter
After your own sense,[18] yea, though our proper son
Stood in your action.[19]

70 **BRABANTIO.**   Humbly I thank your grace.
Here is the man, this Moor, whom now, it seems,
Your special mandate for the state-affairs
Hath hither brought.

DUKE OF VENICE.   We are very sorry for't.

◀ *What does
Brabantio say has
happened to his
daughter? How does
the Duke respond?*

20. **since . . . seven years' pith . . . tented field.** Since my arms had the pith, or strength, of seven years, I have used them on the battleground. In other words, Othello has been a soldier since he was seven years old.

21. **unvarnish'd.** Plain, unembellished

22. **withal.** With

23. **her motion / Blush'd at herself.** She blushed at any stirring of emotion.

24. **vouch.** Claim; swear to be true

25. **dram.** A measure of fluid; a small portion of drink

26. **thin habits.** Thin clothing; that is, superficial appearances

27. **modern seeming.** Everyday assumptions

words for everyday use

con • jur • a • tion (kän´ jü rā´ shən) *n.*, magic spell or trick. *The children were entranced by the magician's conjurations.*

DUKE OF VENICE. [*To* OTHELLO] What, in your own
    part, can you say to this?

75 **BRABANTIO.** Nothing, but this is so.

OTHELLO. Most potent, grave, and reverend signiors,
My very noble and approved good masters,
That I have ta'en away this old man's daughter,
It is most true; true, I have married her:
80 The very head and front of my offending
Hath this extent, no more. Rude am I in my speech,
And little bless'd with the soft phrase of peace:
For since these arms of mine had seven years' pith,
Till now some nine moons wasted, they have used
85 Their dearest action in the tented field,[20]
And little of this great world can I speak,
More than pertains to feats of broil and battle,
And therefore little shall I grace my cause
In speaking for myself. Yet, by your gracious patience,
90 I will a round unvarnish'd[21] tale deliver
Of my whole course of love; what drugs, what charms,
What <u>conjuration</u> and what mighty magic,
For such proceeding I am charged withal,[22]
I won his daughter.

◄ *How does Othello show modesty in his response?*

BRABANTIO.   A maiden never bold;
95 Of spirit so still and quiet, that her motion
Blush'd at herself;[23] and she, in spite of nature,
Of years, of country, credit, every thing,
To fall in love with what she fear'd to look on!
It is a judgment maim'd and most imperfect
100 That will confess perfection so could err
Against all rules of nature, and must be driven
To find out practices of cunning hell,
Why this should be. I therefore vouch[24] again
That with some mixtures powerful o'er the blood,
105 Or with some dram[25] conjured to this effect,
He wrought upon her.

◄ *How does Brabantio describe his daughter? Why does he continue to claim that Othello must have given Desdemona "mixtures powerful o'er the blood"?*

DUKE OF VENICE.   To vouch this, is no proof,
Without more wider and more overt test
Than these thin habits[26] and poor likelihoods
Of modern seeming[27] do prefer against him.

110 **FIRST SENATOR.** But, Othello, speak:
Did you by indirect and forced courses
Subdue and poison this young maid's affections?
Or came it by request and such fair question
As soul to soul affordeth?

28. **Still.** Always

29. **spake.** Spoke

30. **scapes.** Escapes

31. **breach.** A gap in the wall of a fort, caused by enemy fire

32. **portance.** Behavior

33. **antres.** Caverns (from the Latin *antrum*)

34. **idle.** Barren; empty

35. **Anthropophagi.** Man-eaters; cannibals

36. **men whose heads / Do grow beneath their shoulders.** One of the outlandish stories told by ancient travelers. See the picture below. This tribe of people was mentioned by Roman historian Pliny the Elder in his encyclopedic work *Naturalis Historia* (first published in AD 77). Pliny described them as "a tribe who are without necks, and have eyes in their shoulders." The story was repeated by writers and explorers in later centuries, including the medieval writer Sir John Mandeville and travelers to the Americas such as Sir Walter Raleigh. Pliny also wrote about the Anthropophagi, the cannibal tribe, whom he claimed lived north of the Black Sea.

37. **This to hear . . . incline.** Desdemona was inclined, or drawn, to these tales.

38. **But still . . . draw her thence.** But very often Desdemona could not stay to hear the tales, being called away to resolve some household affairs.

39. **Which ever . . . with haste dispatch.** Whenever she could take care of these matters hastily enough

40. **She'ld.** Contraction of *she would*

41. **pliant.** Convenient

Bodleian Library, University of Oxford. Douce MM 489.

"Men Whose Heads Do Grow Beneath Their Shoulders." Woodcut illustration from The Voyages and Travels of Sir John Mandeville *(1582). Mandeville's book first appeared around 1371, and was filled with outlandish tales, many of them borrowed from ancient sources such as Roman historian Pliny the Elder.*

words for everyday use

dis • course (dis´ kō[ə]rs´) *n.*, conversation; verbal expression or exchange of ideas.
The two friends talked frequently, and their <u>discourse</u> was always lively and open.

OTHELLO.   I do beseech you,
115 Send for the lady to the Sagittary,
And let her speak of me before her father:
If you do find me foul in her report,
The trust, the office I do hold of you,
Not only take away, but let your sentence
Even fall upon my life.

120 DUKE OF VENICE.   Fetch Desdemona hither.

OTHELLO. Ancient, conduct them: you best know
     the place.

Exeunt IAGO *and* ATTENDANTS.

And, till she come, as truly as to heaven
I do confess the vices of my blood,
So justly to your grave ears I'll present
125 How I did thrive in this fair lady's love,
And she in mine.

DUKE OF VENICE. Say it, Othello.

OTHELLO. Her father loved me; oft invited me;
Still[28] question'd me the story of my life,
130 From year to year, the battles, sieges, fortunes,
That I have passed.
I ran it through, even from my boyish days,
To the very moment that he bade me tell it;
Wherein I spake[29] of most disastrous chances,
135 Of moving accidents by flood and field
Of hair-breadth scapes[30] i' the imminent deadly
     breach,[31]
Of being taken by the insolent foe
And sold to slavery, of my redemption thence
And portance[32] in my travels' history:
140 Wherein of antres[33] vast and deserts idle,[34]
Rough quarries, rocks and hills whose heads touch
     heaven
It was my hint to speak,—such was the process;
And of the Cannibals that each other eat,
The Anthropophagi[35] and men whose heads
145 Do grow beneath their shoulders.[36] This to hear
Would Desdemona seriously incline:[37]
But still the house-affairs would draw her thence:[38]
Which ever as she could with haste dispatch,[39]
She'ld[40] come again, and with a greedy ear
150 Devour up my discourse: which I observing,
Took once a pliant[41] hour, and found good means
To draw from her a prayer of earnest heart

◄ *Whom does
Othello wish to speak
on his behalf?*

42. **dilate.** Tell at length
43. **by parcels.** In pieces
44. **intentively.** Attentively; with full attention
45. **passing.** Exceptionally; surpassingly
46. **she wish'd . . . heaven had made her such a man.** Some critics have taken this to mean that Desdemona wished she herself had been born a man, and had the adventures Othello had. Or, it could simply mean that she wished she had a man like Othello.
47. **hitherto.** Until now

words for everyday use

pil • gri • mage (pil´ grə mij) n., long journey, often made for religious purposes. *Many Muslims, at some time in their lives, make a pilgrimage to the holy site of Mecca.*

That I would all my <u>pilgrimage</u> dilate,[42]
Whereof by parcels[43] she had something heard,
155　But not intentively:[44] I did consent,
And often did beguile her of her tears,
When I did speak of some distressful stroke
That my youth suffer'd. My story being done,
She gave me for my pains a world of sighs:
She swore, in faith, 'twas strange, 'twas passing[45]
160　　strange,
'Twas pitiful, 'twas wondrous pitiful:
She wish'd she had not heard it, yet she wish'd
That heaven had made her such a man:[46] she
　　thank'd me,
And bade me, if I had a friend that loved her,
165　I should but teach him how to tell my story.
And that would woo her. Upon this hint I spake:
She loved me for the dangers I had pass'd,
And I loved her that she did pity them.
This only is the witchcraft I have used:
170　Here comes the lady; let her witness it.

Enter DESDEMONA, IAGO, *and* ATTENDANTS.

DUKE OF VENICE. I think this tale would win my
　　daughter too.
Good Brabantio,
Take up this mangled matter at the best:
Men do their broken weapons rather use
Than their bare hands.

175　BRABANTIO.　　　　　　I pray you, hear her speak:
If she confess that she was half the wooer,
Destruction on my head, if my bad blame
Light on the man! Come hither, gentle mistress:
Do you perceive in all this noble company
Where most you owe obedience?

180　DESDEMONA.　　　　　　　My noble father,
I do perceive here a divided duty:
To you I am bound for life and education;
My life and education both do learn me
How to respect you; you are the lord of duty;
185　I am hitherto[47] your daughter: but here's my husband,
And so much duty as my mother show'd
To you, preferring you before her father,
So much I challenge that I may profess
Due to the Moor my lord.

BRABANTIO.　　　　　　God be wi' you! I have done.

◀ What hint did
Desdemona give
Othello?

◀ Why, according
to Othello, did
Desdemona fall in
love with him, and
he with her?

◀ Whom does
Desdemona say she
must obey?

48. **get it.** Beget it. In other words, Brabantio wishes he had adopted a child instead of having one of his own.

49. **clogs.** Blocks of wood hung on criminals to keep them from escaping

50. **lay a sentence.** Repeat a saying, or proverb

51. **grise.** Step

52. **Patience . . . makes.** If you bear your injury with patience, you take away its power to hurt you.

53. **bootless.** Vain; pointless

54. **us beguile.** Steal from us

55. **he bears . . . poor patience borrow.** The proverb sounds good to a person who is in a position to be comforted by it; but for one like myself, who is in the midst of grief, it doesn't help. (In other words, he is telling the Duke, "That's easy for you to say.")

56. **These sentences . . . equivocal.** These proverbs are just about as irritating as they are comforting. *Equivocal* here means "equal."

57. **I never yet . . . ear.** Words have no power to hurt (or heal) a person's heart. *Pierced* is sometimes read as *pieced,* in the sense of "to mend, to piece together."

58. **fortitude.** Military fortifications

59. **substitute.** Referring to Montano, the governor of Cyprus

60. **opinion . . . more safer voice on you.** The general opinion is that you, Othello, would be the safer choice. (In other words, Othello will take Montano's place as governor and defender of Cyprus.)

61. **slubber.** Sully; ruin

62. **thrice-driven.** Sifted through three times, to leave only the softest feathers

63. **agnise.** Acknowledge

---

words for everyday use   tyr • an • ny (tir´ ə nē) *n.,* state of being a tyrant, a ruler who exercises absolute power brutally and oppressively. *The tyranny of the dictator was intolerable, and many citizens tried to flee.*

190 Please it your grace, on to the state-affairs:
I had rather to adopt a child than get it.[48]
Come hither, Moor:
I here do give thee that with all my heart
Which, but thou hast already, with all my heart
195 I would keep from thee. For your sake, jewel,
I am glad at soul I have no other child:
For thy escape would teach me tyranny,
To hang clogs[49] on them. I have done, my lord.

DUKE OF VENICE. Let me speak like yourself, and lay
 a sentence,[50]
200 Which, as a grise[51] or step, may help these lovers
Into your favor.
When remedies are past, the griefs are ended
By seeing the worst, which late on hopes depended.
To mourn a mischief that is past and gone
205 Is the next way to draw new mischief on.
What cannot be preserved when fortune takes
Patience her injury a mockery makes.[52]
The robb'd that smiles steals something from the
 thief;
He robs himself that spends a bootless[53] grief.

◀ What advice does the Duke give Brabantio? Does Brabantio appreciate the advice?

210 BRABANTIO. So let the Turk of Cyprus us beguile;[54]
We lose it not, so long as we can smile.
He bears the sentence well that nothing bears
But the free comfort which from thence he hears,
But he bears both the sentence and the sorrow
215 That, to pay grief, must of poor patience borrow.[55]
These sentences, to sugar, or to gall,
Being strong on both sides, are equivocal:[56]
But words are words; I never yet did hear
That the bruised heart was pierced through the ear.[57]
220 I humbly beseech you, proceed to the affairs of state.

DUKE OF VENICE. The Turk with a most mighty
preparation makes for Cyprus. Othello, the
fortitude[58] of the place is best known to you; and
though we have there a substitute[59] of most allowed
225 sufficiency, yet opinion, a sovereign mistress of
effects, throws a more safer voice on you:[60] you
must therefore be content to slubber[61] the gloss of
your new fortunes with this more stubborn and
boisterous expedition.

◀ What expedition must Othello undertake?

230 OTHELLO. The tyrant custom, most grave senators,
Hath made the flinty and steel couch of war
My thrice-driven[62] bed of down: I do agnise[63]

64. **natural . . . hardness.** I have a natural willingness to endure hardness, or hardship [but my wife does not].

65. **fit disposition.** Suitable accommodations

66. **reference of place and exhibition.** Place to stay and an allowance of money

67. **besort . . . breeding.** Suitable company for someone of her breeding, or status

68. **To my unfolding lend your prosperous ear.** Lend a sympathetic ear to what I am about to say.

69. **charter . . . assist my simpleness.** Do me the honor of speaking for me, as I am simple, or unskilled, at stating my case.

70. **My downright violence and storm of fortunes.** My aggressive action in taking my fortune by storm

71. **my heart's subdued / Even to the very quality of my lord.** My heart is in perfect agreement with every quality of my husband.

72. **I saw . . . in his mind.** I saw Othello's beauty in his mind, not in his face.

73. **parts.** Qualities

74. **moth of peace.** An idle creature who feeds off peace without having worked for it.

75. **Vouch.** Swear

76. **Nor to comply with heat . . . defunct.** Not because I want to fulfill my lust—since I'm too old now to have those youthful urges

77. **But . . . bounteous to her mind.** But because I want to be generous to Desdemona's wishes

78. **scant.** Neglect

79. **when light-wing'd toys . . . instruments.** When love and lust get in the way of my senses

80. **disports.** Sports or frolics

words for everyday use

a • lac • ri • ty (ə lak´ rət ē) *n.,* promptness; cheerful readiness. *The plumber responded with alacrity when I called to report a flood in my basement.*

con • se • crate (kän´ sək rāt´) *vt.,* dedicate, as to a sacred purpose. *A portion of land outside the village was consecrated for use as a Catholic cemetery.*

be • reft (bi reft´) *adj.,* deprived or robbed (usually used with *of*). *A terrible accident left the children bereft of their parents.*

in • ter • im (int´ ə rəm) *n.,* intervening time; time in between. *During the interim between semesters, Sandra took a part-time job.*

A natural and prompt <u>alacrity</u>
I find in hardness,[64] and do undertake
235 These present wars against the Ottomites.
Most humbly therefore bending to your state,
I crave fit disposition[65] for my wife.
Due reference of place and exhibition,[66]
With such accommodation and besort
As levels with her breeding.[67]

240 **DUKE OF VENICE.**   If you please,
Be't at her father's.

BRABANTIO.   I'll not have it so.

OTHELLO. Nor I.

DESDEMONA.   Nor I; I would not there reside,
To put my father in impatient thoughts
By being in his eye. Most gracious duke,
245 To my unfolding lend your prosperous ear;[68]
And let me find a charter in your voice,
To assist my simpleness.[69]

DUKE OF VENICE. What would you, Desdemona?

DESDEMONA. That I did love the Moor to live with
        him,
250 My downright violence and storm of fortunes[70]
May trumpet to the world: my heart's subdued
Even to the very quality of my lord:[71]
I saw Othello's visage in his mind,[72]
And to his honor and his valiant parts[73]
255 Did I my soul and fortunes <u>consecrate</u>.
So that, dear lords, if I be left behind,
A moth of peace,[74] and he go to the war,
The rites for which I love him are <u>bereft</u> me,
And I a heavy <u>interim</u> shall support
260 By his dear absence. Let me go with him.

OTHELLO. Let her have your voices.
Vouch[75] with me, heaven, I therefore beg it not
To please the palate of my appetite,
Nor to comply with heat—the young affects
265 In me defunct[76]—and proper satisfaction;
But to be free and bounteous to her mind:[77]
And heaven defend your good souls, that you think
I will your serious and great business scant[78]
For she is with me: no, when light-wing'd toys
270 Of feather'd Cupid seal with wanton dullness
My speculative and officed instruments,[79]
That my disports[80] corrupt and taint my business,

◀ *What does
Desdemona ask of
the Duke?*

81. **helm.** Helmet
82. **indign and base adversities.** Unworthy and evil opponents
83. **Make head against my estimation.** Raise an armed force against my reputation
84. **commission.** Assignment
85. **import.** Concern
86. **ancient.** Iago
87. **To his conveyance . . . wife.** Iago will take care of conveying, or bringing, Desdemona to Cyprus.
88. **If virtue no delighted beauty lack.** If virtue can be said to have beauty
89. **My life upon her faith!** I'd bet my life on her faithfulness.
90. **prithee.** Pray thee
91. **we must obey the time.** We must hurry, as we have not much time.

Let housewives make a skillet of my helm,[81]
And all indign and base adversities[82]
275 Make head against my estimation![83]

DUKE OF VENICE. Be it as you shall privately
        determine,
Either for her stay or going: the affair cries haste,
And speed must answer it.

FIRST SENATOR.   You must away to-night.

DESDEMONA. To-night, my lord?

DUKE OF VENICE.   This night.

OTHELLO.   With all my heart.

DUKE OF VENICE. At nine i' the morning here we'll
280   meet again.
Othello, leave some officer behind,
And he shall our commission[84] bring to you;
With such things else of quality and respect
As doth import[85] you.

OTHELLO.   So please your grace, my ancient;[86]
285 A man he is of honest and trust:
To his conveyance I assign my wife,[87]
With what else needful your good grace shall think
To be sent after me.

DUKE OF VENICE.   Let it be so.
Good night to every one.

[*To* BRABANTIO]

                    And, noble signior,
290 If virtue no delighted beauty lack,[88]
Your son-in-law is far more fair than black.

FIRST SENATOR. Adieu, brave Moor, use Desdemona
        well.

BRABANTIO. Look to her, Moor, if thou hast eyes to see:
She has deceived her father, and may thee.

        Exeunt DUKE OF VENICE, SENATORS, OFFICERS, *etc*.

295 OTHELLO. My life upon her faith![89] Honest Iago,
My Desdemona must I leave to thee:
I prithee,[90] let thy wife attend on her:
And bring them after in the best advantage.
Come, Desdemona: I have but an hour
300 Of love, of worldly matters and direction,
To spend with thee: we must obey the time.[91]

        Exeunt OTHELLO *and* DESDEMONA.

◄ *Who will escort
Desdemona to
Cyprus? What does
Othello say about
this man?*

◄ *What ominous
warning does
Brabantio give
Othello?*

92. **incontinently.** At once
93. **Ere.** Before
94. **guinea-hen.** Slang term for a woman of loose character
95. **fond.** Foolish or overly sentimental
96. **virtue.** Nature
97. **'tis in ourselves . . . thus.** We have the power to determine what kind of people we will be.
98. **hyssop.** A fragrant herb
99. **gender.** Kind
100. **manured with industry.** Fertilized with hard work
101. **corrigible authority.** Ability to correct, or mend, our faults
102. **unbitted.** Uncoiled
103. **sect or scion.** Type or offshoot. Iago sees love as merely an offshoot of lust.
104. **knit to thy deserving.** Devoted to your cause
105. **perdurable.** Extremely durable
106. **stead thee.** Assist you
107. **defeat thy favor.** Spoil your looks, or, hide your appearance
108. **usurped beard.** A beard that you have no right to wear [possibly referring to the fact that Roderigo is too young to wear a beard]. *Usurped* means "taken without any right."

RODERIGO. Iago,—

IAGO. What say'st thou, noble heart?

RODERIGO. What will I do, thinkest thou?

305 IAGO. Why, go to bed, and sleep.

RODERIGO. I will incontinently[92] drown myself.

◄ What does Roderigo say he will do?

IAGO. If thou dost, I shall never love thee after. Why, thou silly gentleman!

RODERIGO. It is silliness to live when to live is
310 torment; and then have we a prescription to die when death is our physician.

IAGO. O villainous! I have looked upon the world for four times seven years; and since I could distinguish betwixt a benefit and an injury, I never found man
315 that knew how to love himself. Ere[93] I would say, I would drown myself for the love of a guinea-hen,[94] I would change my humanity with a baboon.

RODERIGO. What should I do? I confess it is my shame to be so fond;[95] but it is not in my virtue[96] to
320 amend it.

IAGO. Virtue! a fig! 'tis in ourselves that we are thus or thus.[97] Our bodies are our gardens, to the which our wills are gardeners: so that if we will plant nettles, or sow lettuce, set hyssop[98] and weed up
325 thyme, supply it with one gender[99] of herbs, or distract it with many, either to have it sterile with idleness, or manured with industry,[100] why, the power and corrigible authority[101] of this lies in our wills. If the balance of our lives had not one scale of
330 reason to poise another of sensuality, the blood and baseness of our natures would conduct us to most preposterous conclusions. But we have reason to cool our raging motions, our carnal stings, our unbitted[102] lusts, whereof I take this that you call
335 love to be a sect or scion.[103]

◄ What does Iago believe is more powerful: willpower and reason, or emotion and sentiment? What is his opinion of love?

RODERIGO. It cannot be.

IAGO. It is merely a lust of the blood and a permission of the will. Come, be a man. Drown thyself! drown cats and blind puppies. I have professed me thy friend
340 and I confess me knit to thy deserving[104] with cables of perdurable[105] toughness; I could never better stead thee[106] than now. Put money in thy purse; follow thou the wars; defeat thy favor[107] with an usurped beard;[108] I say, put money in thy purse. It cannot be

◄ What does Iago say Roderigo must do?

109. **answerable sequestration.** A separation that is equally rapid (*violent* here means "sudden")

110. **locusts.** The sweet pods of the carob tree

111. **coloquintida.** A bitter fruit used to provoke vomiting

112. **erring barbarian.** Wandering barbarian (referring to Othello). *Barbarian,* meaning "uncivilized person," originated as a term for the people of Barbary, a region in North Africa.

113. **supersubtle.** Super-refined or civilized (referring to Desdemona)

114. **clean out of the way.** Completely out of the question

115. **fast.** True

116. **hearted.** Whole-hearted; deeply felt

117. **be conjunctive.** Work together

118. **cuckold.** Make Othello a cuckold by sleeping with his wife. A cuckold is a man whose lover has cheated on him.

119. **Traverse!** Go forward!

120. **betimes.** At an early hour; or, soon

345   that Desdemona should long continue her love to the
      Moor,—put money in thy purse,—nor he his to her: it
      was a violent <u>commencement</u>, and thou shalt see an
      answerable sequestration:[109]—put but money in thy
      purse. These Moors are changeable in their wills: fill
350   thy purse with money:—the food that to him now is
      as luscious as locusts,[110] shall be to him shortly as
      bitter as coloquintida.[111] She must change for youth:
      when she is sated with his body, she will find the
      error of her choice: she must have change, she must:
355   therefore put money in thy purse. If thou wilt needs
      damn thyself, do it a more delicate way than
      drowning. Make all the money thou canst: if
      <u>sanctimony</u> and a frail vow betwixt an erring
      barbarian[112] and a supersubtle[113] Venetian be not too
360   hard for my wits and all the tribe of hell, thou shalt
      enjoy her; therefore make money. A pox of drowning
      thyself! it is clean out of the way:[114] seek thou rather
      to be hanged in compassing thy joy than to be
      drowned and go without her.

◀ Why, according to Iago, is Othello's marriage destined to fail?

365   RODERIGO. Wilt thou be fast[115] to my hopes, if I
      depend on the issue?

      IAGO. Thou art sure of me:—go, make money:—I
      have told thee often, and I re-tell thee again and
      again, I hate the Moor: my cause is hearted;[116] thine
370   hath no less reason. Let us be conjunctive[117] in our
      revenge against him: if thou canst cuckold[118] him,
      thou dost thyself a pleasure, me a sport. There are
      many events in the womb of time which will be
      delivered. Traverse![119] go, provide thy money. We
375   will have more of this to-morrow. Adieu.

      RODERIGO. Where shall we meet i' the morning?

      IAGO. At my lodging.

      RODERIGO. I'll be with thee betimes.[120]

      IAGO. Go to; farewell. Do you hear, Roderigo?

380   RODERIGO. What say you?

      IAGO. No more of drowning, do you hear?

      RODERIGO. I am changed.

      IAGO. Go to; farewell. Put money enough in your
      purse.

385   RODERIGO. I'll go sell all my land.

                                              Exit.

◀ What will Roderigo do in order to "put money in his purse"?

121. **snipe.** A silly or contemptible person
122. **'twixt my sheets / He has done my office.** He has slept with my wife.
123. **He holds me well.** Othello holds me in high esteem.
124. **proper.** Handsome
125. **plume up my will.** Gratify my ego
126. **knavery.** Mischief; mean-spirited actions
127. **He hath . . . framed to make women false.** A man like Cassio, who is good looking and charming, is made to tempt women into infidelity.
128. **free.** Frank; honest

words for everyday use

en • gen • der (in jen´ dər) vt., bring into being. *The book engendered a flurry of controversy.*

IAGO. Thus do I ever make my fool my purse:
For I mine own gain'd knowledge should profane,
If I would time expend with such a snipe[121]
But for my sport and profit. I hate the Moor:
390 And it is thought abroad, that 'twixt my sheets
He has done my office:[122] I know not if't be true;
But I, for mere suspicion in that kind,
Will do as if for surety. He holds me well;[123]
The better shall my purpose work on him.
395 Cassio's a proper[124] man: let me see now:

◀ How will Iago use Cassio in his plot to get revenge on Othello?

To get his place and to plume up my will[125]
In double knavery[126]—How, how? Let's see:—
After some time, to abuse Othello's ear
That he is too familiar with his wife.
400 He hath a person and a smooth dispose
To be suspected, framed to make women false.[127]
The Moor is of a free[128] and open nature,

◀ What does Iago say of Othello's nature? What can Iago do because of it?

That thinks men honest that but seem to be so,
And will as tenderly be led by the nose
405 As asses are.
I have't. It is <u>engender'd</u>. Hell and night
Must bring this monstrous birth to the world's light.

Exit.

Respond to the Selection

Othello and Desdemona's marriage undergoes a serious challenge in act I. From what you have read so far, what do you think of their relationship? Is it solid, or, as Iago thinks, likely to fail?

Investigate, Inquire, and Imagine

Recall: GATHERING FACTS

1a. What incident has Roderigo upset at the beginning of the play, and why?

2a. What reasons does Iago give for hating Othello?

3a. Why does the Duke send for Othello? How does the Duke resolve the dispute between Brabantio and Othello?

Interpret: FINDING MEANING

➤ 1b. What is Roderigo's relationship with Iago? Is Iago a true friend to him? Explain.

➤ 2b. How does Iago plan to get revenge on Othello? What specifically does he hope to gain through his "monstrous" plot?

➤ 3b. How is Othello regarded by the Duke and the other authorities in Venice? How can you tell?

Analyze: TAKING THINGS APART

4a. In scene i, Othello is never referred to by name. What terms are used to refer to him? Of what does Brabantio accuse him in scene ii? What picture of Othello is created by these references?

Synthesize: BRINGING THINGS TOGETHER

➤ 4b. What impression do you get of Othello when he appears in scene ii? How does the picture of Othello from Iago, Roderigo, and Brabantio's point of view compare to what Othello is really like? Are any of these characters racists?

Evaluate: MAKING JUDGMENTS

5a. What kind of a person is Iago? Does he have any real motive for hating Othello, or is he simply an evil and malicious person? Cite evidence from the text—his own words and his actions—to support your answer.

Extend: CONNECTING IDEAS

➤ 5b. Much has been written about the character of Iago. Some critics say that he is not a believable character, as he seems too transparently evil— almost a caricature of a villain. Do you agree? Do you believe that there are people who are truly pure evil, who have no conscience? How else might you explain the character of Iago?

Understanding Literature

CENTRAL CONFLICT AND INCITING INCIDENT. A **central conflict** is the primary struggle dealt with in the plot of a story or drama. The **inciting incident** is the event that introduces the central conflict. What central conflict is introduced in act I of Othello? What incident introduces this conflict?

CHARACTERIZATION. **Characterization** is the use of literary techniques to create a character. In creating a character, a playwright may use the following techniques: showing what characters themselves say, do, and think; showing what other characters say about him or her; and showing, through stage directions or other references, what physical features, dress, and personality the characters display. What do you learn about *Othello* through his words and actions in act I? What does he say about himself? What do others say about him?

MOTIF. A **motif** is any element that recurs in one or more works of literature or art. One of the motifs running throughout *Othello* is the imagery of animals. What animal images can you find in act I? To whom do they refer? Another motif is the imagery of of light and dark. What images can you find of light and dark, or black and white? What do darkness and the color black signify? What do light and the color white stand for?

ACT II, SCENE i

1. **highwrought flood.** Stirred-up or agitated sea
2. **main.** The sea (any large body of salt water)
3. **ruffian'd.** Raged; stormed
4. **hold the mortise.** Hold its joints together (A *mortise* is the place where two pieces of wood are joined together, as on a ship or building.)
5. **segregation.** Scattering
6. **chidden billow.** The storm-battered sea (*Chidden* actually means "scolded"; we can imagine that the sea was being scolded by the storm.)
7. **mane.** The water could have been spurting up to look like a lion's mane; or, this word could have actually been *main*, meaning "power."
8. **burning bear.** Refers either to the constellation *Ursa major* (the Great Bear, also known as the Big Dipper) or to *Ursa minor* (Little Bear or Little Dipper)
9. **guards . . . pole.** Stars in *Ursa minor* that line up with the North Star (or Pole Star)
10. **enchafed.** Enraged
11. **tempest.** Storm
12. **their designment halts.** Their plans are put to a stop.
13. **Veronesa.** From the city of Verona. The ship may have been built in Verona and sold to the Venetians. Or, it could be that Shakespeare made a mistake here, accidentally calling Cassio a Veronese instead of a Florentine.
14. **in full commission.** With full authority

words for everyday use

quay (kē´) *n.,* structure built as a landing place along water. *The fishing boat docked at the quay to unload two tons of fish.*

cape (kāp´) *n.,* land formation that juts out into the water as a point or a peninsula. *Our family took a trip to Cape Cod in Massachusetts.*

dis • cern (dis ərn´, diz ərn´) *vt.,* detect with the eyes. *Looking through the microscope at the tissue sample, I could discern the outlines of cells.*

des • cry (diz skrī´) *vt.,* catch sight of. *The hiker descried the outline of a person coming toward her in the fog.*

pelt (pelt´) *v.,* strike with blows or with thrown objects; beat or dash repeatedly against. *The angry child pelted the ground with her fists.*

griev • ous (grē´ vəs) *adj.,* serious; characterized by severe pain, suffering, or sorrow. *The criminal had inflicted grievous wrongs on his victims, yet he felt no remorse.*

ACT II

An open place near the quay.

of this scene? What is
happening out at
sea?

Enter MONTANO *and two* GENTLEMEN.

MONTANO. What from the cape can you discern at
    sea?

FIRST GENTLEMAN. Nothing at all: it is a highwrought
    flood.[1]
I cannot, 'twixt the heaven and the main,[2]
Descry a sail.

MONTANO. Methinks the wind hath spoke aloud at
5   land;
A fuller blast ne'er shook our battlements.
If it hath ruffian'd[3] so upon the sea,
What ribs of oak, when mountains melt on them,
Can hold the mortise?[4] What shall we hear of this?

SECOND GENTLEMAN. A segregation[5] of the Turkish
10   fleet:
For do but stand upon the foaming shore,
The chidden billow[6] seems to pelt the clouds;
The wind-shaked surge, with high and monstrous
    mane,[7]
Seems to cast water on the burning bear,[8]
15 And quench the guards of the ever-fixed pole:[9]
I never did like molestation view
On the enchafed[10] flood.

MONTANO.   If that the Turkish fleet
Be not enshelter'd and embay'd, they are drown'd:
It is impossible they bear it out.

Enter a third GENTLEMAN.

20 THIRD GENTLEMAN. News, lads! our wars are done.
The desperate tempest[11] hath so bang'd the Turks,
That their designment halts.[12] A noble ship of Venice
Hath seen a grievous wreck and sufferance
On most part of their fleet.

happened to the
Turkish fleet? Where
is Othello?

MONTANO. How! is this true?

25 THIRD GENTLEMAN.   The ship is here put in,
A Veronesa;[13] Michael Cassio,
Lieutenant to the warlike Moor Othello,
Is come on shore: the Moor himself at sea,
And is in full commission[14] here for Cyprus.

15. **governor.** Commander of a ship [speaking of Othello]

16. **till we make the main and the aerial blue / An indistinct regard.** Until we can no longer tell the difference between the sea and the sky.

17. **His bark is stoutly timber'd.** His ship is made of strong timbers.

18. **pilot.** One who steers the ship

19. **my hopes . . . bold cure.** My hopes, not overindulged, have a good chance of being fulfilled.

20. **brow.** Edge

21. **My hopes . . . governor.** I hope that is Othello's ship.

22. **shot of courtesy.** The ship fired a cannon shot as a signal to the citadel, indicating that it is a Venetian ship, not an enemy ship.

30   MONTANO. I am glad on't; 'tis a worthy governor.[15]

    THIRD GENTLEMAN. But this same Cassio, though he
      speak of comfort
    Touching the Turkish loss, yet he looks sadly,
    And prays the Moor be safe; for they were parted
    With foul and violent tempest.

    MONTANO.   Pray heavens he be;
35 For I have served him, and the man commands
    Like a full soldier. Let's to the seaside, ho!
    As well to see the vessel that's come in
    As to throw out our eyes for brave Othello,
    Even till we make the main and the aerial blue
    An indistinct regard.[16]

◄ *What does
Montano think of
Othello?*

40 THIRD GENTLEMAN.   Come, let's do so:
    For every minute is expectancy
    Of more arrivance.

    Enter CASSIO.

    CASSIO. Thanks, you the valiant of this warlike isle,
    That so approve the Moor! O, let the heavens
45 Give him defense against the elements,
    For I have lost us him on a dangerous sea.

    MONTANO. Is he well shipp'd?

    CASSIO. His bark is stoutly timber'd,[17] his pilot[18]
    Of very expert and approved allowance;
50 Therefore my hopes, not surfeited to death,
    Stand in bold cure.[19]

    A cry within: "A sail, a sail, a sail!"
    Enter a fourth GENTLEMAN.

    CASSIO. What noise?

    FOURTH GENTLEMAN. The town is empty; on the
      brow[20] o' the sea
    Stand ranks of people, and they cry "A sail!"

55 CASSIO. My hopes do shape him for the governor.[21]

    Guns heard.

    SECOND GENTLEMEN. They do discharge their shot of
      courtesy:[22]
    Our friends at least.

    CASSIO.   I pray you, sir, go forth,
    And give us truth who 'tis that is arrived.

    SECOND GENTLEMAN. I shall.

                           Exit.

23. **wived.** Married
24. **paragons description.** Surpasses all description
25. **quirks.** Inventive quips or clever phrases
26. **blazoning.** Proclaiming
27. **in the essential vesture . . . ingener.** Desdemona is so beautifully clothed, or endowed, with virtue by her creator that describing her adequately would exhaust anyone who tried. (*Ingener*, an old spelling of *engineer*, here means an "author.")
28. **put in.** Come into harbor
29. **H'as.** He has
30. **gutter'd.** Jagged
31. **congregated.** Massed together, as in a sandbar
32. **Traitors . . . keel.** The rocks and sands are traitors submerged in the water to hinder or obstruct the innocent ships. (The *keel* of a ship is the central ridge that runs along the bottom of the hull.)
33. **omit / Their mortal natures.** Abandon their deadly ways
34. **footing.** Landing
35. **anticipates . . . se'nnight's speed.** A week (seven nights) ahead of time
36. **Jove.** Another name for Jupiter, the king of the Roman gods, equivalent to Zeus in Greek mythology
37. **extincted.** Extinguished
38. **let her have your knees.** Kneel to her.
39. **Enwheel.** Encircle
40. **How lost you company?** How did you come to be separated from Othello?

MONTANO. But, good lieutenant, is your general
60 wived?[23]

CASSIO. Most fortunately: he hath achieved a maid
That paragons description[24] and wild fame;
One that excels the quirks[25] of blazoning[26] pens,
And in the essential vesture of creation
Does tire the ingener.[27]

Re-enter second GENTLEMAN.

65   How now! who has put in?[28]

SECOND GENTLEMAN. 'Tis one Iago, ancient to the
general.

CASSIO. H'as[29] had most favourable and happy speed:
Tempests themselves, high seas, and howling winds,
The gutter'd[30] rocks and congregated[31] sands—
70 Traitors ensteep'd to clog the guiltless keel,[32]—
As having sense of beauty, do omit
Their mortal natures,[33] letting go safely by
The divine Desdemona.

MONTANO.   What is she?

CASSIO. She that I spake of, our great captain's
captain,
75 Left in the conduct of the bold Iago,
Whose footing[34] here anticipates our thoughts
A se'nnight's speed.[35] Great Jove,[36] Othello guard,
And swell his sail with thine own powerful breath,
That he may bless this bay with his tall ship,
80 Make love's quick pants in Desdemona's arms,
Give renew'd fire to our extincted[37] spirits
And bring all Cyprus comfort!

Enter DESDEMONA, EMILIA, IAGO, RODERIGO, *and*
ATTENDANTS.

                              O, behold,
The riches of the ship is come on shore!
Ye men of Cyprus, let her have your knees.[38]
85 Hail to thee, lady! and the grace of heaven,
Before, behind thee, and on every hand,
Enwheel[39] thee round!

DESDEMONA.   I thank you, valiant Cassio.
What tidings can you tell me of my lord?

CASSIO. He is not yet arrived: nor know I aught
90 But that he's well and will be shortly here.

DESDEMONA. O, but I fear—How lost you company?[40]

◀ What does Cassio
think of Desdemona?

◀ Who has just
arrived with
Desdemona? How
does Cassio greet
Desdemona?

41. **contention of the sea and skies.** Quarrel of the sea and sky; storm
42. **a friend.** That is, not an enemy ship
43. **extend my manners.** Greet your wife with a kiss. (This was a customary greeting.)
44. **she has no speech.** She doesn't talk back (or talk too much).
45. **list.** Desire
46. **before your ladyship.** When you, Desdemona, are present
47. **with thinking.** Without words
48. **Bells.** That is, always making lots of noise, with tongues moving like the clapper of a bell
49. **Saints in your injuries.** Delivering insults in a holier-than-thou manner
50. **housewives.** Hussies

words for everyday use

cit • a • del (sit´ ə del, sit´ əd əl) *n.,* fortress that commands a city; or, a fortified part of a city. *The Acropolis is an ancient citadel in Athens, Greece.*

chide (chīd´) *vt.,* scold or voice disapproval. *I chided myself for the silly error.*

CASSIO. The great contention of the sea and skies[41]
Parted our fellowship—But, hark! a sail.

Within: "A sail, a sail!" *Guns heard.*

SECOND GENTLEMAN. They give their greeting to the
    <u>citadel</u>;
This likewise is a friend.[42]

95 CASSIO.   See for the news.

                       Exit GENTLEMAN.

Good ancient, you are welcome.

To EMILIA.

                     Welcome, mistress.
Let it not gall your patience, good Iago,
That I extend my manners;[43] 'tis my breeding
That gives me this bold show of courtesy.

Kissing her.

How does Cassio greet Emilia?

100 IAGO. Sir, would she give you so much of her lips
As of her tongue she oft bestows on me,
You'll have enough.

DESDEMONA.   Alas, she has no speech.[44]

IAGO. In faith, too much;
I find it still, when I have list[45] to sleep:
105 Marry, before your ladyship,[46] I grant,
She puts her tongue a little in her heart,
And <u>chides</u> with thinking.[47]

EMILIA. You have little cause to say so.

IAGO. Come on, come on; you are pictures out of
    doors,
110 Bells[48] in your parlors, wild-cats in your kitchens,
Saints in your injuries,[49] devils being offended,
Players in your housewifery, and housewives[50] in
    your beds.

What is Iago's opinion of women?

DESDEMONA. O, fie upon thee, slanderer!

IAGO. Nay, it is true, or else I am a Turk:
115 You rise to play and go to bed to work.

EMILIA. You shall not write my praise.

IAGO.   No, let me not.

DESDEMONA. What wouldst thou write of me, if thou
    shouldst praise me?

IAGO. O gentle lady, do not put me to't;
For I am nothing, if not critical.

51. **assay.** Try

52. **I do beguile / The thing I am.** I distract my anxious self

53. **invention / Comes from my pate as birdlime . . . from frize.** Ideas come from my head with as much difficulty as paste is removed from woolen cloth. *Pate:* head; *birdlime:* a sticky paste used to trap birds; *frize* or *frieze:* a coarse woolen cloth. Iago's ideas indeed are akin to birdlime—they are intended to entrap others.

54. **Muse.** In Greek mythology, one of the nine goddesses, daughters of Zeus and Mnemonsyne (Memory), who were said to inspire learning and the arts

55. **black.** Dark-haired or dark-complected; not black as in African

56. **white.** Here, a pun on *wight,* meaning "a person"

57. **folly help'd her to an heir.** Another play on words. *Folly* could mean either "foolishness" or "wantonness." Iago hints that wantonness, or lust, could help a fair woman win a rich husband.

58. **fond.** Silly

59. **thereunto.** In addition

60. **put on the vouch.** Win the approval

61. **Had tongue at will.** Could speak freely

62. **gay.** Showily or gaudily dressed

63. **Fled from her wish . . . "Now I may."** Denied herself something that she could have had free access to

64. **Bade her wrong stay.** Endured her pain [rather than avenge it]

65. **change . . . tail.** Exchange something good for something worthless. Possibly an old proverb that is no longer in use today.

66. **wight.** A person

words for everyday use

par • a • dox (par´ ə däks´) *n.,* seemingly contradictory statement or idea. *The statement "I never tell the truth" is a paradox.*

mal • ice (mal´ əs) *n.,* wickedness. *Although the child claimed that he had broken the toy accidentally, I sensed that he had done it out of malice.*

suit • or (sü´ tər) *n.,* one who courts a woman or seeks to marry her; also, anyone who petitions or entreats. *The popular girl had many suitors, but rejected them all because she was too busy to have a relationship.*

DESDEMONA. Come on, assay.[51] There's one gone to
120   the harbor?

IAGO. Ay, madam.

DESDEMONA. I am not merry; but I do beguile
The thing I am,[52] by seeming otherwise.
Come, how wouldst thou praise me?

125   **IAGO.** I am about it; but indeed my invention
Comes from my pate as birdlime does from frize;[53]
It plucks out brains and all: but my Muse[54] labors,
And thus she is deliver'd.
If she be fair and wise, fairness and wit,
130   The one's for use, the other useth it.

◀ What praise does Iago have for Desdemona? Why is it somewhat of a backhanded compliment?

DESDEMONA. Well praised! How if she be black[55] and
witty?

IAGO. If she be black, and thereto have a wit,
She'll find a white[56] that shall her blackness fit.

◀ Using the footnote, explain the pun on white and wight.

DESDEMONA. Worse and worse.

135   **EMILIA.** How if fair and foolish?

IAGO. She never yet was foolish that was fair;
For even her folly help'd her to an heir.[57]

DESDEMONA. These are old fond[58] paradoxes to make
fools laugh i' the alehouse. What miserable praise
140   hast thou for her that's foul and foolish?

IAGO. There's none so foul and foolish thereunto,[59]
But does foul pranks which fair and wise ones do.

◀ According to Iago, what do all women do, whether foul or fair, foolish or wise?

DESDEMONA. O heavy ignorance! thou praisest the
worst best. But what praise couldst thou bestow on a
145   deserving woman indeed, one that, in the authority
of her merit, did justly put on the vouch[60] of very
malice itself?

IAGO. She that was ever fair and never proud,
Had tongue at will[61] and yet was never loud,
150   Never lack'd gold and yet went never gay,[62]
Fled from her wish and yet said "Now I may,"[63]
She that being anger'd, her revenge being nigh,
Bade her wrong stay[64] and her displeasure fly,
She that in wisdom never was so frail
155   To change the cod's head for the salmon's tail;[65]
She that could think and ne'er disclose her mind,
See suitors following and not look behind,
She was a wight,[66] if ever such wight were,—

DESDEMONA. To do what?

67. **suckle fools . . . beer.** Raise children and keep petty household accounts
68. **liberal.** Here, it means too free with his words, lacking moral restraint.
69. **home.** Directly; bluntly
70. **well said.** Well done
71. **I will gyve thee in thine own courtship.** I will use your very courtly behavior as a means to entrap you. (A gyve was a shackle used on a prisoner's legs.)
72. **kissed your three fingers.** A gesture of admiration
73. **play the sir.** Behave in a courtly manner
74. **clyster-pipes.** Syringes
75. **Olympus-high.** As high as Mount Olympus, a mountain in Greece believed by the ancients to be the home of the gods
76. **Succeeds.** Follows

160 **IAGO.** To suckle fools and chronicle small beer.[67]

DESDEMONA. O most lame and impotent conclusion!
Do not learn of him, Emilia, though he be thy
husband. How say you, Cassio? Is he not a most
profane and liberal[68] counsellor?

165 **CASSIO.** He speaks home,[69] madam: You may relish
him more in the soldier than in the scholar.

IAGO. [*Aside*] He takes her by the palm: ay, well
said,[70] whisper: with as little a web as this will I
ensnare as great a fly as Cassio. Ay, smile upon her,
170 do; I will gyve thee in thine own courtship.[71] You
say true; 'tis so, indeed: if such tricks as these strip
you out of your lieutenantry, it had been better you
had not kissed your three fingers[72] so oft, which
now again you are most apt to play the sir[73] in. Very
175 good; well kissed! an excellent courtesy! 'tis so,
indeed. Yet again your fingers to your lips? Would
they were clyster-pipes[74] for your sake!

[*Trumpet within*]

The Moor! I know his trumpet.

CASSIO. 'Tis truly so.

180 **DESDEMONA.** Let's meet him and receive him.

CASSIO. Lo, where he comes!

Enter OTHELLO *and* ATTENDANTS.

OTHELLO. O my fair warrior!

DESDEMONA.   My dear Othello!

OTHELLO. It gives me wonder great as my content
To see you here before me. O my soul's joy!
185 If after every tempest come such calms,
May the winds blow till they have waken'd death!
And let the laboring bark climb hills of seas
Olympus-high[75] and duck again as low
As hell's from heaven! If it were now to die,
190 'Twere now to be most happy; for, I fear,
My soul hath her content so absolute
That not another comfort like to this
Succeeds[76] in unknown fate.

DESDEMONA.   The heavens forbid
But that our loves and comforts should increase,
Even as our days do grow!

◄ *What will Iago use to snare Cassio?*

◄ *What does Othello say he is likely never to have again? Why might these words be prophetic?*

77. **here.** In my heart
78. **set down the pegs.** Turn the pegs on a stringed instrument, so as to put it out of tune
79. **well desired.** Warmly welcomed
80. **prattle out of fashion.** Chatter on without regard to politeness
81. **coffers.** Trunks
82. **master.** The ship's captain
83. **challenge.** Demand
84. **presently.** Immediately
85. **base men.** Men of low birth
86. **list.** Listen to
87. **court of guard.** A group of soldiers stationed on guard or as sentinels. Cassio will be in charge of watching over this group.
88. **directly.** Completely
89. **thus.** On the lips (in other words, be silent)
90. **the devil.** Refers to Othello, as the devil was said to be black in color.
91. **favor.** Good looks
92. **conveniences.** Agreements; compatibilities

words for everyday use

dis • cord (dis´ kò[ə]rd) *n.*, lack of agreement or harmony. *Family discord tends to increase around the holidays.*

sa • ti • ety (sə tī´ ət ē) *n.*, state of being satisfied fully or to excess. *After the huge meal, the diners let out a groan of satiety.*

195   **OTHELLO.**   Amen to that, sweet powers!
       I cannot speak enough of this content;
       It stops me here;[77] it is too much of joy:
       And this, and this, the greatest <u>discords</u> be

       [*Kissing her*]

       That e'er our hearts shall make!

       IAGO. [*Aside*]   O, you are well tuned now!
200 But I'll set down the pegs[78] that make this music,
       As honest as I am.

       OTHELLO.   Come, let us to the castle.
       News, friends; our wars are done, the Turks are
          drown'd.
       How does my old acquaintance of this isle?
       Honey, you shall be well desired[79] in Cyprus;
205 I have found great love amongst them. O my sweet,
       I prattle out of fashion,[80] and I dote
       In mine own comforts. I prithee, good Iago,
       Go to the bay and disembark my coffers:[81]
       Bring thou the master[82] to the citadel;
210 He is a good one, and his worthiness
       Does challenge[83] much respect. Come, Desdemona,
       Once more, well met at Cyprus.

              Exeunt OTHELLO, DESDEMONA, *and* ATTENDANTS.

       IAGO. [*To an* ATTENDANT *as he goes out*] Do thou meet
       me presently[84] at the harbor. [*To* RODERIGO] Come
215 hither. If thou be'st valiant,—as, they say, base
       men[85] being in love have then a nobility in their
       natures more than is native to them—list[86] me. The
       lieutenant tonight watches on the court of
       guard:[87]—first, I must tell thee this—Desdemona is
220 directly[88] in love with him.

◀ What lie does Iago tell Roderigo?

       RODERIGO. With him! why, 'tis not possible.

       IAGO. Lay thy finger thus,[89] and let thy soul be
       instructed. Mark me with what violence she first
       loved the Moor, but for bragging and telling her
225 fantastical lies: and will she love him still for
       prating? let not thy discreet heart think it. Her eye
       must be fed; and what delight shall she have to look
       on the devil?[90] When the blood is made dull with
       the act of sport, there should be, again to inflame it
230 and to give <u>satiety</u> a fresh appetite, loveliness in
       favor,[91] sympathy in years, manners and beauties; all
       which the Moor is defective in: now, for want of
       these required conveniences,[92] her delicate

◀ According to Iago, why will Desdemona reject Othello? Whom does he claim will be Desdemona's second choice?

93. **heave the gorge.** Feel like vomiting
94. **pregnant.** Clear, obvious, convincing (as of an argument)
95. **no further conscionable . . . humane seeming.** Not really conscientious, or bound by his conscience, but rather just pretending to be civil and polite
96. **salt.** Lusty; lecherous (referring to Cassio's affections)
97. **slipper.** Slippery
98. **counterfeit advantages.** Invent opportunities
99. **green.** Young; inexperienced
100. **condition.** Character
101. **Lechery.** Overindulgence of lust
102. **index.** Table of contents (which, along with the prologue, forms the front matter of Iago's "history of lust")
103. **obscure.** Hidden; secret
104. **mutualities.** Exchanges
105. **hard at hand.** Soon
106. **incorporate.** Carnal; sexual
107. **tainting.** Discrediting
108. **minister.** Provide
109. **haply.** Likely

words for everyday use

em • i • nent (em´ ə nənt) *adj.*, prominent; standing out. *The eminent scientist was often called upon to make television appearances.*

vol • u • ble (väl´ yə bəl) *adj.*, marked by ease and fluency in speech; glib. *Kendra was as voluble as her sister was tongue-tied.*

pes • ti • lent (pes´ tə lənt) *adj.*, causing displeasure or annoyance; extremely disagreeable. *My pestilent neighbor spread foul rumors about me.*

cho • ler (kä´ lər) *n.*, anger, irateness. *Sara was even-tempered, whereas her brother was prone to fits of choler.*

pro • voke (prə vōk´) *vt.*, incite to anger. *The bullfighter provoked his opponent by waving his cape near the animal's nose.*

235 tenderness will find itself abused, begin to heave the
gorge,[93] disrelish and abhor the Moor; very nature
will instruct her in it and compel her to some
second choice. Now, sir, this granted,—as it is a most
pregnant[94] and unforced position—who stands so
eminent in the degree of this fortune as Cassio does?
240 a knave very voluble; no further conscionable than
in putting on the mere form of civil and humane
seeming,[95] for the better compassing of his salt[96]
and most hidden loose affection? why, none; why,
none: a slipper[97] and subtle knave, a finder of
245 occasions, that has an eye can stamp and counterfeit
advantages,[98] though true advantage never present
itself; a devilish knave. Besides, the knave is
handsome, young, and hath all those requisites in
him that folly and green[99] minds look after: a
250 pestilent complete knave; and the woman hath
found him already.

RODERIGO. I cannot believe that in her; she's full of
most blessed condition.[100]

◀ What does
Roderigo refuse to
believe about
Desdemona?

IAGO. Blessed fig's-end! the wine she drinks is made
255 of grapes: if she had been blessed, she would never
have loved the Moor. Blessed pudding! Didst thou
not see her paddle with the palm of his hand? didst
not mark that?

RODERIGO. Yes, that I did; but that was but courtesy.

260 IAGO. Lechery,[101] by this hand; an index[102] and
obscure[103] prologue to the history of lust and foul
thoughts. They met so near with their lips that their
breaths embraced together. Villanous thoughts,
Roderigo! when these mutualities[104] so marshal the
265 way, hard at hand[105] comes the master and main
exercise, the incorporate[106] conclusion, Pish! But, sir,
be you ruled by me: I have brought you from Venice.
Watch you to-night; for the command, I'll lay't
upon you. Cassio knows you not. I'll not be far from
270 you: do you find some occasion to anger Cassio,
either by speaking too loud, or tainting[107] his
discipline; or from what other course you please,
which the time shall more favorably minister.[108]

◀ What is the next
step in Iago's plan?

RODERIGO. Well.

275 IAGO. Sir, he is rash and very sudden in choler, and
haply[109] may strike at you: provoke him, that he
may; for even out of that will I cause these of Cyprus

110. **whose qualification . . . taste again.** Cyprus will not be appeased or brought back into a satisfactory state again.

111. **prefer.** Advance

112. **I warrant thee.** I guarantee you

113. **apt and of great credit.** Likely and credible

114. **howbeit.** Although

115. **peradventure.** Perhaps

116. **I stand accountant . . . sin.** I can be considered guilty of that sin, too (that is, he does lust after Desdemona).

117. **diet.** Feed

118. **leap'd into my seat.** Taken my place, i.e., slept with my wife

119. **inwards.** Innards

120. **this poor trash of Venice.** Roderigo

121. **trash.** In hunting, to *trash* meant to hold back a hound by means of a leash. Iago is holding Roderigo back until the moment is right to set him on Cassio.

122. **stand the putting on.** Respond to my inciting

123. **on the hip.** Where I want him (a wrestling term)

124. **in the rank garb.** In the worst way; using gross terms

125. **I fear Cassio . . . too.** I fear that Cassio has slept with my wife, too.

126. **practicing upon.** Plotting against

127. **Knavery's plain face . . . used.** Critic W. J. Rolfe reads the line thus: "The full design of knavery is never visible until the moment comes for its being put into practice."

words for everyday use

mu • ti • ny (myüt′ ə nē) *n.*, revolt against authority, esp. of a naval crew. *In the novel* Treasure Island, *the villain Long John Silver organizes a* mutiny *against the ship captain.*

im • ped • i • ment (im ped′ ə mənt) *n.*, obstacle; something that impedes. *One of the major* impediments *to our project was lack of sufficient funds.*

egre • gious • ly (i grē′ jəs lē) *adv.*, in a way that is obviously or conspicuously bad: glaringly. *Ryan knew he could never forgive his friend for having insulted him so* egregiously.

to <u>mutiny</u>; whose qualification shall come into no
true taste again[110] but by the displanting of Cassio.

280 So shall you have a shorter journey to your desires
by the means I shall then have to prefer[111] them;
and the <u>impediment</u> most profitably removed,
without the which there were no expectation of our
prosperity.

285 RODERIGO. I will do this, if I can bring it to any
opportunity.

IAGO. I warrant thee.[112] Meet me by and by at the
citadel: I must fetch his necessaries ashore. Farewell.

RODERIGO. Adieu.

Exit.

290 IAGO. That Cassio loves her, I do well believe it;
That she loves him, 'tis apt and of great credit:[113]
The Moor, howbeit[114] that I endure him not,
Is of a constant, loving, noble nature,
And I dare think he'll prove to Desdemona
295 A most dear husband. Now, I do love her too;
Not out of absolute lust, though peradventure[115]
I stand accountant for as great a sin,[116]
But partly led to diet[117] my revenge,
For that I do suspect the lusty Moor
300 Hath leap'd into my seat;[118] the thought whereof
Doth, like a poisonous mineral, gnaw my inwards;[119]
And nothing can or shall content my soul
Till I am even'd with him, wife for wife,
Or failing so, yet that I put the Moor
305 At least into a jealousy so strong
That judgment cannot cure. Which thing to do,
If this poor trash of Venice,[120] whom I trash[121]
For his quick hunting, stand the putting on,[122]
I'll have our Michael Cassio on the hip,[123]
310 Abuse him to the Moor in the rank garb[124]—
For I fear Cassio with my night-cap too[125]—
Make the Moor thank me, love me and reward me.
For making him <u>egregiously</u> an ass
And practicing upon[126] his peace and quiet
315 Even to madness. 'Tis here, but yet confused:
Knavery's plain face is never seen till used.[127]

Exit.

◄ *What is Iago's true opinion of Othello and his marriage to Desdemona? How does he really feel about Desdemona?*

◄ *What does Iago claim, again, as his reason for wanting revenge on Othello? How will he get his revenge?*

ACT II, SCENE ii
1. **mere perdition.** Absolute destruction
2. **addiction.** Inclination or desire
3. **offices.** The parts of a house devoted to household work and service, such as its kitchens, pantries, and cellars, as well as its laundry and stables. "All offices are open" essentially means, "We're ready to serve you."

ACT II, SCENE iii
1. **Not to outsport discretion.** So as not to overdo our sport, or take our partying too far
2. **cast.** Dismissed

SCENE ii: A street.

Enter a HERALD *with a proclamation;* PEOPLE *following.*

HERALD. It is Othello's pleasure, our noble and
valiant general, that, upon certain tidings now
arrived, importing the mere perdition[1] of the
Turkish fleet, every man put himself into triumph;
5 some to dance, some to make bonfires, each man to
what sport and revels his addiction[2] leads him: for,
besides these beneficial news, it is the celebration of
his <u>nuptial</u>. So much was his pleasure should be
proclaimed. All offices[3] are open, and there is full
10 liberty of feasting from this present hour of five till
the bell have told eleven. Heaven bless the isle of
Cyprus and our noble general Othello!

Exeunt.

◀ What two happy
occasions will be
celebrated at
tonight's feast?

SCENE iii: A hall in the castle.

Enter OTHELLO, DESDEMONA, CASSIO, *and* ATTENDANTS.

OTHELLO. Good Michael, look you to the guard to-
night:
Let's teach ourselves that honorable stop,
Not to outsport discretion.[1]

CASSIO. Iago hath direction what to do;
5 But, notwithstanding, with my personal eye
Will I look to't.

OTHELLO.   Iago is most honest.
Michael, good night: to-morrow with your earliest
Let me have speech with you.

[*To* DESDEMONA]

                    Come, my dear love,
The purchase made, the fruits are to ensue;
10 That profit's yet to come 'tween me and you.
Good night.

          Exeunt OTHELLO, DESDEMONA, *and* ATTENDANTS.

Enter IAGO.

CASSIO. Welcome, Iago; we must to the watch.

IAGO. Not this hour, lieutenant; 'tis not yet ten o'
the clock. Our general cast[2] us thus early for the love
15 of his Desdemona; who let us not therefore blame:
he hath not yet made wanton the night with her;
and she is sport for Jove.

◀ Read lines 14–28.
What suggestive
comments does Iago
make about
Desdemona? How does
Cassio respond to his
insinuating comments?

3. **sounds a parley of provocation.** Invites talk of love
4. **alarum.** Trumpet signal
5. **stoup.** A large jar or cask
6. **brace of Cyprus gallants.** A group of young men from Cyprus
7. **would fain.** Would be eager to
8. **a measure.** A drink
9. **craftily qualified.** Diluted, to make it less strong
10. **behold, what innovation it makes here.** Look what effect it has had on me already.
11. **it dislikes me.** I don't like it.
12. **To Desdemona . . . caroused.** Drunk to Desdemona's health
13. **Potations pottle-deep.** Alcoholic drinks by the pottle-full (a *pottle* being a drinking vessel holding about a half a gallon)
14. **swelling.** Prideful

CASSIO. She's a most exquisite lady.

IAGO. And, I'll warrant her, full of game.

20 CASSIO. Indeed, she's a most fresh and delicate creature.

IAGO. What an eye she has! Methinks it sounds a parley of provocation.[3]

CASSIO. An inviting eye; and yet methinks right
25 modest.

IAGO. And when she speaks, is it not an alarum[4] to love?

CASSIO. She is indeed perfection.

IAGO. Well, happiness to their sheets! Come,
30 lieutenant, I have a stoup[5] of wine; and here without are a brace of Cyprus gallants[6] that would fain[7] have a measure[8] to the health of black Othello.

CASSIO. Not to-night, good Iago: I have very poor and unhappy brains for drinking: I could well wish
35 courtesy would invent some other custom of entertainment.

◄ Why does Cassio hesitate to join Iago and the others for drinks?

IAGO. O, they are our friends; but one cup: I'll drink for you.

CASSIO. I have drunk but one cup to-night, and that
40 was craftily qualified[9] too, and, behold, what innovation it makes here:[10] I am unfortunate in the infirmity, and dare not task my weakness with any more.

IAGO. What, man! 'tis a night of revels: the gallants
45 desire it.

CASSIO. Where are they?

IAGO. Here at the door; I pray you, call them in.

CASSIO. I'll do't; but it dislikes me.[11]

Exit.

IAGO. If I can fasten but one cup upon him,
50 With that which he hath drunk to-night already,
He'll be as full of quarrel and offense
As my young mistress' dog. Now, my sick fool Roderigo,
Whom love hath turn'd almost the wrong side out,
To Desdemona hath to-night caroused[12]
55 Potations pottle-deep;[13] and he's to watch:
Three lads of Cyprus, noble swelling[14] spirits,

◄ How will Iago use Cassio's weakness to further his plot?

15. **hold their honors in a wary distance.** Are very sensitive when it comes to their honor

16. **If . . . dream.** If things go as I hope they will

17. **rouse.** A full draught of liquor

18. **canakin.** Diminutive form of *can*: a small can or drinking vessel

19. **span.** A short stretch of time

20. **potent in potting.** Skilled at drinking alcohol

21. **swag-bellied.** Having a big, hanging paunch (caused by drinking too much liquor)

22. **Hollander.** A Dutch soldier. In Shakespeare's time, the English and the Dutch were allies, and Dutch soldiers often fought alongside the British.

23. **Almain.** German soldier (from Old French *aleman*; modern French *allemand*)

24. **I'll do you justice.** I'll drink to your toast.

25. **crown.** An old British coin worth five shillings or about sixty pence

26. **He held them sixpence all too dear.** He believed they were overpriced by six pence.

---

words for everyday use

 fa • ci • li • ty (fə sil´ ət ē) *n.*, ease. *Laura's facility with numbers led her to a career as an accountant.*

That hold their honors in a wary distance,[15]
The very elements of this warlike isle,
Have I to-night fluster'd with flowing cups,
And they watch too. Now, 'mongst this flock of
60   drunkards,
Am I to put our Cassio in some action
That may offend the isle.—But here they come:
If consequence do but approve my dream,[16]
My boat sails freely, both with wind and stream.

Re-enter CASSIO; *with him* MONTANO *and* GENTLEMEN;
SERVANTS *following with wine.*

65 CASSIO. 'Fore God, they have given me a rouse[17]
already.

MONTANO. Good faith, a little one; not past a pint,
as I am a soldier.

IAGO. Some wine, ho!

[*Sings*]

70   "And let me the canakin[18] clink, clink;
And let me the canakin clink
A soldier's a man;
A life's but a span;[19]
Why, then, let a soldier drink."
75 Some wine, boys!

CASSIO. 'Fore God, an excellent song.

IAGO. I learned it in England, where, indeed, they
are most potent in potting:[20] your Dane, your
German, and your swag-bellied[21] Hollander[22]—
80 Drink, ho!—are nothing to your English.

CASSIO. Is your Englishman so expert in his drinking?

IAGO. Why, he drinks you, with <u>facility</u>, your Dane
dead drunk; he sweats not to overthrow your
Almain;[23] he gives your Hollander a vomit, ere the
85 next pottle can be filled.

CASSIO. To the health of our general!

MONTANO. I am for it, lieutenant; and I'll do you
justice.[24]

IAGO. O sweet England!

[*Sings*]

90   "King Stephen was a worthy peer,
His breeches cost him but a crown;[25]
He held them sixpence all too dear,[26]

◀ *How might
Shakespeare's
audience have
reacted on hearing
these lines about
England?*

27. **lown.** A loon, that is, a worthless or roguish person
28. **quality.** High rank
29. **just equinox.** Exact equivalent. That is, his vice is just as great as his virtue.
30. **watch the horologe a double set.** Watch the clock two days in a row; that is, he'll stay up all night.

words for everyday use   vice (vīs´) *n.,* moral fault or failing. *Procrastination is my greatest vice.*

With that he call'd the tailor lown.[27]
He was a wight of high renown,
95   And thou art but of low degree:
'Tis pride that pulls the country down;
    Then take thine auld cloak about thee."
Some wine, ho!

CASSIO. Why, this is a more exquisite song than the
100 other.

IAGO. Will you hear't again?

CASSIO. No; for I hold him to be unworthy of his
place that does those things. Well, God's above all;
and there be souls must be saved, and there be souls
105 must not be saved.

IAGO. It's true, good lieutenant.

CASSIO. For mine own part,—no offense to the
general, nor any man of quality,[28]—I hope to be saved.

IAGO. And so do I too, lieutenant.

110 CASSIO. Ay, but, by your leave, not before me; the
lieutenant is to be saved before the ancient. Let's have
no more of this; let's to our affairs.—Forgive us our
sins!—Gentlemen, let's look to our business. Do not
think, gentlemen, I am drunk: this is my ancient; this
115 is my right hand, and this is my left: I am not drunk
now; I can stand well enough, and speak well enough.

◄ Is Cassio drunk?
How do you know?

ALL. Excellent well.

CASSIO. Why, very well then; you must not think
then that I am drunk.

Exit.

MONTANO. To the platform, masters; come, let's set
120   the watch.

IAGO. You see this fellow that is gone before;
He is a soldier fit to stand by Caesar
And give direction: and do but see his <u>vice</u>;
'Tis to his virtue a just equinox,[29]
125 The one as long as the other: 'tis pity of him.
I fear the trust Othello puts him in.
On some odd time of his infirmity,
Will shake this island.

◄ How does Iago
slyly undermine
Cassio's reputation?

MONTANO.   But is he often thus?

IAGO. 'Tis evermore the prologue to his sleep:
130 He'll watch the horologe a double set,[30]

31. **Should hazard . . . infirmity.** Should risk having as his lieutenant a man with such a habitual weakness
32. **twiggen.** Wicker-covered
33. *Staying him.* Holding him back
34. **mazzard.** Head

If drink rock not his cradle.

MONTANO.   It were well
The general were put in mind of it.
Perhaps he sees it not; or his good nature
Prizes the virtue that appears in Cassio,
135 And looks not on his evils: is not this true?

Enter RODERIGO.

IAGO. [*Aside to him*] How now, Roderigo!
I pray you, after the lieutenant; go.

                              Exit RODERIGO.

MONTANO. And 'tis great pity that the noble Moor
Should hazard such a place as his own second
140 With one of an ingraft infirmity:[31]
It were an honest action to say
So to the Moor.

IAGO.   Not I, for this fair island:
I do love Cassio well; and would do much
To cure him of this evil—But, hark! what noise?

Cry within: "Help! help!"

Re-enter CASSIO, *driving in* RODERIGO.

145 CASSIO. You rogue! you rascal!

MONTANO. What's the matter, lieutenant?

CASSIO. A knave teach me my duty! I'll beat the
knave into a twiggen[32] bottle.

RODERIGO. Beat me!

150 CASSIO. Dost thou prate, rogue?

Striking RODERIGO.

MONTANO. Nay, good lieutenant! [*Staying him*[33]]
I pray you, sir, hold your hand.

CASSIO. Let me go, sir, or I'll knock you o'er the
mazzard.[34]

155 MONTANO. Come, come, you're drunk.

CASSIO. Drunk!

They fight.

IAGO. [*Aside to* RODERIGO] Away, I say; go out, and cry
    a mutiny.

                              Exit RODERIGO.

◄ Who intervenes to stop the fight between Cassio and Roderigo?

35. **Diablo.** Devil (a curse)
36. **Are we turn'd . . . Which heaven hath forbid the Ottomites?** Are we turned into barbarians, doing to ourselves what the Turks could not [i.e., defeat us]?
37. **carve for.** Indulge
38. **Holds his soul light.** Doesn't value his soul
39. **propriety.** Proper self
40. **In quarter.** In close quarters; side by side
41. **Devesting.** Undressing
42. **tilting.** Thrusting
43. **peevish odds.** Foolish quarrel
44. **are thus forgot.** Have so forgotten yourself

Nay, good lieutenant,—alas, gentlemen;—
Help, ho!—Lieutenant,—sir,—Montano,—sir;
160 Help, masters!—Here's a goodly watch indeed!

[*Bell rings*]

Who's that which rings the bell?—Diablo,[35] ho!
The town will rise: God's will, lieutenant, hold!
You will be shamed for ever.

Re-enter OTHELLO *and* ATTENDANTS.

OTHELLO. What is the matter here?

MONTANO.   'Zounds, I bleed still;
I am hurt to the death.

◀ What has happened to Montano?

Faints.

165 OTHELLO.   Hold, for your lives!

IAGO. Hold, ho! Lieutenant,—sir—Montano,—
      gentlemen,—
Have you forgot all sense of place and duty?
Hold! the general speaks to you; hold, hold, for
      shame!

OTHELLO. Why, how now, ho! from whence ariseth
      this?
170 Are we turn'd Turks, and to ourselves do that
Which heaven hath forbid the Ottomites?[36]
For Christian shame, put by this barbarous brawl:
He that stirs next to carve for[37] his own rage
Holds his soul light;[38] he dies upon his motion.
175 Silence that dreadful bell: it frights the isle
From her propriety.[39] What is the matter, masters?
Honest Iago, that look'st dead with grieving,
Speak, who began this? on thy love, I charge thee.

◀ What does Othello call Iago?

IAGO. I do not know: friends all but now, even now,
180 In quarter,[40] and in terms like bride and groom
Devesting[41] them for bed; and then, but now—
As if some planet had unwitted men—
Swords out, and tilting[42] one at other's breast,
In opposition bloody. I cannot speak
185 Any beginning to this peevish odds;[43]
And would in action glorious I had lost
Those legs that brought me to a part of it!

OTHELLO. How comes it, Michael, you are thus
      forgot?[44]

CASSIO. I pray you, pardon me; I cannot speak.

45. **were wont be civil.** Are customarily civil
46. **censure.** Judgment
47. **unlace.** Undo
48. **spend your rich opinion.** Waste your good reputation
49. **something now offends me.** Something hurts me badly
50. **blood begins my safer guides to rule.** Anger is starting to take over my powers of reason.
51. **collied.** Darkened
52. **rout.** Riot; disturbance
53. **approved . . . offense.** Found guilty of this offense
54. **manage.** Carry out
55. **affined.** Biased; that is, influenced by friendship with Cassio
56. **execute upon him.** Use the weapon on him
57. **entreats his pause.** Begs him to stop

190   OTHELLO. Worthy Montano, you were wont be civil;[45]
      The gravity and stillness of your youth
      The world hath noted, and your name is great
      In mouths of wisest censure:[46] what's the matter,
      That you unlace[47] your reputation thus
195   And spend your rich opinion[48] for the name
      Of a night-brawler? Give me answer to it.

      MONTANO. Worthy Othello, I am hurt to danger:
      Your officer, Iago, can inform you,—
      While I spare speech, which something now offends
         me,[49]—
200   Of all that I do know: nor know I aught
      By me that's said or done amiss this night;
      Unless self-charity be sometimes a vice,
      And to defend ourselves it be a sin
      When violence assails us.

      OTHELLO.   Now, by heaven,
205   My blood begins my safer guides to rule;[50]
      And passion, having my best judgment collied,[51]
      Assays to lead the way: if I once stir,
      Or do but lift this arm, the best of you
      Shall sink in my rebuke. Give me to know
210   How this foul rout[52] began, who set it on;
      And he that is approved in this offense,[53]
      Though he had twinn'd with me, both at a birth,
      Shall lose me. What! in a town of war,
      Yet wild, the people's hearts brimful of fear,
215   To manage[54] private and domestic quarrel,
      In night, and on the court and guard of safety!
      'Tis monstrous. Iago, who began't?

      MONTANO. If partially affined,[55] or leagued in office,
      Thou dost deliver more or less than truth,
      Thou art no soldier.

220   IAGO.   Touch me not so near:
      I had rather have this tongue cut from my mouth
      Than it should do offense to Michael Cassio;
      Yet, I persuade myself, to speak the truth
      Shall nothing wrong him. Thus it is, general.
225   Montano and myself being in speech,
      There comes a fellow crying out for help:
      And Cassio following him with determined sword,
      To execute upon him.[56] Sir, this gentleman
      Steps in to Cassio, and entreats his pause:[57]
230   Myself the crying fellow did pursue,
      Lest by his clamor—as it so fell out—

◄ What excuse does Montano give for his involvement in the brawl?

◄ How does Othello feel about the incident? What does he demand to know?

◄ What does Montano warn Iago not to do?

◄ What does Iago say about Cassio?

58. **high in oath.** Using many oaths, or curse words
59. **strange indignity.** Unusually extreme insult
60. **patience . . . pass.** Could not be patiently endured
61. **mince . . . to Cassio.** Making light of the matter in order to protect Cassio
62. **myself . . . surgeon.** That is, I personally will make sure your wounds are treated; Othello himself is not a surgeon.
63. **sense.** Hurt

words for everyday use

vile (vī[ə]lʹ) *adj.*, morally or physically despicable. *The evil wizard wanted to take over the country, but the superhero foiled his vile plot.*

bal • my (bämʹ ē, bälmʹ ē) *adj.*, soothing. *A balmy breeze wafted over us as we lay on the beach.*

strife (strīfʹ) *n.*, conflict or struggle; often bitter and violent. *The country's history was marked by constant strife, and its people longed for peace.*

best • ial (besʹ chəl, beshʹ chəl) *adj.*, of or relating to beasts. *War can bring out people's bestial instincts.*

The town might fall in fright: he, swift of foot,
Outran my purpose; and I return'd the rather
For that I heard the clink and fall of swords,
235 And Cassio high in oath;[58] which till to-night
I ne'er might say before. When I came back—
For this was brief—I found them close together,
At blow and thrust; even as again they were
When you yourself did part them.
240 More of this matter cannot I report:
But men are men; the best sometimes forget:
Though Cassio did some little wrong to him,
As men in rage strike those that wish them best,
Yet surely Cassio, I believe, received
245 From him that fled some strange indignity,[59]
Which patience could not pass.[60]

OTHELLO.   I know, Iago,
Thy honesty and love doth mince this matter,
Making it light to Cassio.[61] Cassio, I love thee
But never more be officer of mine.

◀ What is Othello's
punishment to
Cassio?

Re-enter DESDEMONA, *attended.*

250 Look, if my gentle love be not raised up!
I'll make thee an example.

DESDEMONA.   What's the matter?

OTHELLO. All's well now, sweeting; come away to bed.
[*To* MONTANO] Sir, for your hurts, myself will be your
surgeon.[62] Lead him off.

[MONTANO *is led off.*]

255 Iago, look with care about the town,
And silence those whom this vile brawl distracted.
Come, Desdemona: 'tis the soldiers' life
To have their balmy slumbers waked with strife.

                    Exeunt all but IAGO *and* CASSIO.

IAGO. What, are you hurt, lieutenant?

260 CASSIO. Ay, past all surgery.

IAGO. Marry, heaven forbid!

CASSIO. Reputation, reputation, reputation! O, I
have lost my reputation! I have lost the immortal
part of myself, and what remains is bestial. My
265 reputation, Iago, my reputation!

◀ What does a
ruined reputation
mean to Cassio?
What does Iago say
about reputation?

IAGO. As I am an honest man, I thought you had
received some bodily wound; there is more sense[63]
in that than in reputation. Reputation is an idle and

64. **imposition.** Something imposed by others
65. **recover.** Win back
66. **cast in his mood.** Dismissed because he is angry
67. **sue to him.** Appeal to him
68. **slight.** Worthless
69. **speak parrot.** Speak nonsense
70. **discourse fustian.** Speak in overblown gibberish
71. **Hydra.** A many-headed snake which, in Greek myth, was slain by Hercules as one of his twelve labors

words for everyday use

in • or • di • nate (in òrd´ [ə]n ət) *adj.*, exceeding reasonable limits; excessive. *The vain fashion model spent an inordinate amount of time in front of the mirror.*

most false imposition:[64] oft got without merit, and
270 lost without deserving: you have lost no reputation
at all, unless you repute yourself such a loser. What,
man! There are ways to recover[65] the general again:
you are but now cast in his mood,[66] a punishment
more in policy than in malice, even so as one would
275 beat his offenseless dog to affright an imperious lion:
sue to him[67] again, and he's yours.

CASSIO. I will rather sue to be despised than to
deceive so good a commander with so slight,[68] so
drunken, and so indiscreet an officer. Drunk? and
280 speak parrot?[69] and squabble? swagger? swear? and
discourse fustian[70] with one's own shadow? O thou
invisible spirit of wine, if thou hast no name to be
known by, let us call thee devil!

IAGO. What was he that you followed with your
285 sword? What had he done to you?

CASSIO. I know not.

IAGO. Is't possible?

CASSIO. I remember a mass of things, but nothing
distinctly; a quarrel, but nothing wherefore. O God,
290 that men should put an enemy in their mouths to
steal away their brains! that we should, with joy,
pleasance, revel and applause, transform ourselves
into beasts!

IAGO. Why, but you are now well enough: how
295 came you thus recovered?

◀ Why is Cassio no
longer drunk?

CASSIO. It hath pleased the devil drunkenness to give
place to the devil wrath; one unperfectness shows me
another, to make me frankly despise myself.

IAGO. Come, you are too severe a moraler: as the
300 time, the place, and the condition of this country
stands, I could heartily wish this had not befallen;
but, since it is as it is, mend it for your own good.

CASSIO. I will ask him for my place again; he shall
tell me I am a drunkard! Had I as many mouths as
305 Hydra,[71] such an answer would stop them all. To be
now a sensible man, by and by a fool, and presently
a beast! O strange! Every inordinate cup is unblessed
and the ingredient is a devil.

IAGO. Come, come, good wine is a good familiar
310 creature, if it be well used: exclaim no more against
it. And, good lieutenant, I think you think I love you.

72. **splinter.** Set with splints, as to mend a broken bone

73. **lay.** Wager

74. **I am desperate . . . here.** I despair for my future if my career is ended in this way.

75. **Probal to thinking.** [My advice] will prove to be reasonable and rational to anyone who thinks about it.

76. **subdue.** Win over

77. **honest suit.** Good cause

78. **fruitful.** Generous

79. **baptism . . . seals and symbols of redeemed sin.** The "baptism" refers to Othello's conversion to Christianity. As a Moor, Othello was most likely raised with the Muslim faith, and only as an adult was baptized as a Christian. Here, Iago suggests that Othello would renounce even his Christian faith if Desdemona asked him to do so.

80. **enfetter'd.** Bound or chained to, as if by fetters, or shackles on the feet

81. **what she list.** What she wishes

82. **parallel course.** The course that corresponds with these facts

83. **Divinity.** Theology; that is, the study of religious faith. Iago practices a backwards theology—the "divinity of hell"—by studying Hell rather than Heaven.

84. **put on.** Encourage

85. **suggest . . . heavenly shows.** Tempt people first by pretending to be kind and helpful

words for everyday use

im • por • tune (im´ pər tyün´, im pȯr´ chən) *vt.*, beg or urge with annoying persistence. *The students importuned their teacher to give them less homework.*

CASSIO. I have well approved it, sir. I drunk!

IAGO. You or any man living may be drunk at some time, man. I'll tell you what you shall do. Our
315 general's wife is now the general. I may say so in this respect, for that he hath devoted and given up himself to the contemplation, mark, and denotement of her parts and graces. Confess yourself freely to her; importune her help to put you in your place again.
320 She is of so free, so kind, so apt, so blessed a disposition, she holds it a vice in her goodness not to do more than she is requested. This broken joint between you and her husband entreat her to splinter;[72] and, my fortunes against any lay[73] worth
325 naming, this crack of your love shall grow stronger than it was before.

◄ According to Iago, what should Cassio do to win back the general's favor?

CASSIO. You advise me well.

IAGO. I protest, in the sincerity of love and honest kindness.

330 CASSIO. I think it freely; and betimes in the morning I will beseech the virtuous Desdemona to undertake for me: I am desperate of my fortunes if they cheque me here.[74]

IAGO. You are in the right. Good night, lieutenant; I
335 must to the watch.

CASSIO. Good night, honest Iago.

Exit.

IAGO. And what's he then that says I play the villain? When this advice is free I give and honest, Probal to thinking[75] and indeed the course
340 To win the Moor again? For 'tis most easy The inclining Desdemona to subdue[76] In any honest suit:[77] she's framed as fruitful[78] As the free elements. And then for her To win the Moor—were't to renounce his baptism,
345 All seals and symbols of redeemed sin,[79] His soul is so enfetter'd[80] to her love, That she may make, unmake, do what she list,[81] Even as her appetite shall play the god With his weak function. How am I then a villain
350 To counsel Cassio to this parallel course,[82] Directly to his good? Divinity[83] of hell! When devils will the blackest sins put on,[84] They do suggest at first with heavenly shows,[85]

◄ According to Iago, why is his advice "honest"? Why would it be impossible for anyone to accuse him of being a villain?

86. **Plies.** Appeals to; begs
87. **repeals him.** Asks for Cassio to be reinstated as lieutenant
88. **one that fills up the cry.** One that goes along with the pack
89. **cudgelled.** Beaten
90. **issue.** Result
91. **dilatory.** Slow; tending to cause delay
92. **cashier'd Cassio.** Caused Cassio to be discharged from his position
93. **where thou art billeted.** To your assigned sleeping-quarters
94. **move for Cassio.** Plead Cassio's case
95. **jump.** At the exact moment
96. **device.** Plotting

words for everyday use

pes • ti • lence (pes´ tə len[t]s) *n.,* anything destructive or deadly. *Unclean water can spread pestilence.*

so • lic • it (sə lis´ ət) *vt.,* approach with a request or plea. *The students went door to door to solicit donations for the school.*

As I do now: for whiles this honest fool
355 Plies[86] Desdemona to repair his fortunes
And she for him pleads strongly to the Moor,
I'll pour this <u>pestilence</u> into his ear,
That she repeals him[87] for her body's lust;
And by how much she strives to do him good,
360 She shall undo her credit with the Moor.
So will I turn her virtue into pitch,
And out of her own goodness make the net
That shall enmesh them all.

Re-enter RODERIGO.

How now, Roderigo!

365 **RODERIGO.** I do follow here in the chase, not like a
hound that hunts, but one that fills up the cry.[88] My
money is almost spent; I have been to-night
exceedingly well cudgelled;[89] and I think the issue[90]
will be, I shall have so much experience for my
370 pains, and so, with no money at all and a little more
wit, return again to Venice.

IAGO. How poor are they that have not patience!
What wound did ever heal but by degrees?
Thou know'st we work by wit, and not by witchcraft;
375 And wit depends on dilatory[91] time.
Does't not go well? Cassio hath beaten thee.
And thou, by that small hurt, hast cashier'd Cassio:[92]
Though other things grow fair against the sun,
Yet fruits that blossom first will first be ripe:
380 Content thyself awhile. By the mass, 'tis morning;
Pleasure and action make the hours seem short.
Retire thee; go where thou art billeted:[93]
Away, I say; thou shalt know more hereafter:
Nay, get thee gone.

Exit RODERIGO.

Two things are to be done:
385 My wife must move for Cassio[94] to her mistress;
I'll set her on;
Myself the while to draw the Moor apart,
And bring him jump[95] when he may Cassio find
<u>Soliciting</u> his wife: ay, that's the way!
390 Dull not device[96] by coldness and delay.

Exit.

◄ What "pestilence" will Iago pour into Othello's ear?

◄ How does Iago persuade Roderigo to stay in Cyprus? What makes the hours seem short to Iago?

◄ How will Iago involve Emilia in his plot?

Respond to the Selection

What do you think about the character of Roderigo? Is he a complete fool, or has Iago simply done an excellent job of conning him?

Investigate, Inquire, and Imagine

Recall: GATHERING FACTS

1a. What is the outcome of the battle with the Turks?

2a. Explain the incident that led to Cassio's dismissal.

3a. What report does Iago give to Othello and the others about the incident? What does he say to Cassio privately?

Interpret: FINDING MEANING

1b. Why doesn't Shakespeare spend much time describing the battle? Is the war an important part of the play? Explain.

2b. How has Iago used Roderigo to further his plot against Othello?

3b. How do Iago's words mislead everyone?

Analyze: TAKING THINGS APART

4a. Evaluate Iago's view of women, and of Desdemona in particular. How does Iago's attitude toward Desdemona compare to the way Cassio regards her? Cite lines from the play to support your answer.

Synthesize: BRINGING THINGS TOGETHER

4b. Does either man have a realistic view of women? What do you think Shakespeare's attitudes were toward women? How do you think he intended the audience to feel about Desdemona?

Evaluate: MAKING JUDGMENTS

5a. Cassio's lines, "Reputation, reputation, reputation! O, I have lost my reputation!" (act II, scene iii, 264–67) are among the most famous in the play. Evaluate Cassio's and Iago's stated opinions about reputation. Do you agree with Iago or with Cassio? Explain.

Extend: CONNECTING IDEAS

5b. How important is your reputation to you personally? Do you know of anyone who has a good reputation and does not deserve it? Do you know of anyone who has a bad reputation that has been unfairly imposed upon him or her?

Understanding Literature

ASIDE AND SOLILOQUY. An **aside** is a statement made by a character in a play, intended to be heard by the audience, but not by other characters on the stage. A **soliloquy** is a speech given by a character alone onstage, in which the character reveals his or her thoughts and feelings to the audience. In act II, scene i, Iago delivers several asides and two major soliloquies to the audience. What does he reveal in these asides and soliloquies?

DRAMATIC IRONY. **Irony** is a difference between appearance and reality. **Dramatic irony** occurs when something is known to the reader or audience but not to the characters. How do Iago's asides and soliloquies contribute to the dramatic irony in act II? Why do you suppose Shakespeare chose to make Iago's intentions so clear to the audience?

RISING ACTION. The **rising action,** or **complication,** is the part of a plot that develops the central conflict to a high point of intensity. Summarize the events in act II that make up the rising action.

ACT III, SCENE i

1. **content your pains.** Reward you for your trouble
2. **Good morrow.** Good morning
3. **Naples . . . speak i' the nose.** Could be a reference to the nasally accent of people from Naples, another city and region in Italy. Some editors also believe it is a joke about venereal disease, which was associated with that region.
4. **keep up thy quillets.** Keep your clever quips to yourself.
5. **stirring . . . stir.** The clown is punning on two meanings of *stir:* "to wake up" and "to move."

ACT III

SCENE i: Before the castle.

Enter CASSIO *and some* MUSICIANS.

CASSIO. Masters, play here; I will content your
    pains;[1]
Something that's brief; and bid "Good morrow,[2]
    general."

Music.

Enter CLOWN.

CLOWN. Why masters, have your instruments been
in Naples, that they speak i' the nose[3] thus?

5 FIRST MUSICIAN. How, sir, how!

CLOWN. Are these, I pray you, wind-instruments?

FIRST MUSICIAN. Ay, marry, are they, sir.

CLOWN. O, thereby hangs a tail.

FIRST MUSICIAN. Whereby hangs a tale, sir?

10 CLOWN. Marry, sir, by many a wind-instrument that I
know. But, masters, here's money for you: and the
general so likes your music, that he desires you, for
love's sake, to make no more noise with it.

FIRST MUSICIAN. Well, sir, we will not.

15 CLOWN. If you have any music that may not be
heard, to't again: but, as they say to hear music the
general does not greatly care.

FIRST MUSICIAN. We have none such, sir.

CLOWN. Then put up your pipes in your bag, for I'll
20 away: go; vanish into air; away!

                        Exeunt MUSICIANS.

CASSIO. Dost thou hear, my honest friend?

CLOWN. No, I hear not your honest friend; I hear you.

CASSIO. Prithee, keep up thy quillets.[4] There's a poor
piece of gold for thee: if the gentlewoman that
25 attends the general's wife be stirring, tell her there's
one Cassio entreats her a little favor of speech: wilt
thou do this?

CLOWN. She is stirring, sir: if she will stir[5] hither, I
shall seem to notify unto her.

◀ *Why has Cassio brought the musicians to the castle?*

◀ *Explain the clown's joke about "wind instruments."*

◀ *Whom has Cassio come to see at the castle?*

6. **In happy time.** Just in time; I'm glad I ran into you.

7. **mean.** Means; way

8. **I never knew . . . honest.** Iago is a Venetian, not a Florentine, so this line appears to be an error. However, Cassio is from Florence, so he may be saying here, "I never knew even a Florentine [i.e., one of my own countrymen] to be more kind and honest."

9. **stoutly.** Strongly

10. **great affinity.** Has powerful family connections

11. **wholesome.** Sound; reasonable

12. **He might not but refuse you.** He has no choice but to refuse you.

13. **needs no other suitor but his likings.** He needs no convincing; he's only waiting for the right time.

14. **front.** Forelock, by which he'll pull Cassio in again

15. **bosom.** Innermost thoughts

words for everyday use   pro • cure (prə kyü[ə]r´, prō kyü[ə]r´) *vt.,* obtain; get possession of. *Although it was wartime and supplies were not plentiful, the family was able to procure a ham for the holiday.*

CASSIO. Do, good my friend.

Exit CLOWN.

Enter IAGO.

30   In happy time,[6] Iago.

IAGO. You have not been a-bed, then?

CASSIO. Why, no; the day had broke
Before we parted. I have made bold, Iago,
To send in to your wife: my suit to her
35 Is, that she will to virtuous Desdemona
<u>Procure</u> me some access.

IAGO.   I'll send her to you presently;
And I'll devise a mean[7] to draw the Moor
Out of the way, that your converse and business
May be more free.

CASSIO.   I humbly thank you for't.

Exit IAGO.

40 I never knew a Florentine more kind and honest.[8]

Enter EMILIA.

EMILIA. Good morrow, good Lieutenant: I am sorry
For your displeasure; but all will sure be well.
The general and his wife are talking of it;
And she speaks for you stoutly:[9] the Moor replies,
45 That he you hurt is of great fame in Cyprus,
And great affinity,[10] and that in wholesome[11]
     wisdom
He might not but refuse you;[12] but he protests he
     loves you
And needs no other suitor but his likings[13]
To take the safest occasion by the front[14]
To bring you in again.

50 CASSIO.   Yet, I beseech you,
If you think fit, or that it may be done,
Give me advantage of some brief discourse
With Desdemona alone.

EMILIA.   Pray you, come in;
I will bestow you where you shall have time
To speak your bosom[15] freely.

55 CASSIO.   I am much bound to you.

Exeunt.

◄ *According to Emilia, what does Othello plan to do about Cassio's situation? Is Cassio satisfied with this answer?*

ACT III, SCENE ii

1. **pilot.** The pilot of the ship that is returning to Venice
2. **by him do my duties.** Tell him to pay my respects
3. **walking on the works.** Taking a tour of the fortifications that surround the citadel
4. **Repair.** Return

ACT III, SCENE iii

1. **in strangeness.** In aloofness; as a stranger
2. **polite distance.** Some versions have this as a "politic distance." Either way, the message is the same: Othello is only keeping a distance from Cassio for political reasons.
3. **feed upon such nice and waterish diet.** Need such slight reasons to be continued
4. **Do not doubt that.** Do not be afraid of that.
5. **watch him tame.** Keep him awake until he gives in. Alludes to the practice in falconry of taming hawks by keeping them from sleep. Throughout the play, Shakespeare makes several references to the sport of falconry, which is the practice of training hawks for use in hunting.

SCENE ii: A room in the castle.

Enter OTHELLO, IAGO, *and* GENTLEMEN.

OTHELLO. These letters give, Iago, to the pilot;[1]
And by him do my duties[2] to the senate:
That done, I will be walking on the works;[3]
Repair[4] there to me.

◀ *Where will Othello be?*

IAGO.   Well, my good lord, I'll do't.

5 OTHELLO. This fortification, gentlemen, shall we see't?

GENTLEMEN. We'll wait upon your lordship.

Exeunt.

SCENE iii: The garden of the castle.

Enter DESDEMONA, CASSIO, *and* EMILIA.

DESDEMONA. Be thou assured, good Cassio, I will do
All my abilities in thy behalf.

EMILIA. Good madam, do: I warrant it grieves my
    husband,
As if the case were his.

◀ *What do Emilia and Desdemona believe about Iago?*

DESDEMONA. O, that's an honest fellow. Do not
5   doubt, Cassio,
But I will have my lord and you again
As friendly as you were.

CASSIO.   Bounteous madam,
Whatever shall become of Michael Cassio,
He's never any thing but your true servant.

DESDEMONA. I know't; I thank you. You do love my
10   lord:
You have known him long; and be you well assured
He shall in strangeness[1] stand no further off
Than in a polite distance.[2]

◀ *Of what does Desdemona assure Cassio?*

CASSIO.   Ay, but, lady,
That policy may either last so long,
15 Or feed upon such nice and waterish diet,[3]
Or breed itself so out of circumstance,
That, I being absent and my place supplied,
My general will forget my love and service.

DESDEMONA. Do not doubt that;[4] before Emilia here
20 I give thee warrant of thy place. Assure thee,
If I do vow a friendship, I'll perform it
To the last article. My lord shall never rest;
I'll watch him tame[5] and talk him out of patience;

◀ *What will Desdemona do if Othello is not quick to reinstate Cassio?*

6. **his board a shrift.** The place where he takes his meals will seem like a confessional (where a person goes to confess sins to a priest).

7. **give thy cause away.** Give up your cause

8. **do your discretion.** I leave it to your discretion; do what you think is best.

9. **His present reconciliation take.** Accept his plea to be reconciled with you.

10. **sooth.** True

His bed shall seem a school, his board a shrift;[6]
25 I'll intermingle every thing he does
With Cassio's suit: therefore be merry, Cassio;
For thy solicitor shall rather die
Than give thy cause away.[7]

EMILIA. Madam, here comes my lord.

30 CASSIO. Madam, I'll take my leave.

DESDEMONA. Why, stay, and hear me speak.

CASSIO. Madam, not now: I am very ill at ease,
Unfit for mine own purposes.

DESDEMONA. Well, do your discretion.[8]

Exit CASSIO.

Enter OTHELLO *and* IAGO.

IAGO. Ha! I like not that.

35 OTHELLO.   What dost thou say?

IAGO. Nothing, my lord: or if—I know not what.

OTHELLO. Was not that Cassio parted from my wife?

IAGO. Cassio, my lord! No, sure, I cannot think it,
That he would steal away so guilty-like,
Seeing you coming.

40 OTHELLO.   I do believe 'twas he.

DESDEMONA. How now, my lord!
I have been talking with a suitor here,
A man that <u>languishes</u> in your displeasure.

OTHELLO. Who is't you mean?

DESDEMONA. Why, your lieutenant, Cassio. Good my
45   lord,
If I have any grace or power to move you,
His present reconciliation take;[9]
For if he be not one that truly loves you,
That errs in ignorance and not in cunning,
50 I have no judgment in an honest face:
I prithee, call him back.

OTHELLO.   Went he hence now?

DESDEMONA. Ay, sooth;[10] so humbled
That he hath left part of his grief with me,
To suffer with him. Good love, call him back.

OTHELLO. Not now, sweet Desdemon; some other
55   time.

◄ How might these
lines be ironic?
Whom did
Desdemona call
"honest" at the
beginning of the
scene? Can she really
tell an honest face
when she sees one?

11. **not almost . . . cheque.** Hardly even a fault that would deserve a private reprimand [let alone a public dismissal]

12. **mammering.** Hesitating (as Othello is doing)

13. **ta'en your part.** Defended you

14. **bring him in.** Bring him back into your favor

15. **Why, this is not a boon . . . To your own person.** This is not a favor you are doing for me. I am asking you to do something that would be of particular benefit to your own self. *Peculiar* here means particular or personal.

16. **when I . . . touch your love indeed.** When I really have to rely on your love to grant me a favor

17. **poise.** Weight, importance

18. **fearful to be granted.** Difficult or risky to grant

---

words for everyday use

pen • i • tent (pen´ ə tənt) *adj.*, feeling sorry about offenses; repentant. *After I yelled at him for chewing up my shoes, the dog looked mournful and penitent.*

boon (bün´) *n.*, favor; blessing. *The new library, financed by a rich family in the area, was a real boon for the community.*

DESDEMONA. But shall't be shortly?

OTHELLO.   The sooner, sweet, for you.

DESDEMONA. Shall't be to-night at supper?

OTHELLO.   No, not to-night.

DESDEMONA. To-morrow dinner, then?

OTHELLO.   I shall not dine
  at home;
I meet the captains at the citadel.

DESDEMONA. Why, then, to-morrow night; or
60   Tuesday morn;
On Tuesday noon, or night; on Wednesday morn:
I prithee, name the time, but let it not
Exceed three days: in faith, he's <u>penitent</u>;
And yet his trespass, in our common reason—
65 Save that, they say, the wars must make examples
Out of their best—is not almost a fault
To incur a private cheque.[11] When shall he come?
Tell me, Othello: I wonder in my soul,
What you would ask me, that I should deny,
70 Or stand so mammering[12] on. What! Michael Cassio,
That came a-wooing with you, and so many a time,
When I have spoke of you dispraisingly,
Hath ta'en your part;[13] to have so much to do
To bring him in![14] Trust me, I could do much,—

◄ What has Cassio done to show friendship to Othello?

OTHELLO. Prithee, no more: let him come when he
75   will;
I will deny thee nothing.

◄ What does Othello promise Desdemona?

DESDEMONA.   Why, this is not a <u>boon</u>;
'Tis as I should entreat you wear your gloves,
Or feed on nourishing dishes, or keep you warm,
Or sue to you to do a peculiar profit
80 To your own person.[15] Nay, when I have a suit
Wherein I mean to touch your love indeed,[16]
It shall be full of poise[17] and difficult weight
And fearful to be granted.[18]

OTHELLO.   I will deny thee nothing:
Whereon, I do beseech thee, grant me this,
85 To leave me but a little to myself.

DESDEMONA. Shall I deny you? No: farewell, my lord.

OTHELLO. Farewell, my Desdemona: I'll come to thee
  straight.

DESDEMONA. Emilia, come. Be as your fancies teach
  you;

19. **wretch.** A miserable person; here used as a term of endearment, expressing tenderness mixed with pity

20. **went between us.** Served as a go-between, carrying messages

21. **horrible conceit.** Terrible idea

words for everyday use

per • di • tion (pər dish´ ən) *n.,* damnation; hell. *The preacher shouted that <u>perdition</u> awaited the sinners among us.*

Whate'er you be, I am obedient.

Exeunt DESDEMONA *and* EMILIA.

OTHELLO. Excellent wretch![19] Perdition catch my
90   soul,
But I do love thee! and when I love thee not,
Chaos is come again.

IAGO. My noble lord—

OTHELLO.   What dost thou say, Iago?

◀ What will happen
if Othello loses his
love for Desdemona?

IAGO. Did Michael Cassio, when you woo'd my lady,
95   Know of your love?

OTHELLO. He did, from first to last: why dost thou
    ask?

IAGO. But for a satisfaction of my thought;
No further harm.

OTHELLO.   Why of thy thought, Iago?

◀ What does Iago
ask Othello?

IAGO. I did not think he had been acquainted with
    her.

100   OTHELLO. O, yes; and went between us[20] very oft.

IAGO. Indeed!

OTHELLO. Indeed! ay, indeed: discern'st thou aught in
    that?
Is he not honest?

IAGO.   Honest, my lord!

OTHELLO. Honest! ay, honest.

IAGO.   My lord, for aught I know.

OTHELLO. What dost thou think?

IAGO.   Think, my lord!

105   OTHELLO.   Think, my lord!
By heaven, he echoes me,
As if there were some monster in his thought
Too hideous to be shown. Thou dost mean something:
I heard thee say even now, thou likedst not that,
110   When Cassio left my wife: what didst not like?
And when I told thee he was of my counsel
In my whole course of wooing, thou criedst "Indeed!"
And didst contract and purse thy brow together,
As if thou then hadst shut up in thy brain
115   Some horrible conceit.[21] If thou dost love me,
Show me thy thought.

IAGO. My lord, you know I love you.

22. **these stops of thine.** Your hesitations

23. **such things . . . tricks of custom.** Such things [as exaggerated pauses and hesitations] are tricks customarily used by false and disloyal people who want to mislead a person.

24. **close delations . . . rule.** Hidden accusations or secret thoughts coming out from a heart that cannot control itself during a time of great passionate feeling.

25. **would they might seem none.** It would be better that they not seem like men at all, but like the animals they really are.

26. **to that all slaves are free to.** Even slaves are free to disobey an unjust order.

27. **who has a breast . . . lawful?** Nobody has such a clean mind that some unjustified suspicions do not occasionally enter it, sitting side-by-side with more legitimate thoughts, and leading them to pass unfair judgment on others. *Leets* and *law-days* both mean "days when the court of law is in session."

28. **it is my nature's plague . . . that are not.** It is a flaw in my nature that I am always looking for signs of bad behavior, and often, in my jealousy, I see faults where there are none. *Jealousy* here means "zealous vigilance."

29. **conceits.** Conceives, as in comes up with an idea. The first quarto has "coniects," which some have interpreted as "conjects," meaning "conjectures."

30. **scattering and unsure observance.** Random and uncertain observations

words for everyday use

ru • mi • nate (rü´ mə nāt´) *vi.*, go over in the mind; ponder, reflect. *I sat by the brook, ruminating about the events of the day.*

OTHELLO.   I think thou dost;
And, for I know thou'rt full of love and honesty,
And weigh'st thy words before thou givest them
        breath,
120 Therefore these stops of thine[22] fright me the more:
For such things in a false disloyal knave
Are tricks of custom,[23] but in a man that's just
They are close delations, working from the heart
That passion cannot rule.[24]

IAGO.   For Michael Cassio,
125 I dare be sworn I think that he is honest.

OTHELLO. I think so too.

IAGO.   Men should be what they seem;
Or those that be not, would they might seem none![25]

OTHELLO. Certain, men should be what they seem.

IAGO. Why, then, I think Cassio's an honest man.

130 **OTHELLO.** Nay, yet there's more in this:
I prithee, speak to me as to thy thinkings,
As thou dost <u>ruminate</u>, and give thy worst of
        thoughts
The worst of words.

IAGO.   Good my lord, pardon me:
Though I am bound to every act of duty,
135 I am not bound to that all slaves are free to.[26]
Utter my thoughts? Why, say they are vile and false;
As where's that palace whereinto foul things
Sometimes intrude not? who has a breast so pure,
But some uncleanly apprehensions
140 Keep leets and law-days and in session sit
With meditations lawful?[27]

OTHELLO. Thou dost conspire against thy friend, Iago,
If thou but think'st him wrong'd and makest his ear
A stranger to thy thoughts.

IAGO.   I do beseech you—
145 Though I perchance am vicious in my guess,
As, I confess, it is my nature's plague
To spy into abuses, and oft my jealousy
Shapes faults that are not[28]—that your wisdom yet,
From one that so imperfectly conceits,[29]
150 Would take no notice, nor build yourself a trouble
Out of his scattering and unsure observance.[30]
It were not for your quiet nor your good,
Nor for my manhood, honesty, or wisdom,

◀ *What does Othello think of Iago? What would he think of Iago's behavior, were he not so sure of Iago's honesty?*

◀ *Is Iago really guilty of being "scattering and unsure" in his speech?*

31. **immediate.** Closest; most precious

32. **if.** Even if

33. **mock / The meat it feeds on.** Toys with the jealous person on whom it preys

34. **That cuckold . . . wronger.** A man whose lover is cheating on him can live in bliss, even knowing he is being wronged, if he does not love the woman who wrongs him.

35. **what damnèd minutes . . . yet strongly loves!** What damned, or hellish, times a man has to live through if he loves a woman and suspects her of cheating.

36. **riches fineless.** Infinite riches. *Fine* means "end," so *fineless* means "endless."

37. **make a lie of jealousy.** Invent or imagine things out of sheer jealousy

38. **exsufflicate and blown surmises.** Empty and insubstantial guesses

39. **Matching thy inference.** Such as you have described. Othello means that he would never be mocked by jealousy in the way that Iago has suggested. *He* would never be led on by jealousy to make empty and insubstantial guesses.

40. **Nor from mine . . . revolt.** Just because I may have some imperfect qualities, I see no reason to suspect that she will revolt, or turn against me.

words for everyday use

filch (filch´) *vt.*, steal. *When he thought I was not looking, Dad* filched *a cookie from my plate.*

dote (dōt´) *vi.*, be lavish or excessive in one's attention. *The young parents* doted *on their child, almost to the point of spoiling him.*

To let you know my thoughts.

OTHELLO.   'Zounds, what dost thou mean?

155 IAGO. Good name in man and woman, dear my lord,
Is the immediate[31] jewel of their souls:
Who steals my purse steals trash; 'tis something, nothing;
'Twas mine, 'tis his, and has been slave to thousands:
But he that <u>filches</u> from me my good name
160 Robs me of that which not enriches him
And makes me poor indeed.

OTHELLO. By heaven, I'll know thy thoughts.

IAGO. You cannot, if[32] my heart were in your hand;
Nor shall not, whilst 'tis in my custody.

OTHELLO. Ha!

165 IAGO.   O, beware, my lord, of jealousy!
It is the green-eyed monster which doth mock
The meat it feeds on.[33] That cuckold lives in bliss
Who, certain of his fate, loves not his wronger;[34]
But, O, what damnèd minutes tells he o'er
170 Who <u>dotes</u>, yet doubts, suspects, yet strongly loves![35]

OTHELLO. O misery!

IAGO. Poor and content is rich and rich enough,
But riches fineless[36] is as poor as winter
To him that ever fears he shall be poor.
175 Good heaven, the souls of all my tribe defend
From jealousy!

OTHELLO.   Why, why is this?
Think'st thou I'ld make a lie of jealousy,[37]
To follow still the changes of the moon
With fresh suspicions? No; to be once in doubt
180 Is once to be resolved: exchange me for a goat,
When I shall turn the business of my soul
To such exsufflicate and blown surmises,[38]
Matching thy inference.[39] 'Tis not to make me jealous
To say my wife is fair, feeds well, loves company,
185 Is free of speech, sings, plays and dances well;
Where virtue is, these are more virtuous.
Nor from mine own weak merits will I draw
The smallest fear or doubt of her revolt;[40]
For she had eyes, and chose me. No, Iago;
190 I'll see before I doubt; when I doubt, prove;
And on the proof, there is no more but this—
Away at once with love or jealousy!

◄ What does Iago say about a person's reputation, or "good name"? How does this speech compare with his words to Cassio in act II, scene iii, lines 268–274?

◄ What is the "green-eyed monster"? What is "the meat it feeds on"?

◄ Is Othello a jealous person? Why won't he doubt Desdemona?

41. **not jealous nor secure.** Not too suspicious, but not overly trusting either

42. **self-bounty.** Inherent generosity

43. **give out such a seeming.** Give out such a false appearance. Desdemona kept her love for the Moor secret from her father, as she was afraid of her father's disapproval.

44. **close as oak.** As tightly as the grain of oak (a very close-grained wood)

45. **strain my speech / To grosser issues.** Stretch the meaning of my words in order to come to bigger (or more revolting) conclusions

46. **My speech . . . vile success.** My speech would lead to such terrible consequences (*success* here means "consequence, that which succeeds or follows").

IAGO. I am glad of it; for now I shall have reason
To show the love and duty that I bear you
195   With franker spirit: therefore, as I am bound,
Receive it from me. I speak not yet of proof.
Look to your wife; observe her well with Cassio;
Wear your eye thus, not jealous nor secure:[41]
I would not have your free and noble nature,
200   Out of self-bounty,[42] be abused; look to't.
I know our country disposition well;
In Venice they do let heaven see the pranks
They dare not show their husbands; their best
        conscience
Is not to leave't undone, but keep't unknown.

◀ What does Iago suggest is true of all Venetian women?

205   OTHELLO. Dost thou say so?

IAGO. She did deceive her father, marrying you;
And when she seem'd to shake and fear your looks,
She loved them most.

◀ What "evidence" does Iago have of Desdemona's dishonesty?

OTHELLO.   And so she did.

IAGO.   Why, go to then;
She that, so young, could give out such a seeming,[43]
210   To seal her father's eyes up close as oak[44]—
He thought 'twas witchcraft—but I am much to
        blame;
I humbly do beseech you of your pardon
For too much loving you.

OTHELLO.   I am bound to thee for ever.

IAGO. I see this hath a little dash'd your spirits.

OTHELLO. Not a jot, not a jot.

215   IAGO.   I' faith, I fear it has.
I hope you will consider what is spoke
Comes from my love. But I do see you're moved:
I am to pray you not to strain my speech
To grosser issues[45] nor to larger reach
220   Than to suspicion.

OTHELLO. I will not.

IAGO.   Should you do so, my lord,
My speech should fall into such vile success[46]
As my thoughts aim not at. Cassio's my worthy
        friend—
My lord, I see you're moved.

OTHELLO.   No, not much moved:
225   I do not think but Desdemona's honest.

47. **erring.** Straying

48. **affect.** Take on

49. **of her own clime, complexion, and degree.** Of her own region, race, and social class. *Complexion* here refers to Desdemona's fair skin as contrasted with Othello's dark Moorish skin.

50. **a will most rank.** A foul desire or appetite; *rank* could also mean lustful.

51. **disproportion.** Lack of balance

52. **I do not . . . speak of her.** I do not, in making this argument, speak about Desdemona in particular.

53. **recoiling to.** Going back to

54. **fall to match you . . . repent.** Will begin to compare you to her countrymen (fellow Italians) and perhaps repent of, or regret, her choice in marrying you

55. **Set on thy wife to observe.** Ask your wife, Emilia, to observe Desdemona closely.

56. **strain his entertainment.** Urge his reinstatement

57. **importunity.** The quality of being importunate; that is, overly persistent in request or demand

58. **too busy.** Overactive or overly meddlesome

59. **hold her free.** Consider her to be free from guilt

60. **Fear not my government.** Have faith in my ability to control myself.

61. **learned.** Experienced or intelligent

62. **haggard.** A *haggard* was a wild, untrained hawk.

63. **jesses.** Leather straps attached to the foot of a hawk, by which the falconer held her

64. **whistle her off . . . down the wind.** Another reference to falconry. Critic Samuel Johnson explained this line as follows: "The falconers always let the hawk fly against the wind; if she flies with the wind behind her, she seldom returns. If therefore a hawk was for any reason to be dismissed, she was *let down the wind,* and from that time shifted for herself."

65. **pray at fortune.** Rely on fortune. Some versions of the play read *prey at fortune,* which continues the falconry metaphor.

66. **Haply, for I am black.** Perhaps because I am black. Again, this line does not necessarily mean that Othello is black in our sense of the word. *Black* simply meant dark-haired or dark-complexioned.

67. **soft parts of conversation.** Refined social graces

words for everyday use

ve • he • ment (vē´ ə mənt) *adj.,* intensely emotional; deeply felt or strongly expressed. *I knew there was no use arguing with my mother when she looked me in the eye and gave me a <u>vehement</u> "No!"*

IAGO. Long live she so! and long live you to think so!

OTHELLO. And yet, how nature erring[47] from itself,—

IAGO. Ay, there's the point: as—to be bold with you—
Not to affect[48] many proposèd matches

230 Of her own clime, complexion, and degree,[49]
Whereto we see in all things nature tends—
Foh! one may smell in such a will most rank,[50]
Foul disproportion,[51] thoughts unnatural.
But pardon me; I do not in position

235 Distinctly speak of her;[52] though I may fear
Her will, recoiling to[53] her better judgment,
May fall to match you with her country forms
And happily repent.[54]

OTHELLO.   Farewell, farewell:
If more thou dost perceive, let me know more;

240 Set on thy wife to observe.[55] Leave me, Iago.

IAGO. [Going] My lord, I take my leave.

OTHELLO. Why did I marry? This honest creature doubtless
Sees and knows more, much more, than he unfolds.

IAGO. [Returning] My lord, I would I might entreat
your honor

245 To scan this thing no further; leave it to time:
Though it be fit that Cassio have his place,
For sure, he fills it up with great ability,
Yet, if you please to hold him off awhile,
You shall by that perceive him and his means.

250 Note, if your lady strain his entertainment[56]
With any strong or vehement importunity;[57]
Much will be seen in that. In the mean time,
Let me be thought too busy[58] in my fears—
As worthy cause I have to fear I am—

255 And hold her free,[59] I do beseech your honor.

OTHELLO. Fear not my government.[60]

IAGO. I once more take my leave.

Exit.

OTHELLO. This fellow's of exceeding honesty,
And knows all qualities, with a learned[61] spirit,

260 Of human dealings. If I do prove her haggard,[62]
Though that her jesses[63] were my dear heartstrings,
I'ld whistle her off and let her down the wind,[64]
To pray at fortune.[65] Haply, for I am black[66]
And have not those soft parts of conversation[67]

◀ What does Iago say might be a sign of "foul disproportion" in Desdemona? What does he say she might do?

◀ What does Iago advise Othello to do regarding Cassio? What should Othello watch for?

68. **chamberers.** Courtiers

69. **declined / Into the vale of years.** Fallen into the valley of old age. This and other references in the play suggest that Othello is significantly older than Desdemona, perhaps some twenty years her senior.

70. **keep a corner . . . For others' uses.** Allow even a corner, or a small part, of Desdemona, to be used by others.

71. **the plague of great ones.** The drawback of being a distinguished man

72. **Prerogatived.** Privileged

73. **unshunnable.** Unable to be shunned, or denied

74. **forkèd plague.** The cuckold was always portrayed as having horns, the visible evidence of being played a fool by his wife.

75. **quicken.** Begin to live

76. **generous.** Highborn, or noble (from the Latin *generosus*)

77. **attend.** Await

78. **here.** Referring to spots on both sides of his forehead, where a cuckold's horns would be. Although Desdemona does not understand his meaning, the audience knows that Othello's pain is caused by the horns he imagines are sprouting from his forehead.

79. **that's with watching.** That's from staying up late.

80. **'twill away.** It will go away

81. **bind it.** Wrap your head

82. **napkin.** Handkerchief

83. **a hundred times.** This is apparently inconsistent with the timeframe of the play. The group has only been in Cyprus for two days. However, this and other references give the impression that much more time has elapsed.

84. **Woo'd.** Begged persistently

85. **conjured.** Solemnly or earnestly requested

86. **reserves.** Preserves; keeps

87. **I'll have the work ta'en out.** I'll have the work copied.

88. **I nothing but.** I want nothing but

89. **fantasy.** Fancy, whim

words for everyday use

to • ken (tō´ kən) *n.*, something done or given as a sign of obligation or affection. *"I give you this ring as a token of my affection,"* said Ralph to his girlfriend.

265 That chamberers[68] have, or for I am declined
   Into the vale of years,[69]—yet that's not much—
   She's gone. I am abused; and my relief
   Must be to loathe her. O curse of marriage,
   That we can call these delicate creatures ours,
270 And not their appetites! I had rather be a toad,
   And live upon the vapor of a dungeon,
   Than keep a corner in the thing I love
   For others' uses.[70] Yet, 'tis the plague of great ones;[71]
   Prerogatived[72] are they less than the base;
275 'Tis destiny unshunnable,[73] like death:
   Even then this forkèd plague[74] is fated to us
   When we do quicken.[75] Desdemona comes:

Re-enter DESDEMONA *and* EMILIA.

If she be false, O, then heaven mocks itself!
I'll not believe't.

DESDEMONA.   How now, my dear Othello!
280 Your dinner, and the generous[76] islanders
By you invited, do attend[77] your presence.

OTHELLO. I am to blame.

DESDEMONA.   Why do you speak so faintly?
Are you not well?

OTHELLO. I have a pain upon my forehead here.[78]

DESDEMONA. 'Faith, that's with watching;[79] 'twill
285   away[80] again:
Let me but bind it[81] hard, within this hour
It will be well.

OTHELLO.   Your napkin[82] is too little:
[*He puts the handkerchief from him; and it drops*]
Let it alone. Come, I'll go in with you.

DESDEMONA. I am very sorry that you are not well.

            Exeunt OTHELLO *and* DESDEMONA.

290 EMILIA. I am glad I have found this napkin:
This was her first remembrance from the Moor:
My wayward husband hath a hundred times[83]
Woo'd[84] me to steal it; but she so loves the <u>token</u>,
For he conjured[85] her she should ever keep it,
295 That she reserves[86] it evermore about her
To kiss and talk to. I'll have the work ta'en out,[87]
And give't Iago: what he will do with it
Heaven knows, not I;
I nothing but[88] to please his fantasy.[89]

◀ Reread lines 263–268. What reasons does Othello think Desdemona might have for cheating on him?

◀ Why does Emilia steal the handkerchief?

90. **to the advantage.** Taking advantage of the opportunity

91. **import.** Importance

92. **lack it.** Find it missing

93. **be not acknown on't.** Do not acknowledge that you know where it is.

94. **to the jealous.** To those who are jealous

95. **proofs of holy writ.** Evidence as trustworthy as if it came from God Himself (holy writ refers to the Bible or Holy Scriptures, i.e., the Word of God in Christian belief)

96. **conceits.** Ideas

97. **mines of Sulphur.** Sulphur, also spelled *sulfur*, is a chemical element with a pungent, acidic quality. The Devil was associated with sulphur, so this reference to sulphur mines calls up an image of hell.

98. **I did say so.** Look, I told you so (referring to Othello's reappearance).

99. **Not poppy, nor mandragora.** Poppies are the source of opium; mandragora, or mandrake root, has narcotic properties. Both can induce sleep.

---

words for everyday use

neg • li • gence (neg´ li jən[t]s) n., carelessness or neglect. *When Susan lost her softball jersey, the coach scolded her for her negligence.*

tri • fle (trī´ fəl) n., something of little significance or value. *The gift was only a small trifle, but the child appreciated it immensely.*

Re-enter IAGO.

300 IAGO. How now! what do you here alone?

EMILIA. Do not you chide; I have a thing for you.

IAGO. A thing for me? it is a common thing—

EMILIA. Ha!

IAGO. To have a foolish wife.

305 EMILIA. O, is that all? What will you give me now
For the same handkerchief?

IAGO.   What handkerchief?

EMILIA. What handkerchief?
Why, that the Moor first gave to Desdemona;
That which so often you did bid me steal.

310 IAGO. Hast stol'n it from her?

EMILIA. No, 'faith; she let it drop by <u>negligence</u>.
And, to the advantage,[90] I, being here, took't up.
Look, here it is.

IAGO.   A good wench; give it me.

EMILIA. What will you do with't, that you have been
so earnest
To have me filch it?

315 IAGO. [*Snatching it*] Why, what's that to you?

EMILIA. If it be not for some purpose of import,[91]
Give't me again: poor lady, she'll run mad
When she shall lack it.[92]

IAGO. Be not acknown on't;[93] I have use for it.
320 Go, leave me.

                           Exit EMILIA.

I will in Cassio's lodging lose this napkin,
And let him find it. <u>Trifles</u> light as air
Are to the jealous[94] confirmations strong
As proofs of holy writ:[95] this may do something.
325 The Moor already changes with my poison:
Dangerous conceits[96] are, in their natures, poisons,
Which at the first are scarce found to distaste,
But with a little act upon the blood
Burn like the mines of Sulphur.[97]

Re-enter OTHELLO.

                 I did say so:[98]
Look, where he comes!

330   Not poppy, nor mandragora,[99]

◄ *What will Iago do with the handkerchief?*

100. **owedst.** Owned; had

101. **Avaunt!** Away!

102. **the rack.** An instrument of torture

103. **free.** Carefree

104. **wanting.** Missing

105. **Pioners.** The lowest rank of soldier, usually appointed to that job as a punishment

106. **pomp and circumstance.** Splendor and ceremonies. This phrase has been quoted so often that it is now a cliché.

107. **mortal engines.** Deadly machinery (such as cannons)

108. **immortal Jove's . . . counterfeit.** Imitate the dreaded thunder of the immortal Jove (Jove, or Jupiter, was king of the Roman gods and was believed to cause thunder when angry)

109. **ocular.** Visible to the eye

110. **probation.** Proof

words for everyday use

tran • quil (traŋ ́ kwəl) *adj.*, peaceful. *The vacation cabin was located in a tranquil spot, far from the bustle of the city.*

Nor all the drowsy syrups of the world,
Shall ever medicine thee to that sweet sleep
Which thou owedst[100] yesterday.

OTHELLO.   Ha! ha! false to me?

IAGO. Why, how now, general! no more of that.

OTHELLO. Avaunt![101] be gone! thou hast set me on
335   the rack:[102]
I swear 'tis better to be much abused
Than but to know't a little.

IAGO.   How now, my lord!

OTHELLO. What sense had I of her stol'n hours of lust?
I saw't not, thought it not, it harm'd not me:
340 I slept the next night well, was free[103] and merry;
I found not Cassio's kisses on her lips.
He that is robb'd, not wanting[104] what is stol'n,
Let him not know't, and he's not robb'd at all.

IAGO. I am sorry to hear this.

345 OTHELLO. I had been happy, if the general camp,
Pioners[105] and all, had tasted her sweet body,
So I had nothing known. O, now, for ever
Farewell the <u>tranquil</u> mind! farewell content!
Farewell the plumed troop, and the big wars,
350 That make ambition virtue! O, farewell!
Farewell the neighing steed, and the shrill trump,
The spirit-stirring drum, the ear-piercing fife,
The royal banner, and all quality,
Pride, pomp and circumstance[106] of glorious war!
355 And, O you mortal engines,[107] whose rude throats
The immortal Jove's dread clamours counterfeit,[108]
Farewell! Othello's occupation's gone!

◀ How has Othello already been affected by Iago's poisonous words?

IAGO. Is't possible, my lord?

OTHELLO. Villain, be sure thou prove my love a
      whore,
360 Be sure of it; give me the ocular[109] proof:
Or by the worth of man's eternal soul,
Thou hadst been better have been born a dog
Than answer my waked wrath!

◀ What does Othello demand from Iago?

IAGO.   Is't come to this?

OTHELLO. Make me to see't; or, at the least, so prove it,
365 That the probation[110] bear no hinge nor loop
To hang a doubt on; or woe upon thy life!

IAGO. My noble lord,—

111. **God be wi' you.** Goodbye

112. **this profit.** This lesson

113. **sith.** Since

114. **shouldst be.** Must be (in other words, I believe you to be). Iago plays upon the word in his response.

115. **Dian's visage.** The face of Diana, the Roman goddess of the moon and of hunting. Diana was depicted as a pure and virginal young woman.

116. **begrimed.** Made grimy

117. **If there be cords . . . Would I were satisfied!** I do not care what dangers may befall me, I cannot endure the torment of not knowing the truth. I wish I were satisfied (by learning the truth).

118. **supervisor.** Witness

119. **topp'd.** In other words, with Cassio on top of her (a very vulgar term)

120. **bolster.** Bed down

121. **More than their own.** Other than their own (eyes)

122. **prime.** Lustful

123. **salt.** Lecherous

124. **in pride.** In heat

125. **strong circumstances.** Strong circumstantial evidence

words for everyday use   im • pu • ta • tion (im′ pyə tā′ shən) *n.*, accusation; insinuation. *Carl denied imputations that he'd only gotten the job because he was the boss's son.*

OTHELLO. If thou dost slander her and torture me,
Never pray more; abandon all remorse;
370 On horror's head horrors accumulate;
Do deeds to make heaven weep, all earth amazed;
For nothing canst thou to damnation add
Greater than that.

IAGO. O grace! O heaven forgive me!
Are you a man? have you a soul or sense?
375 God be wi' you;[111] take mine office. O wretched fool,
That livest to make thine honesty a vice!
O monstrous world! Take note, take note, O world,
To be direct and honest is not safe.
I thank you for this profit;[112] and from hence
380 I'll love no friend, sith[113] love breeds such offense.

OTHELLO. Nay, stay: thou shouldst be[114] honest.

IAGO. I should be wise, for honesty's a fool
And loses that it works for.

OTHELLO. By the world,
I think my wife be honest and think she is not;
385 I think that thou art just and think thou art not.
I'll have some proof. Her name, that was as fresh
As Dian's visage,[115] is now begrimed[116] and black
As mine own face. If there be cords, or knives,
Poison, or fire, or suffocating streams,
390 I'll not endure it. Would I were satisfied![117]

◀ How has Desdemona's image changed in Othello's mind?

IAGO. I see, sir, you are eaten up with passion:
I do repent me that I put it to you.
You would be satisfied?

OTHELLO. Would! nay, I will.

IAGO. And may: but, how? how satisfied, my lord?
395 Would you, the supervisor,[118] grossly gape on—
Behold her topp'd?[119]

OTHELLO. Death and damnation! O!

IAGO. It were a tedious difficulty, I think,
To bring them to that prospect: damn them then,
If ever mortal eyes do see them bolster[120]
400 More than their own![121] What then? how then?
What shall I say? Where's satisfaction?
It is impossible you should see this,
Were they as prime[122] as goats, as hot as monkeys,
As salt[123] as wolves in pride,[124] and fools as gross
405 As ignorance made drunk. But yet, I say,
If <u>imputation</u> and strong circumstances,[125]

◀ What kind of proof can Iago offer, if not direct "ocular proof"?

126. **living reason.** Real proof; more than circumstances
127. **Prick'd to't.** Goaded or prodded into it
128. **gripe.** Grip
129. **this denoted a foregone conclusion.** This is further evidence to prove the conclusion we have already come to, i.e., that Desdemona is unfaithful.
130. **shrewd doubt.** Strong reason for suspicion
131. **thicken other proofs . . . thinly.** Give more credence to the other evidence we have, which is still not very substantial.
132. **slave.** Cassio (a term of contempt)

Which lead directly to the door of truth,
Will give you satisfaction, you may have't.

OTHELLO. Give me a living reason[126] she's disloyal.

410 IAGO. I do not like the office:
But, sith I am enter'd in this cause so far,
Prick'd to't[127] by foolish honesty and love,
I will go on. I lay with Cassio lately;
And, being troubled with a raging tooth,
415 I could not sleep.
There are a kind of men so loose of soul,
That in their sleeps will mutter their affairs:
One of this kind is Cassio:
In sleep I heard him say "Sweet Desdemona,

◄ What does Iago claim he heard Cassio say?

420 Let us be wary, let us hide our loves;"
And then, sir, would he gripe[128] and wring my hand,
Cry "O sweet creature!" and then kiss me hard,
As if he pluck'd up kisses by the roots
That grew upon my lips: then laid his leg
425 Over my thigh, and sigh'd, and kiss'd; and then
Cried, "Cursed fate that gave thee to the Moor!"

OTHELLO. O monstrous! monstrous!

IAGO.   Nay, this was but
    his dream.

OTHELLO. But this denoted a foregone conclusion:[129]
'Tis a shrewd doubt,[130] though it be but a dream.

430 IAGO. And this may help to thicken other proofs
That do demonstrate thinly.[131]

OTHELLO.   I'll tear her all to pieces.

IAGO. Nay, but be wise: yet we see nothing done;
She may be honest yet. Tell me but this,
Have you not sometimes seen a handkerchief
435 Spotted with strawberries in your wife's hand?

OTHELLO. I gave her such a one; 'twas my first gift.

IAGO. I know not that; but such a handkerchief—
I am sure it was your wife's—did I to-day
See Cassio wipe his beard with.

◄ What final piece of "evidence" convinces Othello of his wife's infidelity?

OTHELLO.   If it be that—

440 IAGO. If it be that, or any that was hers,
It speaks against her with the other proofs.

OTHELLO. O, that the slave[132] had forty thousand lives!
One is too poor, too weak for my revenge.
Now do I see 'tis true. Look here, Iago;

133. **fond.** Foolish

134. **hearted throne.** The throne in my heart, on which I had Desdemona sit (she was the queen of his heart)

135. **fraught.** Freight, load

136. **aspics' tongues.** The tongues of asps, or poisonous snakes, whose bites could cause swelling (as in the previous line, "Swell, bosom...")

137. **Pontic sea.** The Black Sea, north of Turkey

138. **compulsive.** Relentless

139. **Ne'er feels retiring ebb.** Its tide continually flows, without ebbing, or receding backward, as the tide normally does.

140. **Propontic and the Hellespont.** The Propontic is the Sea of Marmara, in northwest Turkey. The Hellespont is another name for the Strait of Dardanelles, which connects the Sea of Marmara with the Aegean.

141. **capable.** Capacious, ample

142. **yond.** Yonder, distant

143. **engage.** Pledge

144. **clip us.** Enclose us

145. **execution.** Use, employment

146. **to obey . . . ever.** To obey him will be an act of pity and kindness, not of cruelty, however bloody the business may be. Critic Samuel Johnson explained the line thus: "It shall be an act, not of cruelty, but *of tenderness to obey him;* not of malice to others, but of *tenderness* to him."

147. **lewd minx.** Sexually unchaste woman. *Lewd* meant unchaste or wicked; *minx* meant a wanton woman.

445 All my fond[133] love thus do I blow to heaven.
'Tis gone.
Arise, black vengeance, from thy hollow cell!
Yield up, O love, thy crown and hearted throne[134]
To tyrannous hate! Swell, bosom, with thy fraught,[135]
For 'tis of aspics' tongues![136]

450 IAGO.   Yet be content.

OTHELLO. O, blood, blood, blood!

IAGO. Patience, I say; your mind perhaps may change.

OTHELLO. Never, Iago: Like to the Pontic sea,[137]
Whose icy current and compulsive[138] course
455 Ne'er feels retiring ebb,[139] but keeps due on
To the Propontic and the Hellespont,[140]
Even so my bloody thoughts, with violent pace,
Shall ne'er look back, ne'er ebb to humble love,
Till that a capable[141] and wide revenge
460 Swallow them up. Now, by yond[142] marble heaven,
[Kneels]
In the due reverence of a sacred vow
I here engage[143] my words.

IAGO.   Do not rise yet.
[Kneels]
Witness, you ever-burning lights above,
You elements that clip us[144] round about,
465 Witness that here Iago doth give up
The execution[145] of his wit, hands, heart,
To wrong'd Othello's service! Let him command,
And to obey shall be in me remorse,
What bloody business ever.[146]

They rise.

OTHELLO.   I greet thy love,
470 Not with vain thanks, but with acceptance bounteous,
And will upon the instant put thee to't:
Within these three days let me hear thee say
That Cassio's not alive.

◄ What will Iago do for Othello?

IAGO. My friend is dead; 'tis done at your request.
475 But let her live.

OTHELLO. Damn her, lewd minx![147] O, damn her!
Come, go with me apart; I will withdraw,
To furnish me with some swift means of death
For the fair devil. Now art thou my lieutenant.

◄ How will Othello reward Iago? What will he do to Desdemona?

480 IAGO. I am your own for ever.

Exeunt.

ACT III, SCENE iv

1. **sirrah.** Form of address indicating inferiority of the person being spoken to

2. **lies.** Lodges

3. **to say a soldier lies, is stabbing.** To accuse a soldier of lying is tantamount to stabbing him.

4. **Go to.** Come on! (Stop your kidding!)

5. **lie in mine own throat.** Tell an outright lie

6. **catechise.** To give religious instruction by questions, answers, and corrections to the answers. Plays on another meaning of *edify*, which is "to instruct in moral and religious knowledge."

7. **make questions . . . answer.** Here he extends his joke about catechizing the world. He will ask questions, and from the information he learns, he will be able to answer Desdemona's question.

8. **moved my lord on his behalf.** Attempted to influence Othello in his favor. Othello is indeed moved on Cassio's behalf, but not in the way Desdemona thinks.

9. **compass.** Scope, range. The Clown uses flowery language to humorous effect. The entire sentence could be reworded as: "To do this is doable, and therefore I will attempt to do it."

10. **Where should I lose.** Where could I have lost

11. **crusadoes.** Portuguese gold coins, which were valid currency in England in Shakespeare's day. They had a cross stamped on one side, and thus the term *crusado*, from Portuguese *cruzado*, meaning "crossed."

12. **baseness.** The quality of being base, or low. *Base* meant lacking noble qualities. Desdemona thinks that Othello has no baseness in him.

13. **humors.** Inclinations; states of mind

words for everyday use

ed • i • fy (ed´ ə fī´) *vi.,* inform or enlighten. *The pupils were all eager to be edified by the learned teacher.*

SCENE iv: Before the castle.

Enter DESDEMONA, EMILIA, *and* CLOWN.

DESDEMONA. Do you know, sirrah,[1] where
Lieutenant Cassio lies?[2]

CLOWN. I dare not say he lies any where.

DESDEMONA. Why, man?

5 CLOWN. He's a soldier, and for one to say a soldier
lies, is stabbing.[3]

DESDEMONA. Go to:[4] where lodges he?

CLOWN. To tell you where he lodges, is to tell you
where I lie.

10 DESDEMONA. Can any thing be made of this?

CLOWN. I know not where he lodges, and for me to
devise a lodging and say he lies here or he lies there,
were to lie in mine own throat.[5]

DESDEMONA. Can you inquire him out, and be
15 edified by report?

CLOWN. I will catechise[6] the world for him; that is,
make questions, and by them answer.[7]

DESDEMONA. Seek him, bid him come hither: tell
him I have moved my lord on his behalf,[8] and hope
20 all will be well.

CLOWN. To do this is within the compass[9] of man's
wit: and therefore I will attempt the doing it.

Exit.

DESDEMONA. Where should I lose[10] that
   handkerchief, Emilia?

EMILIA. I know not, madam.

DESDEMONA. Believe me, I had rather have lost my
25   purse
Full of crusadoes:[11] and, but my noble Moor
Is true of mind and made of no such baseness[12]
As jealous creatures are, it were enough
To put him to ill thinking.

EMILIA.   Is he not jealous?

DESDEMONA. Who, he? I think the sun where he was
30   born
Drew all such humors[13] from him.

EMILIA.   Look, where he comes.

◄ *What different meanings of "lie" does the Clown play on?*

◄ *Does Desdemona view Othello as jealous?*

14. **hardness.** Anger; hardheartedness
15. **fruitfulness and liberal heart.** Generosity; but here, Othello means *overly* generous. He implies that she is too giving—that she gives herself to others.
16. **sequester from liberty.** A period of being sequestered, or kept secluded apart from others, as nuns in a convent
17. **exercise devout.** Performance of religious duties
18. **frank.** Honest, open—but again, Othello implies that she has been *too* open.
19. **Our new heraldry is hands, not hearts.** Our new way of doing things is to give up our hands in marriage, but not our hearts. (Hearts and hands were common symbols in heraldry, or coats of arms.)
20. **chuck.** A term of endearment, related to *chick*
21. **salt and sorry rheum.** Sharp and painful head cold. *Rheum* also meant "tears." Othello is probably trying to explain away the fact that he is crying.
22. **Egyptian.** Gypsy
23. **charmer.** Enchantress or witch; one who casts spells

words for everyday use	dis • sem • ble (dis em´ bəl) *vt.*, hide under a false appearance. *Laura <u>dissembled</u> her annoyance by smiling cheerfully.*	cas • ti • ga • tion (kas´ tə gā´ shən) *n.*, punishment. *Slaves could be severely beaten and even killed as <u>castigation</u> for running away.*

DESDEMONA. I will not leave him now till Cassio
Be call'd to him.

Enter OTHELLO.

                      How is't with you, my lord?

OTHELLO. Well, my good lady. [*Aside*] O, hardness[14]
    to <u>dissemble</u>!—
How do you, Desdemona?

35 **DESDEMONA.**   Well, my good lord.

OTHELLO. Give me your hand. This hand is moist,
    my lady.

DESDEMONA. It yet hath felt no age nor known no
    sorrow.

OTHELLO. This argues fruitfulness and liberal heart:[15]
Hot, hot, and moist: this hand of yours requires
40 A sequester from liberty,[16] fasting and prayer,
Much <u>castigation</u>, exercise devout;[17]
For here's a young and sweating devil here,
That commonly rebels. 'Tis a good hand,
A frank[18] one.

◄ What does Othello say about Desdemona's hand?

DESDEMONA.   You may, indeed, say so;
45 For 'twas that hand that gave away my heart.

OTHELLO. A liberal hand: the hearts of old gave hands;
But our new heraldry is hands, not hearts.[19]

DESDEMONA. I cannot speak of this. Come now, your
    promise.

OTHELLO. What promise, chuck?[20]

DESDEMONA. I have sent to bid Cassio come speak
50   with you.

OTHELLO. I have a salt and sorry rheum[21] offends me;
Lend me thy handkerchief.

DESDEMONA.   Here, my lord.

OTHELLO. That which I gave you.

DESDEMONA.   I have it not about me.

OTHELLO. Not?

DESDEMONA. No, indeed, my lord.

OTHELLO.   That is a fault.
55 That handkerchief
Did an Egyptian[22] to my mother give;
She was a charmer,[23] and could almost read
The thoughts of people: she told her, while she kept it,

◄ What magic charm does the handkerchief possess? What does Othello say will happen if the handkerchief is lost or given away?

24. **amiable.** Lovable
25. **wive.** Take a wife
26. **give it her.** Give it to my wife.
27. **perdition.** Here, it could mean either a loss or a disaster
28. **web.** Fabric or weave
29. **sibyl.** A female prophet or fortune-teller
30. **The sun to course two hundred compasses.** The sun had gone two hundred times around the earth; that is, the sibyl was two hundred years old.
31. **prophetic fury.** A frenzy or trance into which a prophet goes when attempting to receive messages from the spirits or gods
32. **dyed in mummy . . . maidens' hearts.** Dyed with the embalming fluid taken from the hearts of mummified virgins. *Mummy* itself, the fluid taken from mummies, was said to have medicinal qualities and in Shakespeare's day, could be purchased at a pharmacy. The fact that this *mummy* came from virgins' hearts is highly significant, since it adds to the symbolism of the handkerchief as a sign of Desdemona's chastity.
33. **rash.** Hastily; without thought
34. **what an if.** What if
35. **put me from.** Distract me from
36. **misgives.** Is giving in to doubts and fears
37. **sufficient.** Able; deserving

'Twould make her amiable[24] and subdue my father
60 Entirely to her love, but if she lost it
Or made gift of it, my father's eye
Should hold her loathed and his spirits should hunt
After new fancies. She, dying, gave it me;
And bid me, when my fate would have me wive,[25]
65 To give it her.[26] I did so: and take heed on't;
Make it a darling like your precious eye;
To lose't or give't away were such perdition[27]
As nothing else could match.

DESDEMONA.   Is't possible?

OTHELLO. 'Tis true: there's magic in the web[28] of it.
70 A sibyl,[29] that had number'd in the world
The sun to course two hundred compasses,[30]
In her prophetic fury[31] sew'd the work;
The worms were hallow'd that did breed the silk;
And it was dyed in mummy which the skillful
Conserved of maidens' hearts.[32]

◀ What dye was used on the handkerchief?

75 DESDEMONA.   Indeed! is't true?

OTHELLO. Most <u>veritable</u>; therefore look to't well.

DESDEMONA. Then would to God that I had never
    seen't!

OTHELLO. Ha! wherefore?

DESDEMONA. Why do you speak so startingly and
    rash?[33]

OTHELLO. Is't lost? is't gone? speak, is it out o' the
80   way?

DESDEMONA. Heaven bless us!

OTHELLO. Say you?

DESDEMONA. It is not lost; but what an if[34] it were?

OTHELLO. How!

DESDEMONA. I say, it is not lost.

85 OTHELLO.   Fetch't, let me see't.

DESDEMONA. Why, so I can, sir, but I will not now.
This is a trick to put me from[35] my suit:
Pray you, let Cassio be received again.

◀ What does Desdemona think is the reason for Othello's questioning?

OTHELLO. Fetch me the handkerchief: my mind
    misgives.[36]

90 DESDEMONA. Come, come;
You'll never meet a more sufficient[37] man.

38. **but.** Nothing but
39. **hungerly.** Hungrily
40. **'tis she must do't.** She, Desdemona, is the one who must help you win back Othello's favor
41. **the happiness!** Good luck!
42. **virtuous.** Powerful
43. **If my offense be of such mortal kind.** If my offense is so deadly serious
44. **Nor purposed merit in futurity.** Nor any promise to serve well in the future
45. **shut myself up in.** Confine myself to
46. **advocation . . . in tune.** My advocacy, or pleading, is not now pleasing to Othello's ears (but is rather like an instrument out of tune).
47. **nor should . . . in humour alter'd.** If he were as changed in appearance as he is in personality and mood, I would not recognize him.
48. **sanctified.** Holy

words for everyday use

alms (ä[l]mz´) n., something (as money or food) given as charity. *It was our custom to give alms to the poor during the holiday season.*

OTHELLO. The handkerchief!

DESDEMONA.   I pray, talk me of Cassio.

OTHELLO. The handkerchief!

DESDEMONA.   A man that all his time
Hath founded his good fortunes on your love,
95 Shared dangers with you,—

OTHELLO. The handkerchief!

DESDEMONA. In sooth, you are to blame.

OTHELLO. Away!

Exit.

EMILIA. Is not this man jealous?

100 DESDEMONA. I ne'er saw this before.
Sure, there's some wonder in this handkerchief:
I am most unhappy in the loss of it.

EMILIA. 'Tis not a year or two shows us a man:
They are all but[38] stomachs, and we all but food;
105 They eat us hungerly,[39] and when they are full,
They belch us. Look you, Cassio and my husband!

◄ *What view does
Emilia have of men?*

Enter CASSIO and IAGO.

IAGO. There is no other way; 'tis she must do't:[40]
And, lo, the happiness![41] go, and importune her.

DESDEMONA. How now, good Cassio! what's the news
with you?

110 CASSIO. Madam, my former suit: I do beseech you
That by your virtuous[42] means I may again
Exist, and be a member of his love
Whom I with all the office of my heart
Entirely honour. I would not be delay'd.
115 If my offense be of such mortal kind[43]
That nor my service past, nor present sorrows,
Nor purposed merit in futurity,[44]
Can ransom me into his love again,
But to know so must be my benefit;
120 So shall I clothe me in a forced content,
And shut myself up in[45] some other course,
To fortune's <u>alms</u>.

DESDEMONA.   Alas, thrice-gentle Cassio!
My advocation is not now in tune;[46]
My lord is not my lord; nor should I know him,
125 Were he in favor as in humor alter'd.[47]
So help me every spirit sanctified,[48]

49. **blank.** Bull's eye, on a target

50. **ranks.** Soldiers under his command

51. **Puff'd his own brother.** Blew away his own brother. The implication here is that even when his brother was killed in battle, Othello was able to remain cool and calm.

52. **Something of moment.** Something very important

53. **Something, sure, of state.** Something relating to matters of the state, or politics

54. **unhatch'd practice.** A plot that has yet to be hatched, or carried out

55. **puddled.** Muddied

56. **wrangle with inferior things.** Pick fights about smaller issues

57. **it indues . . . pain.** It brings pain to the other parts of the body

58. **observances / As fit the bridal.** Niceties or politenesses that would be more conducive to a happy marriage

59. **Beshrew me.** A very mild oath

60. **unhandsome warrior.** Unfair assailant

61. **Arraigning . . . with my soul.** Charging him with unkindness in the courtroom of my soul

62. **I find I had suborn'd the witness.** I find that I have forced the witness to lie on the stand; that is, I forced the evidence to fit my own false conclusions. *Witness* could mean an actual person who witnessed the crime, or it could mean evidence of any kind.

63. **toy.** Fancy; idea

64. **Begot upon itself.** Made by itself, without any outside cause

---

words for everyday use

suf • fice (sə fīs´) *vi., vt.,* to meet or satisfy a need; to be enough or be enough for. *The supplies in the cupboard were not plentiful, but they would suffice to get the family through the long winter.*

in • dict (in dīt´) *vt.,* criticize; accuse; charge with a crime. *Three men were indicted by a federal grand jury on charges they tried to rob a bank.*

As I have spoken for you all my best
And stood within the blank[49] of his displeasure
For my free speech! you must awhile be patient:
130 What I can do I will; and more I will
Than for myself I dare: let that <u>suffice</u> you.

IAGO. Is my lord angry?

EMILIA.   He went hence but now,
And certainly in strange unquietness.

IAGO. Can he be angry? I have seen the cannon,
135 When it hath blown his ranks[50] into the air,
And, like the devil, from his very arm
Puff'd his own brother:[51]—and can he be angry?
Something of moment[52] then: I will go meet him:
There's matter in't indeed, if he be angry.

DESDEMONA. I prithee, do so.

Exit IAGO.

140   Something, sure, of state,[53]
Either from Venice, or some unhatch'd practice[54]
Made demonstrable here in Cyprus to him,
Hath puddled[55] his clear spirit: and in such cases
Men's natures wrangle with inferior things,[56]
145 Though great ones are their object. 'Tis even so;
For let our finger ache, and it indues
Our other healthful members even to that sense
Of pain.[57] Nay, we must think men are not gods,
Nor of them look for such observances
150 As fit the bridal.[58] Beshrew me[59] much, Emilia,
I was, unhandsome warrior[60] as I am,
Arraigning his unkindness with my soul;[61]
But now I find I had suborn'd the witness,[62]
And he's <u>indicted</u> falsely.

◀ *On what does
Desdemona blame
Othello's odd
behavior?*

155 EMILIA. Pray heaven it be state-matters, as you think,
And no conception nor no jealous toy[63]
Concerning you.

DESDEMONA. Alas the day! I never gave him cause.

EMILIA. But jealous souls will not be answer'd so;
160 They are not ever jealous for the cause,
But jealous for they are jealous: 'tis a monster
Begot upon itself,[64] born on itself.

DESDEMONA. Heaven keep that monster from
    Othello's mind!

EMILIA. Lady, amen.

65. **'Save you.** God save you (a common greeting)

66. **What make you from home?** What are you doing away from home?

67. **Eight score eight hours.** One hundred sixty-eight hours, the number of hours in a week. (A *score* is twenty.) Here is another reference that suggests that more time has elapsed. Going by Bianca's words, we must conclude that the group has been in Cyprus for at least a week.

68. **lovers' absent . . . times.** The hours in which a lover is gone are one hundred sixty times more slow and agonizing than regular clock-hours. *Dial* means "clock."

69. **weary reckoning.** Tiresome mathematics

70. **leaden.** Heavy, as made of lead

71. **continuate.** Uninterrupted

72. **Strike off this score.** Pay off this debt (playing on another meaning of score)

73. **Take me this work out.** Copy this needlework for me.

74. **in good troth.** In good truth

75. **ere it be demanded.** Before someone comes to demand it back

76. **think it no addition.** I think it would not add anything to my image

DESDEMONA. I will go seek him. Cassio, walk
165   hereabout:
If I do find him fit, I'll move your suit
And seek to effect it to my uttermost.

CASSIO. I humbly thank your ladyship.

Exeunt DESDEMONA *and* EMILIA.

Enter BIANCA.

BIANCA. 'Save you,[65] friend Cassio!

CASSIO.   What make you
from home?[66]
170 How is it with you, my most fair Bianca?
I' faith, sweet love, I was coming to your house.

BIANCA. And I was going to your lodging, Cassio.
What, keep a week away? seven days and nights?
Eight score eight hours?[67] and lovers' absent hours,
175 More tedious than the dial eight score times?[68]
O weary reckoning![69]

CASSIO.   Pardon me, Bianca:
I have this while with leaden[70] thoughts been press'd:
But I shall, in a more continuate[71] time,
Strike off this score[72] of absence. Sweet Bianca,

[*Giving her* DESDEMONA's *handkerchief*]

Take me this work out.[73]

180 **BIANCA.**   O Cassio, whence came this?
This is some token from a newer friend:
To the felt absence now I feel a cause:
Is't come to this? Well, well.

CASSIO.   Go to, woman!
Throw your vile guesses in the devil's teeth,
185 From whence you have them. You are jealous now
That this is from some mistress, some remembrance:
No, in good troth,[74] Bianca.

BIANCA.   Why, whose is it?

CASSIO. I know not, sweet: I found it in my chamber.
I like the work well: ere it be demanded[75]—
190 As like enough it will—I'ld have it copied:
Take it, and do't; and leave me for this time.

BIANCA. Leave you! wherefore?

CASSIO. I do attend here on the general;
And think it no addition,[76] nor my wish,
To have him see me woman'd.

◀ *What excuse does Cassio give for his long absence? What does he give to Bianca?*

77. **bring me on the way.** Lead me on
78. **I must be circumstanced.** I must yield to circumstances.

195 **BIANCA.** Why, I pray you?

CASSIO. Not that I love you not.

BIANCA. But that you do not
love me.
I pray you, bring me on the way[77] a little,
And say if I shall see you soon at night.

CASSIO. 'Tis but a little way that I can bring you;
200 For I attend here: but I'll see you soon.

BIANCA. 'Tis very good; I must be circumstanced.[78]

Exeunt.

Respond to the Selection

At this point in the play, Iago's "poison" has worked quite well—Othello believes his wife has been unfaithful. Desdemona, having no idea of his suspicions, is completely bewildered by Othello's anger regarding the misplaced handkerchief. What would you do at this point if you were Othello? if you were Desdemona?

Investigate, Inquire, and Imagine

Recall: GATHERING FACTS

1a. To whom does Cassio appeal for help in regaining his position? At the beginning of the act, what does Othello say he plans to do about Cassio?

2a. How does Iago get Desdemona's handkerchief? What does he do with it?

3a. At the end of act III, scene iii, what does Othello say he will do about Cassio? about Desdemona? Who will be his lieutenant now?

Interpret: FINDING MEANING

➤ 1b. How does this fit into Iago's plan?

➤ 2b. Explain the significance of the handkerchief. Why is it special?

➤ 3b. Explain Othello's change of heart.

Analyze: TAKING THINGS APART

4a. In act III, scene iii, Desdemona is "tried" and found guilty, with Iago as the prosecutor and nobody to act as her defense. Analyze Iago's arguments against Desdemona. What "evidence" does he present?

Synthesize: BRINGING THINGS TOGETHER

➤ 4b. How convincing is the evidence? What flaws do you see in Iago's case? Given the evidence presented, is Othello right to condemn Desdemona?

Evaluate: MAKING JUDGMENTS

5a. Analyze the role that jealousy plays in this act. What is the nature of jealousy, according to Iago and Emilia? Is Othello a naturally jealous person? How does jealousy change Othello's view of the world?

Extend: CONNECTING IDEAS

➤ 5b. Is Othello right that "'tis better to be much abused / Than but to know't a little?" Is ignorance bliss?

Understanding Literature

CLIMAX AND CRISIS. The **climax** of a play is the high point of interest or suspense in the plot. The **crisis,** or **turning point,** often the same event as the crisis, is the point in the plot where something decisive happens to determine the future course of events and the eventual working out of the conflict. All throughout act III, the suspense has been building as Iago feeds Othello more lies and insinuations. Identify the high point of the suspense—the climatic moment in which Othello is finally and irrevocably convinced of Desdemona's guilt. What does he resolve to do?

DRAMATIC IRONY. **Irony** is a difference between appearance and reality. **Dramatic irony** occurs when something is known to the reader or audience but not to the characters. The dramatic irony builds throughout act III, as Iago continues to gain the trust and esteem of others even while the effects of his poison are being seen. What examples can you find of Iago being called "honest"? Who is being called "dishonest"? What irony can you find in Iago's line "Men should be what they seem" (act III, scene iii, line 126)? (Recall Iago's line from act I, scene i: "I am not what I am.")

COMIC RELIEF AND PUN. Writers sometimes insert into a serious work of fiction or drama a humorous scene that is said to provide **comic relief** because it relieves the seriousness or emotional intensity felt by the audience. A **pun** is a play on words, one that wittily exploits a double meaning. What character is introduced in act III to provide comic relief? What puns does this character employ?

SYMBOL. A **symbol** is a thing that stands for or represents both itself and something else. Othello is extremely upset when he believes that Desdemona has given away her handkerchief. What does the handkerchief symbolize to Othello?

ACT IV, SCENE i

1. **hypocrisy against the devil.** Hypocrisy against God is pretending to be virtuous when you are not. Hypocrisy against the devil, then, is giving the appearance of being sinful when you are not. Othello is being ironic here.

2. **The devil . . . heaven.** As explained by the poet and critic W. E. Henley: *"The devil tempts their virtue* by stirring up their passions, and *they tempt heaven* by placing themselves in such a situation [i.e., naked in bed] as makes it scarcely possible to avoid falling [into sinful behavior] by the gratification of them."

3. **venial slip.** A sin that is forgivable or slight (as opposed to a mortal sin)

4. **They have it very oft . . . not.** People who have the honor and respect of others often do not deserve it.

5. **As doth the raven . . . house.** It was believed that the raven hovered near a house in which sickness or infection existed.

6. **Who having . . . blab.** Who, having convinced a woman to sleep with them (or supplied the woman with the sex that she wanted), feel the need to blab about it.

ACT IV

SCENE i: Cyprus. Before the castle.

Enter OTHELLO *and* IAGO.

IAGO. Will you think so?

OTHELLO.   Think so, Iago!

IAGO.   What,
To kiss in private?

OTHELLO.   An unauthorized kiss.

IAGO. Or to be naked with her friend in bed
An hour or more, not meaning any harm?

5   OTHELLO. Naked in bed, Iago, and not mean harm!
It is hypocrisy against the devil:[1]
They that mean virtuously, and yet do so,
The devil their virtue tempts, and they tempt
     heaven.[2]

IAGO. So they do nothing, 'tis a venial slip:[3]
10   But if I give my wife a handkerchief,—

OTHELLO. What then?

IAGO. Why, then, 'tis hers, my lord; and, being hers,
She may, I think, bestow't on any man.

OTHELLO. She is protectress of her honor too:
15   May she give that?

IAGO. Her honor is an essence that's not seen;
They have it very oft that have it not:[4]
But, for the handkerchief,—

OTHELLO. By heaven, I would most gladly have
     forgot it.
20   Thou said'st, it comes o'er my memory,
As doth the raven o'er the infected house,[5]
Boding to all—he had my handkerchief.

IAGO. Ay, what of that?

OTHELLO.   That's not so good now.

IAGO.   What
If I had said I had seen him do you wrong?
25   Or heard him say—as knaves be such abroad,
Who having, by their own importunate suit,
Or voluntary dotage of some mistress,
Convinced or supplied them, cannot choose
But they must blab[6]—

◄ *What does Iago say about honor? How is this true of him?*

7. **belie her.** Show her to be false or wrong

8. **fulsome.** Too much, overdone; also, morally offensive

9. **Nature . . . instruction.** It would not be natural for me to be taken over by such a strong and foreboding emotion unless there were some reason for it. *Shadowing passion* could mean passion, or strong emotion, that comes over Othello like a shadow. *Instruction* refers to a cause or reason.

10. **Noses, ears, and lips.** Othello is probably imagining Cassio and Desdemona kissing each other's noses, ears, and lips

11. *Falls in a trance.* Some directors interpret this to mean that Othello literally falls down to the ground while in a trancelike state. This would make sense considering that Iago, in the next lines, tells Cassio that Othello is having an epileptic fit.

12. **epilepsy.** Epileptic fit

13. **lethargy.** State of unconsciousness

14. **his.** Its

OTHELLO. Hath he said any thing?

30 **IAGO.** He hath, my lord; but be you well assured,
No more than he'll unswear.

OTHELLO. What hath he said?

IAGO. 'Faith, that he did—I know not what he did.

OTHELLO. What? what?

IAGO. Lie—

OTHELLO. With her?

IAGO. With her, on her; what you will.

◀ According to Iago, what has Cassio said?

35 **OTHELLO.** Lie with her! lie on her! We say lie on her,
when they belie her.[7] Lie with her! that's fulsome.[8]
—Handkerchief—confessions—handkerchief!—To
confess, and be hanged for his labor;—first, to be
hanged, and then to confess.—I tremble at it. Nature
40 would not invest herself in such shadowing passion
without some instruction.[9] It is not words that shake
me thus. Pish! Noses, ears, and lips.[10]—Is't
possible?—Confess—handkerchief!—O devil!—

◀ How does this news affect Othello?

Falls in a trance.[11]

IAGO. Work on,
45 My medicine, work! Thus credulous fools are caught;
And many worthy and chaste dames even thus,
All guiltless, meet reproach. What, ho! my lord!
My lord, I say! Othello!

[*Enter* CASSIO]

How now, Cassio!

CASSIO. What's the matter?

50 **IAGO.** My lord is fall'n into an epilepsy:[12]
This is his second fit; he had one yesterday.

CASSIO. Rub him about the temples.

IAGO. No, forbear;
The lethargy[13] must have his[14] quiet course:
If not, he foams at mouth and by and by
55 Breaks out to savage madness. Look, he stirs.
Do you withdraw yourself a little while,
He will recover straight: when he is gone,
I would on great occasion speak with you.

Exit CASSIO.

How is it, general? have you not hurt your head?

OTHELLO. Dost thou mock me?

15. **hornèd man's.** A cuckold's
16. **civil.** Civilized
17. **but yoked.** Married
18. **May draw with you.** Has the same luck as you (with a pun on *draw*, meaning pull a load, as oxen do under a yoke)
19. **unproper beds . . . peculiar.** Beds that are not exclusively their own, which they would swear are private, or theirs alone
20. **arch-mock.** The worst mock of all
21. **lip a wanton.** Kiss a wanton, or unchaste, woman
22. **secure couch.** A bed that's safe, or free from any suspicion
23. **in a patient list.** In the bounds of patience
24. **laid . . . ecstasy.** Gave a good excuse for your fit of emotion
25. **encave.** Hide
26. **fleers.** Mocks
27. **notable scorns.** Easily noted expressions of scorn
28. **cope.** To meet with or come into contact with
29. **all and all in spleen.** Totally overtaken by anger; out of control
30. **housewife.** Hussy
31. **It.** Bianca. Iago calls her "it" instead of "she" to show his contempt
32. **strumpet's . . . one.** The curse of prostitutes is that they seduce many men, but fall in love with one who does not love them back.

60 IAGO.   I mock you! no, by heaven.
Would you would bear your fortune like a man!

OTHELLO. A hornèd man's[15] a monster and a beast.

IAGO. There's many a beast then in a populous city,
And many a civil[16] monster.

OTHELLO. Did he confess it?

65 IAGO.   Good sir, be a man;
Think every bearded fellow that's but yoked[17]
May draw with you:[18] there's millions now alive
That nightly lie in those unproper beds
Which they dare swear peculiar:[19] your case is better.
70 O, 'tis the spite of hell, the fiend's arch-mock,[20]
To lip a wanton[21] in a secure couch,[22]
And to suppose her chaste! No, let me know;
And knowing what I am, I know what she shall be.

OTHELLO. O, thou art wise; 'tis certain.

IAGO.   Stand you awhile apart;
75 Confine yourself but in a patient list.[23]
Whilst you were here o'erwhelmed with your grief—
A passion most unsuiting such a man—
Cassio came hither: I shifted him away,
And laid good 'scuse upon your ecstasy,[24]
80 Bade him anon return and here speak with me;
The which he promised. Do but encave[25] yourself,
And mark the fleers,[26] the gibes, and notable scorns,[27]
That dwell in every region of his face;
For I will make him tell the tale anew,
85 Where, how, how oft, how long ago, and when
He hath, and is again to cope[28] your wife:
I say, but mark his gesture. Marry, patience;
Or I shall say you are all in all in spleen,[29]
And nothing of a man.

OTHELLO.   Dost thou hear, Iago?
90 I will be found most cunning in my patience;
But—dost thou hear?—most bloody.

IAGO.   That's not amiss;
But yet keep time in all. Will you withdraw?

[OTHELLO *retires*]

Now will I question Cassio of Bianca,
A housewife[30] that by selling her desires
95 Buys herself bread and clothes. It[31] is a creature
That dotes on Cassio; as 'tis the strumpet's plague
To beguile many and be beguiled by one:[32]

◀ What does Iago prepare Othello to hear?

◀ Bianca first appeared in the previous scene. Who is Bianca, and what is Cassio's opinion of her? Why will Iago ask Cassio about her?

33. **unbookish.** Ignorant

34. **worser . . . kills me.** Worse now that you give me the title [of lieutenant], the lack of which is killing me

35. **Ply.** Urge

36. **caitiff.** Despicable wretch

37. **Do you triumph, Roman?** Alluding to the Roman conquerors, who seized foreign lands in order to enlarge their empire

38. **customer.** Prostitute

words for everyday use

con • strue (kən strü´) *vt.*, understand or explain the intention of a word or action, usually in a particular way given a set of circumstances. *The CEO claimed that he had done nothing wrong, although he could see how his actions "could be construed as violating the law."*

He, when he hears of her, cannot refrain
From the excess of laughter. Here he comes.

Re-enter CASSIO.

100 As he shall smile, Othello shall go mad;
And his unbookish[33] jealousy must <u>construe</u>
Poor Cassio's smiles, gestures and light behavior,
Quite in the wrong. How do you now, lieutenant?

CASSIO. The worser that you give me the addition
105 Whose want even kills me.[34]

IAGO. Ply[35] Desdemona well, and you are sure on't.

[*Speaking lower*]

Now, if this suit lay in Bianca's power,
How quickly should you speed!

CASSIO.   Alas, poor caitiff![36]

OTHELLO. Look, how he laughs already!

110 IAGO. I never knew woman love man so.

CASSIO. Alas, poor rogue! I think, i' faith, she loves
me.

OTHELLO. Now he denies it faintly, and laughs it out.

IAGO. Do you hear, Cassio?

OTHELLO.   Now he importunes him
To tell it o'er: go to; well said, well said.

115 IAGO. She gives it out that you shall marry her:
Do you intend it?

CASSIO. Ha, ha, ha!

OTHELLO. Do you triumph, Roman?[37] do you
triumph?

CASSIO. I marry her! what? a customer![38] Prithee,
120 bear some charity to my wit: do not think it so
unwholesome. Ha, ha, ha!

OTHELLO. So, so, so, so: they laugh that win.

IAGO. 'Faith, the cry goes that you shall marry her.

CASSIO. Prithee, say true.

125 IAGO. I am a very villain else.

OTHELLO. Have you scored me? Well.

CASSIO. This is the monkey's own giving out: she is
persuaded I will marry her, out of her own love and
flattery, not out of my promise.

39. **beckons.** Signals with a hand gesture
40. **hales.** Hauls
41. **fitchew.** Polecat, an animal (related to the ferret) known for having a bad smell. Cassio goes on to say that although Bianca is a fitchew, at least she is a "perfumed one."
42. **devil and his dam.** The devil and his mother
43. **likely piece of work.** Likely story
44. **hobby-horse.** Harlot
45. **should.** Must
46. **An.** If

130   **OTHELLO.** Iago beckons[39] me; now he begins the story.

  CASSIO. She was here even now; she haunts me in every place. I was the other day talking on the sea-bank with certain Venetians; and thither comes the <u>bauble</u>, and, by this hand, she falls me thus about
135 my neck—

  OTHELLO. Crying "O dear Cassio!" as it were: his gesture imports it.

◀ *What does Othello think Cassio is talking about?*

  CASSIO. So hangs, and <u>lolls</u>, and weeps upon me; so hales,[40] and pulls me: ha, ha, ha!

140   **OTHELLO.** Now he tells how she plucked him to my chamber. O, I see that nose of yours, but not that dog I shall throw it to.

  CASSIO. Well, I must leave her company.

  IAGO. Before me! look, where she comes.

145   **CASSIO.** 'Tis such another fitchew![41] marry a perfumed one.

Enter BIANCA.

What do you mean by this haunting of me?

  BIANCA. Let the devil and his dam[42] haunt you! What did you mean by that same handkerchief you
150 gave me even now? I was a fine fool to take it. I must take out the work?—A likely piece of work,[43] that you should find it in your chamber, and not know who left it there! This is some minx's token, and I must take out the work? There; give it your hobby-
155 horse:[44] wheresoever you had it, I'll take out no work on't.

  CASSIO. How now, my sweet Bianca! how now! how now!

  OTHELLO. By heaven, that should[45] be my
160 handkerchief!

◀ *What does Othello see?*

  BIANCA. An[46] you'll come to supper to-night, you may; an you will not, come when you are next prepared for.

Exit.

  IAGO. After her, after her.

165   **CASSIO.** 'Faith, I must; she'll <u>rail</u> in the street else.

  IAGO. Will you sup there?

  CASSIO. 'Faith, I intend so.

47. **very fain.** Very much like to

48. **vice.** Sinful behavior

49. **I would . . . nine years a-killing.** I wish I could make his killing last nine years (so prolonged do I want his pain to be)

50. **condition.** Disposition

51. **too gentle.** Too generous with her affections

52. **fond.** Foolishly doting

53. **Give her patent.** Give her permission, or license

IAGO. Well, I may chance to see you; for I would very fain[47] speak with you.

170 CASSIO. Prithee, come; will you?

IAGO. Go to; say no more.

Exit CASSIO.

OTHELLO. [*Advancing*] How shall I murder him, Iago?

IAGO. Did you perceive how he laughed at his vice?[48]

OTHELLO. O Iago!

175 IAGO. And did you see the handkerchief?

OTHELLO. Was that mine?

IAGO. Yours by this hand: and to see how he prizes the foolish woman your wife! she gave it him, and he hath given it his whore.

180 OTHELLO. I would have him nine years a-killing.[49] A fine woman! a fair woman! a sweet woman!

IAGO. Nay, you must forget that.

OTHELLO. Ay, let her rot, and perish, and be damned to-night; for she shall not live: no, my heart is
185 turned to stone; I strike it, and it hurts my hand. O, the world hath not a sweeter creature: she might lie by an emperor's side and command him tasks.

IAGO. Nay, that's not your way.

OTHELLO. Hang her! I do but say what she is: so
190 delicate with her needle: an admirable musician: O! she will sing the savageness out of a bear: of so high and plenteous wit and invention:—

IAGO. She's the worse for all this.

OTHELLO. O, a thousand thousand times: and then,
195 of so gentle a condition![50]

IAGO. Ay, too gentle.[51]

OTHELLO. Nay, that's certain: but yet the pity of it, Iago! O Iago, the pity of it, Iago!

IAGO. If you are so fond[52] over her iniquity, give her
200 patent[53] to offend; for, if it touch not you, it comes near nobody.

OTHELLO. I will chop her into messes: cuckold me!

IAGO. O, 'tis foul in her.

OTHELLO. With mine officer!

◀ What is Othello now determined to do?

◀ How is Othello conflicted?

54. **unprovide my mind.** Cause me to lose my resolve
55. **his undertaker.** The one who undertakes his killing
56. **With all my heart.** I thank you with all my heart; or, I welcome you with all my heart
57. **instrument of their pleasures.** Said while kissing his hand, as if to blow a kiss: his hand is the instrument, or tool, ready to do whatever the duke and senators wish.
58. **cousin.** Lodovico is a kinsman to Desdemona's father. *Cousin* was a general term meaning "relative."

words for everyday use

ex • pos • tu • late (ik späs´ chə lāt´) *vi.*, express objection in the form of earnest reasoning. *The senators expostulated with one another all day, but never came to a decision about the issue.*

breach (brēch´) *n.*, break in relations. *A breach developed between the leadership of both countries, and diplomats attempted to repair the broken relationship.*

205 IAGO. That's fouler.

OTHELLO. Get me some poison, Iago; this night. I'll
not <u>expostulate</u> with her, lest her body and beauty
unprovide my mind[54] again: this night, Iago.

◀ What has Othello
decided?

IAGO. Do it not with poison, strangle her in her bed,
210 even the bed she hath contaminated.

OTHELLO. Good, good: the justice of it pleases: very
good.

IAGO. And for Cassio, let me be his undertaker:[55]
you shall hear more by midnight.

215 OTHELLO. Excellent good.

[*A trumpet within*]

What trumpet is that same?

IAGO. Something from Venice, sure. 'Tis Lodovico
Come from the duke: and, see, your wife is with
  him.

◀ Who has arrived?

Enter LODOVICO, DESDEMONA, *and* ATTENDANTS.

LODOVICO. 'Save you, worthy general!

OTHELLO.   With all my
  heart,[56] sir.

220 LODOVICO. The duke and senators of Venice greet you.

Gives him a letter.

OTHELLO. I kiss the instrument of their pleasures.[57]

Opens the letter and reads.

DESDEMONA. And what's the news, good cousin[58]
  Lodovico?

IAGO. I am very glad to see you, signior.
Welcome to Cyprus.

LODOVICO. I thank you. How does Lieutenant
225   Cassio?

◀ What does
Desdemona tell
Lodovico?

IAGO. Lives, sir.

DESDEMONA. Cousin, there's fall'n between him and
  my lord
An unkind <u>breach</u>: but you shall make all well.

OTHELLO. Are you sure of that?

230 DESDEMONA. My lord?

OTHELLO. [*Reads*] "This fail you not to do, as you
  will—"

59. **atone.** Reconcile

60. **Deputing.** Substituting

61. **glad . . . mad.** Could be an error, as it would be more likely he was "mad to see her glad," or perhaps Othello is being sarcastic.

62. **If that the earth could teem . . . a crocodile.** If the Earth could teem, or bring forth life, at the touch of a woman's tears, each drop shed by Desdemona would turn into a crocodile. An allusion to the false tears supposedly shed by crocodiles upon eating their victims.

LODOVICO. He did not call; he's busy in the paper.
Is there division 'twixt my lord and Cassio?

DESDEMONA. A most unhappy one: I would do much
235 To atone[59] them, for the love I bear to Cassio.

OTHELLO. Fire and brimstone!

DESDEMONA.   My lord?

OTHELLO.   Are you wise?

DESDEMONA. What, is he angry?

LODOVICO.   May be the letter
    moved him;
For, as I think, they do command him home,
Deputing[60] Cassio in his government.

◀ What did the letter say? How does Desdemona feel about the news?

DESDEMONA. Trust me, I am glad on't.

OTHELLO.   Indeed!

240 DESDEMONA.   My lord?

OTHELLO. I am glad to see you mad.[61]

DESDEMONA.   Why, sweet Othello,—

OTHELLO. [Striking her] Devil!

DESDEMONA. I have not deserved this.

◀ What does Othello do that shocks Desdemona and Lodovico?

LODOVICO. My lord, this would not be believed in
    Venice,
245 Though I should swear I saw't. 'Tis very much:
Make her amends; she weeps.

OTHELLO.   O devil, devil!
If that the earth could teem with woman's tears,
Each drop she falls would prove a crocodile.[62]
Out of my sight!

DESDEMONA. I will not stay to offend you. [Going]

250 LODOVICO. Truly, an obedient lady:
I do beseech your lordship, call her back.

OTHELLO. Mistress!

DESDEMONA.   My lord?

OTHELLO.   What would you with
    her, sir?

LODOVICO. Who, I, my lord?

OTHELLO. Ay; you did wish that I would make her
    turn:

63. **Concerning this.** Referring to the letter given him by Lodovico

64. **well-painted passion.** Well-acted emotion (said to Desdemona; whose tears he believes are false and hypocritical)

65. **safe.** Sound

66. **censure.** Opinion; judgment

67. **Is it his use?** Is this his usual behavior?

68. **work upon his blood.** Make him angry

69. **honesty.** Proper behavior

255 Sir, she can turn, and turn, and yet go on,
And turn again; and she can weep, sir, weep;
And she's obedient, as you say, obedient,
Very obedient. Proceed you in your tears.
Concerning this,[63] sir,—O well-painted passion![64]—
260 I am commanded home. Get you away;
I'll send for you anon. Sir, I obey the mandate,
And will return to Venice.—Hence, avaunt!

Exit DESDEMONA.

Cassio shall have my place. And, sir, tonight,
I do entreat that we may sup together:
265 You are welcome, sir, to Cyprus.—Goats and monkeys!

Exit.

◀ Which of these lines are spoken to Lodovico, and which to Desdemona?

LODOVICO. Is this the noble Moor whom our full senate
Call all in all sufficient? Is this the nature
Whom passion could not shake? whose solid virtue
The shot of accident, nor dart of chance,
Could neither graze nor pierce?

◀ Whose reputation is suffering now as a result of Iago's plots and schemes?

270 IAGO.   He is much changed.

LODOVICO. Are his wits safe?[65] is he not light of brain?

IAGO. He's that he is: I may not breathe my censure[66]
What he might be: if what he might he is not,
I would to heaven he were!

LODOVICO.   What, strike his wife!

275 IAGO. 'Faith, that was not so well; yet would I knew
That stroke would prove the worst!

LODOVICO.   Is it his use?[67]
Or did the letters work upon his blood,[68]
And new-create this fault?

IAGO.   Alas, alas!
It is not honesty[69] in me to speak
280 What I have seen and known. You shall observe him,
And his own courses will denote him so
That I may save my speech: do but go after,
And mark how he continues.

LODOVICO. I am sorry that I am deceived in him.

Exeunt.

ACT IV, SCENE ii

1. **durst . . . wager.** I dare lay a bet
2. **the serpent's curse.** The curse placed by God on the serpent in the Bible
3. **she's a simple bawd . . . as much.** A bawd was a female pimp, or brothel-keeper. Othello is saying that any brothel-keeper will protect her whores, just as Emilia defends the "whore" Desdemona.
4. **subtle whore.** Sneaky whore (speaking of Desdemona)
5. **Some of your function.** Do what you do best (that is, stand outside the door and watch for someone coming, as you do when Desdemona meets with Cassio)

words for everyday use   re • quite (ri kwīt´) *vt.*, repay or return; avenge. *Trinh vowed to requite the abuse she had suffered.*

SCENE ii: A room in the castle.

Enter OTHELLO *and* EMILIA.

OTHELLO. You have seen nothing then?

EMILIA. Nor ever heard, nor ever did suspect.

OTHELLO. Yes, you have seen Cassio and she together.

EMILIA. But then I saw no harm, and then I heard
5 Each syllable that breath made up between them.

OTHELLO. What, did they never whisper?

EMILIA.   Never, my lord.

OTHELLO. Nor send you out o' the way?

EMILIA. Never.

OTHELLO. To fetch her fan, her gloves, her mask, nor
   nothing?

10 EMILIA. Never, my lord.

OTHELLO. That's strange.

EMILIA. I durst, my lord, to wager[1] she is honest,
Lay down my soul at stake: if you think other,
Remove your thought; it doth abuse your bosom.
15 If any wretch have put this in your head,
Let heaven <u>requite</u> it with the serpent's curse![2]
For, if she be not honest, chaste, and true,
There's no man happy; the purest of their wives
Is foul as slander.

OTHELLO.   Bid her come hither: go.

Exit EMILIA.

20 She says enough; yet she's a simple bawd
That cannot say as much.[3] This is a subtle whore,[4]
A closet lock and key of villainous secrets
And yet she'll kneel and pray; I have seen her do't.

Enter DESDEMONA *with* EMILIA.

DESDEMONA. My lord, what is your will?

OTHELLO.   Pray, chuck,
   come hither.

DESDEMONA. What is your pleasure?

25 OTHELLO.   Let me see your eyes;
Look in my face.

DESDEMONA.   What horrible fancy's this?

OTHELLO. [*To* EMILIA] Some of your function,[5] mistress;

◄ About what does Othello question Emilia?

◄ What does Emilia say about Desdemona? Why doesn't Othello believe her?

6. **procreants.** Those who procreate, i.e., lovers
7. **your mystery.** Your business or occupation
8. **dispatch.** Go off and perform your duty
9. **what doth . . . import.** What do you mean by these words?
10. **being like one of heaven.** Looking like an angel
11. **honest.** Chaste
12. **If haply you . . . calling back.** If you suspect my father is responsible for you being called back to Venice
13. **fixed figure . . . finger at.** A disputed passage. Probably means "a person who the scornful world points its finger at." The image is one of the hand on a clock pointing at an unmoving number.
14. **garner'd up.** Stored, as if in a grain bin
15. **cistern.** A tank for storing water

Leave procreants[6] alone and shut the door;
Cough, or cry "hem," if any body come:
30 Your mystery, your mystery:[7] nay, dispatch.[8]

Exit EMILIA.

DESDEMONA. Upon my knees, what doth your
speech import?[9]
I understand a fury in your words,
But not the words.

OTHELLO. Why, what art thou?

DESDEMONA.   Your wife, my lord; your true
And loyal wife.

35 OTHELLO.   Come, swear it, damn thyself
Lest, being like one of heaven,[10] the devils themselves
Should fear to seize thee: therefore be double damn'd:
Swear thou art honest.[11]

DESDEMONA.   Heaven doth truly know it.

OTHELLO. Heaven truly knows that thou art false as
hell.

DESDEMONA. To whom, my lord? with whom? how
40   am I false?

OTHELLO. O Desdemona! away! away! away!

DESDEMONA. Alas the heavy day! Why do you weep?
Am I the motive of these tears, my lord?
If haply you my father do suspect
45 An instrument of this your calling back,[12]
Lay not your blame on me. If you have lost him,
Why, I have lost him too.

OTHELLO.   Had it pleased heaven
To try me with affliction; had they rain'd
All kinds of sores and shames on my bare head,
50 Steep'd me in poverty to the very lips,
Given to captivity me and my utmost hopes,
I should have found in some place of my soul
A drop of patience: but, alas, to make me
A fixed figure for the time of scorn
55 To point his slow unmoving finger at![13]
Yet could I bear that too; well, very well:
But there, where I have garner'd up[14] my heart,
Where either I must live, or bear no life;
The fountain from the which my current runs,
60 Or else dries up; to be discarded thence!
Or keep it as a cistern[15] for foul toads

◀ *What does
Desdemona think
could be the reason
for Othello's anger?*

◀ *What afflictions
could Othello bear?
What can't he bear?*

16. **knot and gender.** Mate

17. **Turn thy complexion there . . . hell.** Patience, which is depicted as a rosy angel, would pale and look grim with the knowledge of what Desdemona has done.

18. **shambles.** Slaughterhouse

19. **quicken even with blowing.** Come to life as soon as the eggs are deposited

20. **commoner.** Harlot

21. **forges.** Furnaces where metal is wrought

22. **moon winks.** Closes her eyes, as not to see. The moon is associated with chastity.

23. **Impudent strumpet.** Indecent or immodest prostitute

24. **this vessel.** This body

25. **cry you mercy.** Beg your pardon

To knot and gender[16] in! Turn thy complexion there,
Patience, thou young and rose-lipp'd cherubin,—
Ay, there, look grim as hell![17]

65 DESDEMONA. I hope my noble lord esteems me honest.

OTHELLO. O, ay; as summer flies are in the shambles,[18]
That quicken even with blowing.[19] O thou weed,
Who art so lovely fair and smell'st so sweet
That the sense aches at thee, would thou hadst ne'er
    been born!

DESDEMONA. Alas, what ignorant sin have I
70   committed?

OTHELLO. Was this fair paper, this most goodly book,
Made to write "whore" upon? What committed!
Committed! O thou public commoner![20]
I should make very forges[21] of my cheeks,
75 That would to cinders burn up modesty,
Did I but speak thy deeds. What committed!
Heaven stops the nose at it and the moon winks,[22]
The bawdy wind that kisses all it meets
Is hush'd within the hollow mine of earth,
80 And will not hear it. What committed!
Impudent strumpet![23]

DESDEMONA.   By heaven, you do me wrong.

OTHELLO. Are you not a strumpet?

DESDEMONA.   No, as I am a Christian:
If to preserve this vessel[24] for my lord
From any other foul unlawful touch
85 Be not to be a strumpet, I am none.

OTHELLO. What, not a whore?

DESDEMONA.   No, as I shall be saved.

OTHELLO. Is't possible?

DESDEMONA. O, heaven forgive us!

OTHELLO.   I cry you mercy,[25] then:
I took you for that cunning whore of Venice
That married with Othello.

[Raising his voice]

90   You, mistress,
That have the office opposite to Saint Peter,
And keep the gate of hell!

Re-enter EMILIA.

                You, you, ay, you!

◄ What does Othello
call Desdemona?
What does he call
Emilia?

26. **keep our counsel.** Keep our conversation secret

27. **answer . . . go by water.** The only answer I could give you would come in the form of tears.

28. **wedding sheets.** Some critics have cited this line as evidence that Othello and Desdemona's marriage may still not have been consummated, owing to the interruptions on previous nights. If this is true, perhaps Desdemona means to prove her chastity to Othello by giving up her virginity to him. Or, the sheets may just foreshadow the tragedy that is to come, since wives were sometimes buried in their wedding sheets.

29. **small'st opinion . . . misuse.** Harshest judgment on my smallest mistake

30. **bewhored her.** Called her "whore." Apparently Emilia did hear their conversation when listening at the door.

31. **Thrown such despite.** Showed so much scorn

We have done our course; there's money for your
    pains:
I pray you, turn the key and keep our counsel.[26]

Exit.

95 EMILIA. Alas, what does this gentleman conceive?
How do you, madam? how do you, my good lady?

DESDEMONA. 'Faith, half asleep.

EMILIA. Good madam, what's the matter with my
    lord?

DESDEMONA. With who?

100 EMILIA. Why, with my lord, madam.

DESDEMONA. Who is thy lord?

EMILIA.   He that is yours, sweet lady.

DESDEMONA. I have none: do not talk to me, Emilia;
I cannot weep; nor answer have I none,
But what should go by water.[27] Prithee, tonight
105 Lay on my bed my wedding sheets:[28] remember;
And call thy husband hither.

◄ *Whose advice does Desdemona seek?*

EMILIA.   Here's a change indeed!

Exit.

DESDEMONA. 'Tis meet I should be used so, very meet.
How have I been behaved, that he might stick
The small'st opinion on my least misuse?[29]

Re-enter EMILIA *with* IAGO.

110 IAGO. What is your pleasure, madam?
How is't with you?

DESDEMONA. I cannot tell. Those that do teach
    young babes
Do it with gentle means and easy tasks:
He might have chid me so; for, in good faith,
I am a child to chiding.

115 IAGO.   What's the matter, lady?

EMILIA. Alas, Iago, my lord hath so bewhored her.[30]
Thrown such despite[31] and heavy terms upon her,
As true hearts cannot bear.

DESDEMONA. Am I that name, Iago?

IAGO.   What name, fair lady?

120 DESDEMONA. Such as she says my lord did say I was.

EMILIA. He call'd her whore: a beggar in his drink

32. **callat.** Coarse or lewd woman
33. **forsook . . . matches.** Desdemona turned down so many noble suitors
34. **Beshrew.** Curse
35. **trick.** Foolish behavior
36. **cogging, cozening.** Lying, cheating. Note that Emilia does not suspect her husband of being this "eternal villain."
37. **to get some office.** To earn some position
38. **halter.** A hangman's noose
39. **notorious.** Notable
40. **scurvy.** Worthless; contemptible
41. **companions.** Rascals
42. **unfold.** Uncover; expose
43. **Speak within door.** Keep your voice down.
44. **squire.** Servant or attendant (used contemptuously)
45. **seamy side without.** Wrong side out
46. **made you to . . . Moor.** Refers to Iago's suspicion that Emilia slept with Othello

words for everyday use

in • sin • u • ating (in sin´ yə wā´ tiŋ) *adj.*, ingratiating: winning favor and confidence by imperceptible degrees. *The manipulative boy tried to become popular by kissing up to the older kids, but they saw through his insinuating ways and ignored him.*

Could not have laid such terms upon his callat.[32]

IAGO. Why did he so?

DESDEMONA. I do not know; I am sure I am none
    such.

125 IAGO. Do not weep, do not weep. Alas the day!

EMILIA. Hath she forsook so many noble matches,[33]
Her father and her country and her friends,
To be call'd whore? would it not make one weep?

DESDEMONA. It is my wretched fortune.

IAGO.   Beshrew[34] him for't!
How comes this trick[35] upon him?

DESDEMONA.   Nay, heaven doth
130   know.

EMILIA. I will be hang'd, if some eternal villain,
Some busy and <u>insinuating</u> rogue,
Some cogging, cozening[36] slave, to get some office,[37]
Have not devised this slander; I'll be hang'd else.

135 IAGO. Fie, there is no such man; it is impossible.

DESDEMONA. If any such there be, heaven pardon
    him!

EMILIA. A halter[38] pardon him! and hell gnaw his
    bones!
Why should he call her whore? who keeps her
    company?
What place? what time? what form? what
    likelihood?
140 The Moor's abused by some most villainous knave,
Some base notorious[39] knave, some scurvy[40] fellow.
O heaven, that such companions[41] thou'ldst
    unfold,[42]
And put in every honest hand a whip
To lash the rascals naked through the world
Even from the east to the west!

145 IAGO.   Speak within door.[43]

EMILIA. O, fie upon them! Some such squire[44] he was
That turn'd your wit the seamy side without,[45]
And made you to suspect me with the Moor.[46]

IAGO. You are a fool; go to.

DESDEMONA.   O good Iago,
150 What shall I do to win my lord again?
Good friend, go to him; for, by this light of heaven,

◀ What does Emilia
guess is the cause of
Othello's behavior?
How does Iago
respond?

47. **discourse of thought.** In the course of thought; or, could be a misprint for "discourse or thought"

48. **defeat.** Destroy

49. **To do . . . addition earn.** To actually earn the title of "whore" by behaving like one

50. **'tis but his humor.** It is just his mood

51. **chide with.** Quarrel with

52. **I warrant.** I guarantee it

53. **stay the meat.** Are waiting to have supper

54. **What in the contrary?** What reason do you have to say that I am unjust?

55. **daffest me.** Put me off

56. **device.** Trick or excuse

57. **keepest . . . hope.** You keep me from Desdemona, rather than supplying me with any hope.

58. **put up in peace.** Peacefully put up with

59. **your words and performances are no kin together.** Your words do not match up with your actions.

---

words for everyday use

for • swear (fôr swa[ə]r´, fōr swa[ə]r´) vt., reject or renounce. *"From this day forward, I forswear candy,"* Don said after he discovered he had three cavities.

taint (tānt´) vt., spoil; contaminate. *The water supply was tainted by chemicals that had leached into the soil.*

I know not how I lost him. Here I kneel:
If e'er my will did trespass 'gainst his love,
Either in discourse of thought[47] or actual deed,
155 Or that mine eyes, mine ears, or any sense,
Delighted them in any other form;
Or that I do not yet, and ever did,
And ever will—though he do shake me off
To beggarly divorcement—love him dearly,
160 Comfort <u>forswear</u> me! Unkindness may do much;
And his unkindness may defeat[48] my life,
But never <u>taint</u> my love. I cannot say "whore."
It does abhor me now I speak the word;
To do the act that might the addition earn[49]
165 Not the world's mass of vanity could make me.

IAGO. I pray you, be content; 'tis but his humor:[50]
The business of the state does him offense,
And he does chide with[51] you.

DESDEMONA. If 'twere no other—

IAGO.   'Tis but so, I warrant.[52]

[*Trumpets within*]

170 Hark, how these instruments summon to supper!
The messengers of Venice stay the meat;[53]
Go in, and weep not; all things shall be well.

                    Exeunt DESDEMONA *and* EMILIA.

Enter RODERIGO.

How now, Roderigo!

RODERIGO. I do not find that thou dealest justly with
    me.

175 IAGO. What in the contrary?[54]

RODERIGO. Every day thou daffest me[55] with some
device,[56] Iago; and rather, as it seems to me now,
keepest from me all conveniency than suppliest me
with the least advantage of hope.[57] I will indeed no
180 longer endure it, nor am I yet persuaded to put up in
peace[58] what already I have foolishly suffered.

IAGO. Will you hear me, Roderigo?

RODERIGO. 'Faith, I have heard too much, for your
words and performances are no kin together.[59]

185 IAGO. You charge me most unjustly.

◄ *What complaint
does Roderigo have
about Iago?*

60. **votarist.** Nun
61. **sudden respect.** Forthcoming attention [from her]
62. **fobbed.** Duped
63. **give over.** Give up
64. **You have said now.** You've had your say.
65. **protest intendment of doing.** What I intend to do
66. **taken . . . exception.** Voiced a fair objection to my behavior
67. **engines for.** Plots against
68. **compass.** Ability

words for everyday use

met • tle (met´ əl) *n.,* strength of spirit; courage. *The tough times tested Li's mettle, but her spirit was not broken.*

RODERIGO. With nought but truth. I have wasted myself out of my means. The jewels you have had from me to deliver to Desdemona would half have corrupted a votarist:[60] you have told me she hath
190 received them and returned me expectations and comforts of sudden respect[61] and acquaintance, but I find none.

IAGO. Well; go to; very well.

RODERIGO. Very well! go to! I cannot go to, man; nor
195 'tis not very well: nay, I think it is scurvy, and begin to find myself fobbed[62] in it.

IAGO. Very well.

RODERIGO. I tell you 'tis not very well. I will make myself known to Desdemona: if she will return me
200 my jewels, I will give over[63] my suit and repent my unlawful solicitation; if not, assure yourself I will seek satisfaction of you.

IAGO. You have said now.[64]

RODERIGO. Ay, and said nothing but what I protest
205 intendment of doing.[65]

IAGO. Why, now I see there's <u>mettle</u> in thee, and even from this instant to build on thee a better opinion than ever before. Give me thy hand, Roderigo: thou hast taken against me a most just
210 exception;[66] but yet, I protest, I have dealt most directly in thy affair.

RODERIGO. It hath not appeared.

IAGO. I grant indeed it hath not appeared, and your suspicion is not without wit and judgment. But,
215 Roderigo, if thou hast that in thee indeed, which I have greater reason to believe now than ever, I mean purpose, courage and valour, this night show it: if thou the next night following enjoy not Desdemona, take me from this world with treachery
220 and devise engines for[67] my life.

RODERIGO. Well, what is it? is it within reason and compass?[68]

IAGO. Sir, there is especial commission come from Venice to depute Cassio in Othello's place.

225 RODERIGO. Is that true? why, then Othello and Desdemona return again to Venice.

◄ How has Iago tricked Roderigo out of his jewels?

69. **Mauritania.** The Roman name for Barbary, the region in northern Africa, including parts of modern-day Morocco and Algeria, which was considered to be the homeland of the Moors (generally spelled *Mauretania*). Not to be confused with the modern African nation of Mauritania in northwest Africa.

70. **abode.** Stay

71. **lingered.** Prolonged; extended

72. **determinate.** Effective

73. **harlotry.** Harlot

74. **honorable fortune.** The fact that he will take Othello's place in Cyprus

75. **watch his going thence.** Watch for him as he leaves Bianca's house

76. **high suppertime.** High time for supper

ACT IV, SCENE iii

1. **forthwith.** Immediately

IAGO. O, no; he goes into Mauritania[69] and takes away with him the fair Desdemona, unless his abode[70] be lingered[71] here by some accident:
230 wherein none can be so determinate[72] as the removing of Cassio.

◀ What does Iago instruct Roderigo to do?

RODERIGO. How do you mean, removing of him?

IAGO. Why, by making him uncapable of Othello's place; knocking out his brains.

235 **RODERIGO.** And that you would have me to do?

IAGO. Ay, if you dare do yourself a profit and a right. He sups tonight with a harlotry,[73] and thither will I go to him: he knows not yet of his honorable fortune.[74] If you will watch his going thence,[75] which I will
240 fashion to fall out between twelve and one, you may take him at your pleasure: I will be near to second your attempt, and he shall fall between us. Come, stand not amazed at it, but go along with me; I will show you such a necessity in his death that you shall think
245 yourself bound to put it on him. It is now high suppertime,[76] and the night grows to waste: about it.

RODERIGO. I will hear further reason for this.

IAGO. And you shall be satisfied.

Exeunt.

SCENE iii: Another room in the castle.

Enter OTHELLO, LODOVICO, DESDEMONA, EMILIA *and* ATTENDANTS.

LODOVICO. I do beseech you, sir, trouble yourself no further.

OTHELLO. O, pardon me: 'twill do me good to walk.

LODOVICO. Madam, good night; I humbly thank your ladyship.

DESDEMONA. Your honor is most welcome.

OTHELLO.   Will you walk, sir?
5 O,—Desdemona,—

DESDEMONA. My lord?

OTHELLO. Get you to bed on the instant; I will be returned forthwith:[1] dismiss your attendant there: look it be done.

10 **DESDEMONA.** I will, my lord.

2. **incontinent.** Immediately
3. **nightly wearing.** Nightgown
4. **cheques.** Scoldings
5. **unpin me.** Unpin my gown
6. **All's one.** All the same; very well.
7. **shroud.** Cover with a shroud, that is, a winding-sheet for the dead. Wives were sometimes shrouded in their wedding sheets.
8. **you talk.** You talk nonsense
9. **Barbary.** A name reminiscent of the Barbary coast, the area where Othello was born.
10. **proved mad.** Turned out to be insane, or went insane
11. **I have much to do . . . Barbary.** It is hard for me to resist hanging my head down and singing the song like poor Barbary. Note that the willow is symbolic of weeping and death. The garland in the song could be interpreted as a funeral wreath.
12. **nether.** Bottom

Exeunt OTHELLO, LODOVICO, *and* ATTENDANTS.

EMILIA. How goes it now? he looks gentler than he
did.

DESDEMONA. He says he will return incontinent:[2]
He hath commanded me to go to bed,
And bade me to dismiss you.

EMILIA.   Dismiss me!

DESDEMONA. It was his bidding: therefore, good
15   Emilia,
Give me my nightly wearing,[3] and adieu:
We must not now displease him.

EMILIA. I would you had never seen him!

◀ What do Emilia and Desdemona wish?

DESDEMONA. So would not I. My love doth so
     approve him,
20 That even his stubbornness, his cheques,[4] his frowns—
Prithee, unpin me,[5]—have grace and favor in them.

EMILIA. I have laid those sheets you bade me on the
bed.

DESDEMONA. All's one.[6] Good faith, how foolish are
     our minds!
If I do die before thee prithee, shroud[7] me
In one of those same sheets.

◀ What does Desdemona ask Emilia to do if she dies before Emilia?

25 EMILIA.   Come, come you talk.[8]

DESDEMONA. My mother had a maid call'd Barbary:[9]
She was in love, and he she loved proved mad[10]
And did forsake her: she had a song of "willow;"
An old thing 'twas, but it express'd her fortune,
30 And she died singing it: that song to-night
Will not go from my mind; I have much to do,
But to go hang my head all at one side,
And sing it like poor Barbary.[11] Prithee, dispatch.

◀ Who was Barbary? What happened to her?

EMILIA. Shall I go fetch your night-gown?

DESDEMONA.   No, unpin me here.
35 This Lodovico is a proper man.

EMILIA. A very handsome man.

DESDEMONA. He speaks well.

EMILIA. I know a lady in Venice would have walked
barefoot to Palestine for a touch of his nether[12] lip.

DESDEMONA. [*Singing*] "The poor soul sat sighing by
40   a sycamore tree,
Sing all a green willow;

13. **Lay by these.** Set these [clothes] aside
14. **hie thee.** Hurry away
15. **next.** The full lyrics are as follows, as recorded by Samuel Pepys:

> The poor soul sat sighing by a sycamore tree
> Sing all a green willow;
> Her hand on her bosom, her head on her knee,
> Sing willow, willow, willow!
>
> The fresh streams ran by her, and murmur'd her moans;
> Sing willow, willow, willow;
> Her salt tears fell from her and soften'd the stones;
> Sing willow, willow, willow!
>
> Let nobody blame him, his scorn I approve,
> Sing willow, willow, willow,
> He was born to be fair, I to die for his love.
> Sing willow, willow, willow!
>
> I called my love false love, but what said he then?
> Sing willow, willow, willow
> If I court moe women, you'll couch with moe men.
> Sing willow, willow, willow!
>
> Chorus to be sung between verses:
> Sing willow, willow, willow
> My garland shall be;
> Sing all a green willow,
> Willow, willow, willow,
> Sing all a green willow my garland shall be.

16. **moe.** More
17. **abuse . . . gross kind.** Cheat on their husbands
18. **joint-ring.** A ring made in separable halves, often with the man's name on one half, and the woman's on the other. A common love-token in Shakespeare's time.
19. **measures of lawn.** Lengths of fabric
20. **petty exhibition.** Small gift

Her hand on her bosom, her head on her knee,
Sing willow, willow, willow:
The fresh streams ran by her, and murmur'd her
    moans;
45 Sing willow, willow, willow;
Her salt tears fell from her, and soften'd the stones"—
Lay by these[13]—
[*Singing*] "Sing willow, willow, willow"—
Prithee, hie thee;[14] he'll come anon—
50 [*Singing*] "Sing all a green willow must be my garland.
Let nobody blame him; his scorn I approve"—
Nay, that's not next.[15]—Hark! who is't that knocks?

EMILIA. It's the wind.

DESDEMONA. [*Singing*] "I call'd my love false love;
    but what said he then?
55 Sing willow, willow, willow;
If I court moe[16] women, you'll couch with moe men!"
So, get thee gone; good night. Mine eyes do itch;
Doth that bode weeping?

EMILIA.   'Tis neither here nor there.

DESDEMONA. I have heard it said so. O, these men,
    these men!
60 Dost thou in conscience think,—tell me, Emilia,—
That there be women do abuse their husbands
In such gross kind?[17]

◀ What question does Desdemona have for Emilia?

EMILIA.   There be some such, no question.

DESDEMONA. Wouldst thou do such a deed for all the
    world?

EMILIA. Why, would not you?

DESDEMONA.   No, by this heavenly light!

65 EMILIA. Nor I neither by this heavenly light;
I might do't as well i' the dark.

DESDEMONA. Wouldst thou do such a deed for all the
    world?

EMILIA. The world's a huge thing: it is a great price
For a small vice.

70 DESDEMONA. In troth, I think thou wouldst not.

EMILIA. In troth, I think I should; and undo't when I
had done. Marry, I would not do such a thing for a
joint-ring,[18] nor for measures of lawn,[19] nor for
gowns, petticoats, nor caps, nor any petty
75 exhibition;[20] but for the whole world,—why, who

◀ How does Emilia justify the idea of cheating on her husband for "all the world"?

21. **a monarch.** If a woman won the whole world for the sin of cheating, then she could make her husband king of the world.

22. **purgatory.** According to Roman Catholic doctrine, an intermediary state of punishment where souls go to be purged of sin before going to Heaven. Emilia would risk being sent to purgatory if it meant she could get the whole world.

23. **the wrong is but . . . make it right.** Cheating is only a sin according to the rules of the world. If you win the world for your cheating, then you can simply change the rules.

24. **to the vantage.** More, to boot

25. **store . . . played for.** Would populate the world they played for (by continuing to sleep around)

26. **foreign.** Other women's

27. **peevish.** Foolish (today, it means fretful, overly obstinate, or ill-tempered)

28. **restraint.** Restrictions

29. **scant . . . in despite.** Reduce our allowance out of spite

30. **galls.** Bitter feelings

31. **sense.** Senses

32. **doth affection breed it?** Is it affection that causes it?

33. **The ills we do . . . instruct us so.** Whatever bad things we do, we learned them from men.

34. **heaven me such uses send.** Heaven keep me away from such bad behavior

35. **Not to . . . mend!** In seeing bad behavior, not to imitate it, but rather to see a lesson in what *not* to do

would not make her husband a cuckold to make him
a monarch?[21] I should venture purgatory[22] for't.

DESDEMONA. Beshrew me, if I would do such a wrong
For the whole world.

80 EMILIA. Why, the wrong is but a wrong i' the world:
and having the world for your labor, 'tis a wrong in
your own world, and you might quickly make it
right.[23]

DESDEMONA. I do not think there is any such
woman.

85 EMILIA. Yes, a dozen; and as many to the vantage[24]
as would store the world they played for.[25]
But I do think it is their husbands' faults
If wives do fall: say that they slack their duties,
And pour our treasures into foreign[26] laps,
90 Or else break out in peevish[27] jealousies,
Throwing restraint[28] upon us; or say they strike us,
Or scant our former having in despite;[29]
Why, we have galls,[30] and though we have some
grace,
Yet have we some revenge. Let husbands know
Their wives have sense[31] like them: they see and
95   smell
And have their palates both for sweet and sour,
As husbands have. What is it that they do
When they change us for others? Is it sport?
I think it is. And doth affection breed it?[32]
100 I think it doth. Is't frailty that thus errs?
It is so too. And have not we affections,
Desires for sport, and frailty, as men have?
Then let them use us well: else let them know,
The ills we do, their ills instruct us so.[33]

DESDEMONA. Good night, good night: heaven me
105   such uses send,[34]
Not to pick bad from bad, but by bad mend![35]

                                        Exeunt.

◀ Whom does Emilia
say is to blame for
women's infidelities,
and why?

◀ How does
Desdemona think
women should
respond to men's bad
behavior?

Respond to the Selection

Which character do you sympathize with more—Othello or Desdemona? Why?

Investigate, Inquire, and Imagine

Recall: GATHERING FACTS

1a. While Othello watches from the sidelines, whom does Iago question Cassio about? Who approaches while they are talking, and what does she give to Cassio?

2a. What news does Lodovico bring from the Duke? How does Desdemona react to the news?

3a. What plan do Iago and Roderigo devise at the end of scene ii?

Interpret: FINDING MEANING

➤ 1b. How does Othello interpret what he sees? What does he resolve to do as a result?

➤ 2b. Why does Othello slap Desdemona? How might he have interpreted her reaction to the news?

➤ 3b. How does Iago convince Roderigo to go through with this plan?

Analyze: TAKING THINGS APART

4a. Gather evidence from act IV of Othello's decline into savage madness. What do other characters, in particular Emilia and Lodovico, say about his behavior?

Synthesize: BRINGING THINGS TOGETHER

➤ 4b. How has Iago's poison changed Othello?

Evaluate: MAKING JUDGMENTS

5a. After Othello has slapped her in public, yelled at her, and called her a whore, Desdemona insists, "Unkindness may do much; / And his unkindness may defeat my life, / But never taint my love" (act IV, scene ii, 160–62). What do you think of Desdemona and her response to Othello's treatment? Do you pity her? respect her? How might you explain her behavior?

Extend: CONNECTING IDEAS

➤ 5b. How does Cassio treat Bianca? Why do you think Bianca puts up with this treatment? Compare Bianca's situation to Desdemona's.

Understanding Literature

FALLING ACTION. The **falling action** of a plot is all of the events that happen as a result of the crisis. Ever since the turning point in act III, in which Othello was won over by Iago's lies, the action of the play has been falling to its inevitable tragic conclusion. Summarize the falling action in act IV. Are things turning out the way Iago planned?

DRAMATIC IRONY. **Irony** is a difference between appearance and reality. **Dramatic irony** occurs when something is known to the reader or audience but not to the characters. Discuss the irony in act IV, scene ii, lines 131–145. What do we know that Emilia does not?

FOIL. A **foil** is a character whose attributes, or characteristics, contrast with and therefore throw into relief the attributes of another character. How does Emilia act as a foil for Desdemona in act IV, scene iii? In other words, what do we learn about Desdemona by seeing her interact with Emilia?

FORESHADOWING. **Foreshadowing** is the act of presenting materials that hint at events to occur later in the story. Discuss the use of foreshadowing in act IV, scene iii.

ACT V, SCENE i

1. **bulk.** A part of a building jutting out
2. **rapier bare.** A straight two-edged sword with a narrow, pointed blade; bare: unsheathed.
3. **put it home.** Drive it straight into your target (Cassio's breast)
4. **mars.** Harms or destroys
5. **miscarry in't.** Carry it out poorly
6. **quat.** Pimple; contemptuous term for a young person
7. **to the sense.** To the quick
8. **bobb'd from him.** Fooled him out of
9. **beauty in his life.** Unclear. Perhaps refers to Cassio's virtue or good looks, of which Iago is envious
10. **had been mine enemy indeed.** Would have proved a worthy, and deadly, enemy
11. **coat.** A shirt of mail worn underneath his outer garments
12. **I will make proof of thine.** Now, I'll test your armor

words for everyday use

res • ti • tu • tion (res´ tə t[y]ü´ shən) *n.*, making up for an injury or restoring something to its rightful owner. *The thieving employee was ordered to pay restitution for the money he stole.*

gait (gāt´) *n.*, manner of walking. *The animal's gait was hampered by a crippled foot.*

maim (mām´) *vt.*, mutilate or disfigure. *The drunk driver was maimed when her car hit a telephone pole.*

ACT V

SCENE i: Cyprus. A street.

Enter OTHELLO *and* IAGO.

IAGO. Here, stand behind this bulk;[1] straight will he
    come:
Wear thy good rapier bare,[2] and put it home:[3]
Quick, quick; fear nothing; I'll be at thy elbow:
It makes us, or it mars[4] us; think on that,
5 And fix most firm thy resolution.

RODERIGO. Be near at hand; I may miscarry in't.[5]

IAGO. Here, at thy hand: be bold, and take thy stand.

                                    Retires.

RODERIGO. I have no great devotion to the deed;
And yet he hath given me satisfying reasons.
10 'Tis but a man gone. Forth, my sword: he dies.

IAGO. I have rubb'd this young quat[6] almost to the
    sense,[7]
And he grows angry. Now, whether he kill Cassio,
Or Cassio him, or each do kill the other,
Every way makes my gain: live Roderigo,
15 He calls me to a <u>restitution</u> large
Of gold and jewels that I bobb'd from him,[8]
As gifts to Desdemona;
It must not be. If Cassio do remain,
He hath a daily beauty in his life[9]
20 That makes me ugly; and, besides, the Moor
May unfold me to him; there stand I in much peril:
No, he must die. But so: I hear him coming.

◀ *What reasons
does Iago have for
wanting both Cassio
and Roderigo dead?*

Enter CASSIO.

RODERIGO. I know his <u>gait</u>, 'tis he.—Villain, thou diest!

Makes a pass at CASSIO.

CASSIO. That thrust had been mine enemy indeed,[10]
25 But that my coat[11] is better than thou know'st
I will make proof of thine.[12]

◀ *What is the result
of Roderigo's attack
on Cassio? Who
wounds Cassio?
Who kills Roderigo?*

Draws, and wounds RODERIGO.

RODERIGO.   O, I am slain!

IAGO *from behind wounds* CASSIO *in the leg, and exits.*

CASSIO. I am <u>maim'd</u> for ever. Help, ho! murder!
    murder! [*Falls*]

13. **your unblest fate hies.** Your cursed fate is approaching rapidly.

14. **blotted.** Blotted out

15. **no passage?** No passers-by?

16. **heavy.** Dark or foggy

17. **counterfeits.** Impostors; men who are pretending to be hurt but are actually muggers or thieves trying to lure in a victim

18. **shirt.** Nightshirt

Enter OTHELLO.

OTHELLO. The voice of Cassio: Iago keeps his word.

RODERIGO. O, villain that I am!

OTHELLO.   It is even so.

30 CASSIO. O, help, ho! light! a surgeon!

OTHELLO. 'Tis he:—O brave Iago, honest and just,
That hast such noble sense of thy friend's wrong!
Thou teachest me. <u>Minion</u>, your dear lies dead,
And your unblest fate hies:[13] strumpet, I come.
Forth of my heart those charms, thine eyes, are
35   blotted;[14]
Thy bed, lust-stain'd, shall with lust's blood be
     spotted.

                         Exit OTHELLO.

Enter LODOVICO *and* GRATIANO.

CASSIO. What, ho! no watch? no passage?[15] murder!
     murder!

GRATIANO. 'Tis some mischance; the cry is very direful.

CASSIO. O, help!

40 LODOVICO. Hark!

RODERIGO. O wretched villain!

LODOVICO. Two or three groan: it is a heavy[16] night:
These may be counterfeits:[17] let's think't unsafe
To come in to the cry without more help.

RODERIGO. Nobody come? then shall I bleed to
45   death.

LODOVICO. Hark!

Re-enter IAGO, *with a light.*

GRATIANO. Here's one comes in his shirt,[18] with light
     and weapons.

IAGO. Who's there? whose noise is this that cries on
     murder?

LODOVICO. We do not know.

IAGO.   Did not you hear a cry?

CASSIO. Here, here! for heaven's sake, help me!

50 IAGO.   What's the matter?

GRATIANO. This is Othello's ancient, as I take it.

LODOVICO. The same indeed; a very valiant fellow.

◀ How does Othello still regard Iago? What does he say Desdemona can expect?

19. **make away.** Get away
20. **As you shall prove us, praise us.** See for yourself that we are good.

Iago. What are you here that cry so grievously?

Cassio. Iago? O, I am spoil'd, undone by villains!
55 Give me some help.

Iago. O me, lieutenant! what villains have done this?

Cassio. I think that one of them is hereabout,
And cannot make away.[19]

Iago. O treacherous villains!
[*To* Lodovico *and* Gratiano]
What are you there? Come in, and give some help.

60 **Roderigo.** O, help me here!

Cassio. That's one of them.

Iago. O murderous slave! O villain!

◄ *Who kills Roderigo?*

Stabs Roderigo.

Roderigo. O damn'd Iago! O inhuman dog!

Iago. Kill men i' the dark!—Where be these bloody
thieves?—
How silent is this town!—Ho! murder! murder!—
65 What may you be? are you of good or evil?

Lodovico. As you shall prove us, praise us.[20]

Iago. Signior Lodovico?

Lodovico. He, sir.

Iago. I cry you mercy. Here's Cassio hurt by villains.

70 **Gratiano.** Cassio!

Iago. How is't, brother!

Cassio. My leg is cut in two.

Iago. Marry, heaven forbid!
Light, gentlemen; I'll bind it with my shirt.

Enter Bianca.

Bianca. What is the matter, ho? who is't that cried?

75 **Iago.** Who is't that cried!

Bianca. O my dear Cassio! my sweet Cassio!
O Cassio, Cassio, Cassio!

Iago. O notable strumpet! Cassio, may you suspect
Who they should be that have thus many led you?

80 **Cassio.** No.

Gratiano. I am to find you thus: I have been to seek
you.

21. **garter.** A band used to hold up a stocking. Iago will use it to bind Cassio's wounded leg.

22. **chair.** A sedan chair, one that is designed to be carried by poles

23. **this trash.** Bianca

24. **gastness.** Ghastliness, or terror. Iago is attempting to suggest that Bianca's fear is actually a fear of being implicated in the plot against Cassio. Actually, of course, Bianca is in love with Cassio and is simply horrified that he is hurt.

Iago. Lend me a garter.[21] So. O, for a chair,[22]
To bear him easily hence!

Bianca. Alas, he faints! O Cassio, Cassio, Cassio!

85 **Iago.** Gentlemen all, I do suspect this trash[23]
To be a party in this injury.
Patience awhile, good Cassio. Come, come;
Lend me a light. Know we this face or no?
Alas my friend and my dear countryman
90 Roderigo! no:—yes, sure: O heaven! Roderigo.

Gratiano. What, of Venice?

Iago. Even he, sir; did you know him?

Gratiano.   Know him! ay.

Iago. Signior Gratiano? I cry you gentle pardon;
These bloody accidents must excuse my manners,
That so neglected you.

95 **Gratiano.**   I am glad to see you.

Iago. How do you, Cassio? O, a chair, a chair!

Gratiano. Roderigo!

Iago. He, he, 'tis he.

A chair brought in.

                         O, that's well said; the chair!

Gratiano. Some good man bear him carefully from
        hence;
I'll fetch the general's surgeon.

[*To* Bianca]

100   For you, mistress,
Save you your labor. He that lies slain here, Cassio,
Was my dear friend: what malice was between you?

Cassio. None in the world; nor do I know the man.

Iago. [*To* Bianca] What, look you pale? O, bear him
    out o' the air.

Cassio *and* Roderigo *are borne off.*

105 Stay you, good gentlemen. Look you pale, mistress?
Do you perceive the gastness[24] of her eye?
Nay, if you stare, we shall hear more anon.
Behold her well; I pray you, look upon her:
Do you see, gentlemen? nay, guiltiness will speak,
110 Though tongues were out of use.

Enter Emilia.

◀ *Whom does Iago say might be to blame for Cassio's being attacked?*

◀ *What does Iago suggest is a sign of Bianca's guilt? What is a more likely explanation of this "sign"?*

25. **'Las.** Alas

26. **This is the fruit of whoring.** This is what Cassio gets for sleeping with whores.

27. **tell's another tale.** Tell us what really happened (i.e., we know that you have something to do with Cassio's being attacked)

28. **fordoes.** Destroys

ACT V, SCENE ii

1. **the cause.** The cause of justice

2. **monumental alabaster.** Alabaster is a fine-textured, translucent white material often used to make monuments such as those found in cemeteries.

3. **flaming minister.** Fiery servant (i.e., the candle)

4. **thy light . . . excelling nature.** Desdemona's light, the wondrously clever creation of nature that she is

5. **Promethean heat.** The fire of Prometheus; that is, the fire of the gods. In Greek mythology, Prometheus stole fire from the gods and gave it to mankind.

EMILIA. 'Las,[25] what's the matter? what's the matter, husband?

IAGO. Cassio hath here been set on in the dark
By Roderigo and fellows that are scaped:
He's almost slain, and Roderigo dead.

115 EMILIA. Alas, good gentleman! alas, good Cassio!

IAGO. This is the fruit of whoring.[26] Prithee, Emilia,
Go know of Cassio where he supp'd to-night.

[*To* BIANCA]

What, do you shake at that?

BIANCA. He supp'd at my house; but I therefore shake not.

120 IAGO. O, did he so? I charge you, go with me.

EMILIA. Fie, fie upon thee, strumpet!

BIANCA. I am no strumpet; but of life as honest
As you that thus abuse me.

EMILIA.   As I! foh! fie upon thee!

IAGO. Kind gentlemen, let's go see poor Cassio dress'd.
125 Come, mistress, you must tell's another tale.[27]
Emilia, run you to the citadel,
And tell my lord and lady what hath happ'd.
Will you go on? I pray. [*Aside*] This is the night
That either makes me or fordoes[28] me quite.

Exeunt.

SCENE ii: A bedchamber in the castle:
Desdemona in bed asleep; a light burning.

Enter OTHELLO.

OTHELLO. It is the cause,[1] it is the cause, my soul,—
Let me not name it to you, you chaste stars!—
It is the cause. Yet I'll not shed her blood;
Nor scar that whiter skin of hers than snow,
5 And smooth as monumental alabaster.[2]
Yet she must die, else she'll betray more men.
Put out the light, and then put out the light:
If I quench thee, thou flaming minister,[3]
I can again thy former light restore,
10 Should I repent me: but once put out thy light,
Thou cunning'st pattern of excelling nature,[4]
I know not where is that Promethean heat[5]

◀ Whose "light" will
Othello put out?

6. **relume.** Light up again

7. **walk by.** Stand by; wait

8. **forfend.** Forbid

9. **kill thy soul.** According to traditional Christian belief, repenting and asking God's forgiveness for one's sins is the only way to get into heaven.

words
for
everyday
use

vi • tal (vī´ təl) *adj.*, having to do with life; characteristic of life. *The accident victim had lost a lot of blood and other* <u>*vital*</u> *fluids.*

That can thy light relume.[6] When I have pluck'd the
    rose,
I cannot give it <u>vital</u> growth again.
15 It must needs wither: I'll smell it on the tree.

[*Kissing her*]

Ah balmy breath, that dost almost persuade
Justice to break her sword! One more, one more.
Be thus when thou art dead, and I will kill thee,
And love thee after. One more, and this the last:
20 So sweet was ne'er so fatal. I must weep,
But they are cruel tears: this sorrow's heavenly;
It strikes where it doth love. She wakes.

DESDEMONA. Who's there? Othello?

OTHELLO.   Ay, Desdemona.

DESDEMONA. Will you come to bed, my lord?

OTHELLO. Have you pray'd to-night, Desdemona?

25 DESDEMONA.   Ay, my lord.

OTHELLO. If you bethink yourself of any crime
Unreconciled as yet to heaven and grace,
Solicit for it straight.

DESDEMONA. Alas, my lord, what do you mean by
    that?

30 OTHELLO. Well, do it, and be brief; I will walk by:[7]
I would not kill thy unprepared spirit;
No; heaven forfend![8] I would not kill thy soul.[9]

DESDEMONA. Talk you of killing?

OTHELLO.   Ay, I do.

DESDEMONA.   Then heaven
Have mercy on me!

OTHELLO.   Amen, with all my heart!

35 DESDEMONA. If you say so, I hope you will not kill me.

OTHELLO. Hum!

DESDEMONA. And yet I fear you; for you are fatal
    then
When your eyes roll so: why I should fear I know not,
Since guiltiness I know not; but yet I feel I fear.

OTHELLO. Think on thy sins.

40 DESDEMONA.   They are loves I bear to you.

OTHELLO. Ay, and for that thou diest.

◀ What does Othello
want to make sure of
before he kills
Desdemona?

◀ What sins does
Desdemona say she
has committed?

10. **strong conception.** Strong conviction that you are guilty

11. **That I do groan withal.** Which makes me groan in pain.

12. **But with such . . . I might love.** In an innocent and chaste way, which was permitted by heaven.

13. **thou dost stone my heart.** You turn my heart to stone (with your lies)

words
for
everyday
use

por • tent (pȯ[ə]r´ tənt) *n.,* sign of things to come: omen. *The cry of an owl was once thought a portent of death.*

per • jur • y (pərj´ ə rē) *n.,* violation of an oath; often, referring to a person lying on the stand in court. *The defendant was convicted of perjury when it was discovered that he lied about his involvement in the crime.*

Desdemona. That death's unnatural that kills for loving.
Alas, why gnaw you so your nether lip?
Some bloody passion shakes your very frame:
45 These are <u>portents</u>; but yet I hope, I hope,
They do not point on me.

Othello.   Peace, and be still!

Desdemona. I will so. What's the matter?

Othello. That handkerchief which I so loved and gave thee
Thou gavest to Cassio.

Desdemona.   No, by my life and soul!
Send for the man, and ask him.

50 **Othello.**   Sweet soul, take heed,
Take heed of <u>perjury</u>; thou art on thy deathbed.

Desdemona. Ay, but not yet to die.

Othello.   Yes, presently:
Therefore confess thee freely of thy sin;
For to deny each article with oath
55 Cannot remove nor choke the strong conception[10]
That I do groan withal.[11] Thou art to die.

Desdemona. Then Lord have mercy on me!

Othello.   I say, amen.

Desdemona. And have you mercy too! I never did
Offend you in my life; never loved Cassio
60 But with such general warranty of heaven
As I might love:[12] I never gave him token.

Othello. By heaven, I saw my handkerchief in's hand.
O perjured woman! thou dost stone my heart,[13]
And makest me call what I intend to do
65 A murder, which I thought a sacrifice:
I saw the handkerchief.

Desdemona.   He found it then;
I never gave it him: send for him hither;
Let him confess a truth.

Othello.   He hath confess'd.

Desdemona. What, my lord?

Othello. That he hath used thee.

Desdemona.   How? unlawfully?

◀ *How does Desdemona defend herself in response to Othello's accusations?*

14. **ta'en order for't.** Taken measures to have him killed.
15. **strive.** Struggle
16. **Being done.** Since all is over
17. **So, so.** Said as he is strangling her again to make sure she is completely dead
18. **like.** Likely

70 OTHELLO. Ay.

DESDEMONA. He will not say so.

OTHELLO. No, his mouth is stopp'd;
Honest Iago hath ta'en order for't.[14]

DESDEMONA. O! my fear interprets: what, is he dead?

OTHELLO. Had all his hairs been lives, my great
revenge
75 Had stomach for them all.

DESDEMONA. Alas! he is betray'd and I undone.

OTHELLO. Out, strumpet! weep'st thou for him to
my face?

◄ How does
Othello interpret
Desdemona's tears?

DESDEMONA. O, banish me, my lord, but kill me not!

OTHELLO. Down, strumpet!

80 **DESDEMONA.** Kill me to-morrow: let me live to-night!

OTHELLO. Nay, if you strive[15]—

DESDEMONA. But half an hour!

OTHELLO. Being done,[16] there is no
pause.

DESDEMONA. But while I say one prayer!

OTHELLO. It is too late.

◄ How does Othello
kill Desdemona?

He stifles her.

EMILIA. [*Within*] My lord, my lord! what, ho! my
lord, my lord!

OTHELLO. What noise is this? Not dead? not yet
85 quite dead?
I that am cruel am yet merciful;
I would not have thee linger in thy pain: So, so.[17]

EMILIA. [*Within*] What, ho! my lord, my lord!

OTHELLO. Who's there?

EMILIA. [*Within*] O, good my lord, I would speak a
word with you!

90 **OTHELLO.** Yes: 'tis Emilia. By and by. She's dead.
'Tis like[18] she comes to speak of Cassio's death.—
The noise was here. Ha! no more moving?
Still as the grave. Shall she come in? were't good?—
I think she stirs again:—no. What's best to do?
95 If she come in, she'll sure speak to my wife:
My wife! my wife! what wife? I have no wife.
O insupportable! O heavy hour!

19. **the affrighted globe . . . alteration.** The frightened earth should gape open, as with an earthquake, at this change (now that she is dead)
20. **Soft.** Wait a moment
21. **error.** Aberration; odd behavior
22. **than she was wont.** Than it customarily does

Methinks it should be now a huge eclipse
Of sun and moon, and that the affrighted globe
Should yawn at alteration.[19]

100 EMILIA. [*Within*]   I do beseech you
That I may speak with you, O, good my lord!

OTHELLO. I had forgot thee: O, come in, Emilia;
Soft;[20] by and by. Let me the curtains draw.
Where art thou? [*Unlocks the door*]

Enter EMILIA.

What's the matter with thee now?

EMILIA. O, my good lord, yonder's foul murders
105   done!

OTHELLO. What, now?

EMILIA. But now, my lord.

OTHELLO. It is the very error[21] of the moon;
She comes more nearer earth than she was wont,[22]
110 And makes men mad.

EMILIA. Cassio, my lord, hath kill'd a young Venetian
Call'd Roderigo.

◄ What news does Emilia report? What surprises Othello?

OTHELLO.   Roderigo kill'd!
And Cassio kill'd!

EMILIA.   No, Cassio is not kill'd.

OTHELLO. Not Cassio kill'd! then murder's out of tune,
115 And sweet revenge grows harsh.

DESDEMONA. O, falsely, falsely murder'd!

EMILIA.   Alas, what cry is that?

OTHELLO. That! what?

EMILIA. Out, and alas! that was my lady's voice.
Help! help, ho! help! O lady, speak again!
120 Sweet Desdemona! O sweet mistress, speak!

DESDEMONA. A guiltless death I die.

◄ Whom does Desdemona say is guilty of her death?

EMILIA. O, who hath done this deed?

DESDEMONA. Nobody; I myself. Farewell!
Commend me to my kind lord: O, farewell!

Dies.

OTHELLO. Why, how should she be murder'd?

125 EMILIA.   Alas, who knows?

OTHELLO. You heard her say herself, it was not I.

23. **folly.** Wantonness, unchastity
24. **belie.** Tell a lie about; slander
25. **false as water.** Probably an idiom in Shakespeare's day. Refers to the fact that water is fluid and changeable, rather than fixed and reliable.
26. **such another world.** Another world like this one (echoes Desdemona's claim in the previous act)
27. **chrysolite.** Topaz, a precious gem
28. **iteration.** Repetition
29. **too fond . . . bargain.** Too devoted to her wedding vows

---

words for everyday use

per • ni • cious (pər nish′ əs) *adj.*, destructive; deadly. *The _pernicious_ disease only got worse when doctors attempted to treat it.*

EMILIA. She said so: I must needs report the truth.

OTHELLO. She's, like a liar, gone to burning hell:
'Twas I that kill'd her.

EMILIA.   O, the more angel she,
130 And you the blacker devil!

OTHELLO. She turn'd to folly,[23] and she was a whore.

EMILIA. Thou dost belie[24] her, and thou art a devil.

OTHELLO. She was false as water.[25]

EMILIA.   Thou art rash as fire, to say
That she was false: O, she was heavenly true!

135 OTHELLO. Cassio did top her; ask thy husband else.
O, I were damn'd beneath all depth in hell,
But that I did proceed upon just grounds
To this extremity. Thy husband knew it all.

EMILIA. My husband!

140 OTHELLO. Thy husband.

EMILIA. That she was false to wedlock?

OTHELLO. Ay, with Cassio. Nay, had she been true,
If heaven would make me such another world[26]
Of one entire and perfect chrysolite,[27]
I'ld not have sold her for it.

145 EMILIA.   My husband!

OTHELLO. Ay, 'twas he that told me first:
An honest man he is, and hates the slime
That sticks on filthy deeds.

EMILIA.   My husband!

OTHELLO. What needs this iteration,[28] woman? I say
      thy husband.

EMILIA. O mistress, villainy hath made mocks with
150   love,
My husband say that she was false!

OTHELLO.   He, woman;
I say thy husband: dost understand the word?
My friend, thy husband, honest, honest Iago.

EMILIA. If he say so, may his <u>pernicious</u> soul
155 Rot half a grain a day! he lies to the heart:
She was too fond of her most filthy bargain.[29]

OTHELLO. Ha!

EMILIA. Do thy worst:

◄ What phrase does
Emilia repeat? What
is she only now
realizing?

30. **to be hurt.** To endure hurt
31. **apt.** Credible
32. **I thought so then.** I thought so earlier (i.e., in IV, ii, lines 131–148)

words **for** **everyday** **use**	**gull** (gəl´) *n.*, person who is easily deceived or cheated. *The swindler was always looking for a gull to involve in his latest scheme.*

odi • ous (ō´ dē əs) *adj.*, hateful. *To get revenge on his ex-best friend, Brian spread odious gossip about him.*

This deed of thine is no more worthy heaven
Than thou wast worthy her.

160 OTHELLO.   Peace, you were best.

EMILIA. Thou hast not half that power to do me harm
As I have to be hurt.[30] O gull! O dolt!
As ignorant as dirt! thou hast done a deed—
I care not for thy sword; I'll make thee known,
165 Though I lost twenty lives.—Help! help, ho! help!
The Moor hath kill'd my mistress! Murder! murder!

◀ Who responds to Emilia's screams?

Enter MONTANO, GRATIANO, IAGO, *and others.*

MONTANO. What is the matter? How now, general!

EMILIA. O, are you come, Iago? you have done well,
That men must lay their murders on your neck.

170 GRATIANO. What is the matter?

EMILIA. Disprove this villain, if thou be'st a man:
He says thou told'st him that his wife was false:
I know thou didst not, thou'rt not such a villain:
Speak, for my heart is full.

◀ What does Emilia demand to know from Iago? What does she conclude by his answer?

175 IAGO. I told him what I thought, and told no more
Than what he found himself was apt[31] and true.

EMILIA. But did you ever tell him she was false?

IAGO. I did.

EMILIA. You told a lie, an odious, damned lie;
180 Upon my soul, a lie, a wicked lie.
She false with Cassio!—did you say with Cassio?

IAGO. With Cassio, mistress. Go to, charm your
tongue.

EMILIA. I will not charm my tongue; I am bound to
speak:
My mistress here lies murder'd in her bed,—

185 ALL. O heavens forfend!

EMILIA. And your reports have set the murder on.

OTHELLO. Nay, stare not, masters: it is true, indeed.

GRATIANO. 'Tis a strange truth.

MONTANO. O monstrous act!

EMILIA.   Villainy, villainy, villainy!
190 I think upon't, I think: I smell't: O villainy!—
I thought so then:[32]—I'll kill myself for grief:—
O villainy, villainy!

33. **uncle.** Gratiano is Brabantio's brother

34. **Shore his old thread in twain.** Cut the thread of his life in half

35. **desperate turn.** A desperate act (of revenge against Othello)

36. **curse his better angel . . . reprobation.** Brabantio would ignore his conscience and kill Othello in revenge, even if it meant condemning his own soul to hell in the process.

37. **gratify.** Reward

38. **recognizance.** Token

39. **My father gave my mother.** Note that this does not match what he told Desdemona in act III, scene iv. Earlier, he was probably telling a tall tale to Desdemona in order to scare her.

40. **liberal as the north.** As freely as the north wind blows

words for everyday use

am • o • rous (am´ ə rəs) *adj.*, indicative of love. *Liz was embarrassed by the amorous notes she received from the boy in her class.*

IAGO. What, are you mad? I charge you, get you
　　home.

EMILIA. Good gentlemen, let me have leave to speak:
195 'Tis proper I obey him, but not now.
Perchance, Iago, I will ne'er go home.

OTHELLO. O! O! O!

He falls on the bed.

EMILIA.　　　　　　Nay, lay thee down and roar;
For thou hast kill'd the sweetest innocent
That e'er did lift up eye.

OTHELLO.　　　　　[*Rising*] O, she was foul!
200 I scarce did know you, uncle:[33] there lies your niece,
Whose breath, indeed, these hands have newly
　　stopp'd:
I know this act shows horrible and grim.

GRATIANO. Poor Desdemona! I am glad thy father's
　　dead:
Thy match was mortal to him, and pure grief
205 Shore his old thread in twain:[34] did he live now,
This sight would make him do a desperate turn,[35]
Yea, curse his better angel from his side,
And fall to reprobation.[36]

OTHELLO. 'Tis pitiful; but yet Iago knows
210 That she with Cassio hath the act of shame
A thousand times committed; Cassio confess'd it:
And she did gratify[37] his amorous works
With that recognizance[38] and pledge of love
Which I first gave her; I saw it in his hand:
215 It was a handkerchief, an antique token
My father gave my mother.[39]

EMILIA. O heaven! O heavenly powers!

IAGO. Come, hold your peace.

EMILIA.　　　　　　'Twill out, 'twill out: I peace?
No, I will speak as liberal as the north:[40]
220 Let heaven and men and devils, let them all,
All, all, cry shame against me, yet I'll speak.

IAGO. Be wise, and get you home.

EMILIA.　　　　　　I will not.

IAGO *offers to stab* EMILIA.

GRATIANO.　　　　　　Fie!
Your sword upon a woman?

◄ How does Iago answer Emilia? What does she say about her obedience to him?

◄ What happened to Brabantio? What would he do if he could hear of this?

41. **coxcomb.** Fool (referring to Othello)

42. **Are there no stones . . . thunder?** Are all the stones in heaven used to create thunder? Why doesn't heaven drop stones on this villain?

43. **notorious.** Notable; egregious (not the modern sense of infamous)

44. **But kill him rather.** Kill Othello if he tries to escape

45. **that same villain.** Iago

46. **'tis.** It is; again showing contempt by calling Iago an "it." He is not a person, but an animal.

47. **whipster.** Nimble little fellow; a whippersnapper (said with contempt)

48. **play the swan, / And die in music.** Imitate the swan, who is said to sing a particularly sweet song (a swansong) just before dying.

EMILIA. O thou dull Moor! That handkerchief thou speak'st of

225 I found by fortune and did give my husband;
For often, with a solemn earnestness,
More than indeed belong'd to such a trifle,
He begg'd of me to steal it.

IAGO.   Villainous whore!

EMILIA. She give it Cassio! no, alas! I found it,
And I did give't my husband.

230 **IAGO.**   Filth, thou liest!

EMILIA. By heaven, I do not, I do not, gentlemen.
O murderous coxcomb![41] What should such a fool
Do with so good a woman?

OTHELLO.   Are there no stones in heaven
But what serve for the thunder?[42]—Precious villain!

He runs at IAGO *but is disarmed by* MONTANO. IAGO,
from behind, stabs EMILIA, *and exits.*

GRATIANO. The woman falls; sure, he hath kill'd his
235 wife.

EMILIA. Ay, ay: O, lay me by my mistress' side.

GRATIANO. He's gone, but his wife's kill'd.

MONTANO. 'Tis a notorious[43] villain. Take you this
weapon,
Which I have here recover'd from the Moor:
240 Come, guard the door without; let him not pass,
But kill him rather.[44] I'll after that same villain,[45]
For 'tis[46] a damned slave.

                    Exeunt MONTANO *and* GRATIANO.

OTHELLO.   I am not valiant neither,
But every puny whipster[47] gets my sword:
But why should honor outlive honesty?
Let it go all.

245 **EMILIA.**   What did thy song bode, lady?
Hark, canst thou hear me? I will play the swan,
And die in music.[48]

[Singing]

                    "Willow, willow, willow,"—
Moor, she was chaste; she loved thee, cruel Moor;
So come my soul to bliss, as I speak true;
250 So speaking as I think, I die, I die.

Dies.

◀ What does Emilia reveal?

◀ What happens to Emilia?

49. **sword . . . ice-brook's temper.** Swords from Spain were famous for their quality. The "ice-brook" might refer to the fact that steel is tempered by plunging it red-hot into ice-cold water; however, some editors read this as an error for "Innsbruck," a place noted for its superior steel.

50. **perforce.** By necessity

51. **naked.** Unarmed

52. **more impediments . . . your stop.** Impediments, or obstacles, that had twenty times your power to stop me

53. **butt.** Goal

54. **sea-mark.** Beacon or other elevated marker on a harbor that serves as a guide to mariners; hence, something that marks a journey's end.

55. **my utmost sail.** My last journey

56. **lost.** Wasted

57. **Man but a rush . . . retires.** Come after me with a rush (a tufted grass) and I will give in.

58. **how dost thou look now?** Said while looking at Desdemona

59. **ill-starr'd.** Ill-fated

60. **compt.** Judgment Day

61. **steep-down gulfs.** Deep gulfs

OTHELLO. I have another weapon in this chamber;
It is a sword of Spain, the ice-brook's temper:[49]—
O, here it is. Uncle, I must come forth.

GRATIANO. [*Within*] If thou attempt it, it will cost
    thee dear:
255 Thou hast no weapon, and perforce[50] must suffer.

OTHELLO. Look in upon me then and speak with me,
Or, naked[51] as I am, I will assault thee.

Re-enter GRATIANO.

GRATIANO. What is the matter?

OTHELLO.   Behold, I have a weapon;
A better never did itself sustain
260 Upon a soldier's thigh: I have seen the day,
That, with this little arm and this good sword,
I have made my way through more impediments
Than twenty times your stop:[52] but, O vain boast!
Who can control his fate? 'tis not so now.
265 Be not afraid, though you do see me weapon'd;
Here is my journey's end, here is my butt,[53]
And very sea-mark[54] of my utmost sail.[55]
Do you go back dismay'd? 'tis a lost[56] fear;
Man but a rush against Othello's breast,
270 And he retires.[57] Where should Othello go?
Now, how dost thou look now?[58] O ill-starr'd[59]
    wench!
Pale as thy smock! when we shall meet at compt,[60]
This look of thine will hurl my soul from heaven,
And fiends will snatch at it. Cold, cold, my girl!
275 Even like thy chastity. O cursed slave!
Whip me, ye devils,
From the possession of this heavenly sight!
Blow me about in winds! roast me in sulphur!
Wash me in steep-down gulfs[61] of liquid fire!
280 O Desdemona! Desdemona! dead!
Oh! Oh! Oh!

Enter LODOVICO, MONTANO, CASSIO *carried in a chair,
and* OFFICERS *with* IAGO, *prisoner.*

LODOVICO. Where is this rash and most unfortunate
    man?

OTHELLO. That's he that was Othello: here I am.

LODOVICO. Where is that viper? bring the villain
    forth.

◀ What does Othello
say will happen when
he and Desdemona
meet at Judgment
Day?

62. **I look . . . a fable.** I look down to see if Iago's feet are cloven-hoofed [as the devil's were fabled to be].

63. **If that thou be'st a devil.** If you be a devil

64. **wert.** Were

65. **practice.** Plot

66. **consent in.** Conspire together in

67. **demand that demi-devil.** Demand an answer from that half devil

68. **Torments.** Torture

OTHELLO. I look down towards his feet; but that's a
285   fable.[62]
If that thou be'st a devil,[63] I cannot kill thee.

Wounds IAGO.

LODOVICO. Wrench his sword from him.

IAGO.   I bleed, sir;
    but not kill'd.

OTHELLO. I am not sorry neither: I'ld have thee live;
For, in my sense, 'tis happiness to die.

290 **LODOVICO.** O thou Othello, thou wert[64] once so good,
Fall'n in the practice[65] of a damned slave,
What shall be said to thee?

OTHELLO.   Why, any thing:
An honorable murderer, if you will;
For nought I did in hate, but all in honor.

◄ What does Othello have to say for himself?

LODOVICO. This wretch hath part confess'd his
295   villainy:
Did you and he consent in[66] Cassio's death?

OTHELLO. Ay.

CASSIO. Dear general, I never gave you cause.

OTHELLO. I do believe it, and I ask your pardon.
300 Will you, I pray, demand that demi-devil[67]
Why he hath thus ensnared my soul and body?

◄ What does Othello ask of Cassio? What does he want to know from Iago? What is Iago's response?

IAGO. Demand me nothing: what you know, you
    know:
From this time forth I never will speak word.

LODOVICO. What, not to pray?

GRATIANO.   Torments[68] will ope
    your lips.

305 **OTHELLO.** Well, thou dost best.

LODOVICO. Sir, you shall understand what hath
    befall'n,
Which, as I think, you know not. Here is a letter
Found in the pocket of the slain Roderigo;
And here another: the one of them imports
310 The death of Cassio to be undertook
By Roderigo.

OTHELLO. O villain!

◄ What does the group learn from the letters found in the dead Roderigo's pocket?

CASSIO.   Most heathenish and most gross!

69. **another discontented . . . villain.** Here's another discontented letter found in Roderigo's pocket, which Roderigo was apparently planning to give to Iago.

70. **belike.** Likely

71. **wrought to.** Worked toward

72. **Brave me.** Confront me

73. **whereon . . . I was cast.** For which I was dismissed from my position

74. **he spake.** Roderigo spoke

75. **You shall close prisoner rest.** You, Othello, shall be kept prisoner, in close custody.

76. **nothing extenuate.** Leave nothing out

77. **set down.** Record

78. **but being wrought.** But once wrought upon, or manipulated

79. **Perplex'd.** Bewildered; distressed

80. **base Indian . . . tribe.** Indians were seen as ignorant savages, who would throw away a pearl because they had no knowledge of its value. Base means "low," in the sense of uncivilized. The First Folio edition has this as, not Indian, but Iudean, which could be a reference to the Judean king Herod, who, in a fit of blind jealousy, threw away Marianne, his "jewel" of a wife, or, to the Jews who killed Jesus, not recognizing his value.

81. **subdued.** Downcast

words for everyday use

al • be • it (òl bē′ ət) *conj.*, even though; although. *The chocolate mousse torte was a rich dessert, albeit a small one.*

LODOVICO. Now here's another discontented paper,
Found in his pocket too; and this, it seems,
315 Roderigo meant to have sent this damnèd villain;[69]
But that belike[70] Iago in the interim
Came in and satisfied him.

OTHELLO.   O the pernicious caitiff!
How came you, Cassio, by that handkerchief
That was my wife's?

CASSIO.   I found it in my chamber:
320 And he himself confess'd but even now
That there he dropp'd it for a special purpose
Which wrought to[71] his desire.

OTHELLO.   O fool! fool! fool!

CASSIO. There is besides in Roderigo's letter,
How he upbraids Iago, that he made him
325 Brave me[72] upon the watch; whereon it came
That I was cast:[73] and even but now he spake,[74]
After long seeming dead, Iago hurt him,
Iago set him on.

◀ What did Roderigo
himself say as he lay
dying?

LODOVICO. You must forsake this room, and go with
    us:
330 Your power and your command is taken off,
And Cassio rules in Cyprus. For this slave,
If there be any cunning cruelty
That can torment him much and hold him long,
It shall be his. You shall close prisoner rest,[75]
335 Till that the nature of your fault be known
To the Venetian state. Come, bring him away.

◀ What will happen
to Othello? to Iago
and Cassio?

OTHELLO. Soft you; a word or two before you go.
I have done the state some service, and they know't.
No more of that. I pray you, in your letters,
340 When you shall these unlucky deeds relate,
Speak of me as I am; nothing extenuate,[76]
Nor set down[77] aught in malice: then must you speak
Of one that loved not wisely but too well;
Of one not easily jealous, but being wrought[78]
345 Perplex'd[79] in the extreme; of one whose hand,
Like the base Indian, threw a pearl away
Richer than all his tribe;[80] of one whose subdued[81]
    eyes,
Albeit unused to the melting mood,
Drop tears as fast as the Arabian trees
350 Their medicinal gum. Set you down this;

82. **Aleppo.** A city in the Ottoman Empire (modern-day Syria)

83. **circumcised dog.** Circumcision was and still is today a strictly observed religious practice by Muslims in Turkey and elsewhere. At the time, Christians in Europe were not generally circumcised. Circumcision, and turbans, were a mark of the enemy Turk.

84. **period.** End; conclusion

85. **Spartan dog.** The dogs of Sparta (a city in Greece) were bred as attack dogs.

86. **fell.** Cruel

87. **Let it be hid.** Let the bodies be hid by the curtain.

88. **they succeed on you.** Gratiano, as kinsman to Othello and Desdemona, will inherit the Moor's fortunes.

89. **censure.** Sentence; condemnation

90. **Myself will straight aboard.** I will immediately get on board ship and return to Venice.

words for everyday use

tra • duce (trə düs´, trə dyüs´) *vt.*, destroy the reputation of someone or cause shame by misrepresenting or telling falsehoods. *The author traduced his family in a shocking memoir that turned out to be a pack of lies.*

And say besides, that in Aleppo[82] once,
Where a malignant and a turban'd Turk
Beat a Venetian and <u>traduced</u> the state,
I took by the throat the circumcised dog,[83]
And smote him, thus.

Stabs himself.

355 LODOVICO.   O bloody period![84]

GRATIANO. All that's spoke is marr'd.

OTHELLO. I kiss'd thee ere I kill'd thee: no way but
     this;
Killing myself, to die upon a kiss.

Falls on the bed, and dies.

CASSIO. This did I fear, but thought he had no
     weapon;
For he was great of heart.

360 LODOVICO. [*To* IAGO]   O Spartan dog,[85]
More fell[86] than anguish, hunger, or the sea!
Look on the tragic loading of this bed;
This is thy work: the object poisons sight;
Let it be hid.[87] Gratiano, keep the house,
365 And seize upon the fortunes of the Moor,
For they succeed on you.[88] To you, lord governor,
Remains the censure[89] of this hellish villain;
The time, the place, the torture: O, enforce it!
Myself will straight aboard,[90] and to the state
370 This heavy act with heavy heart relate.

                                        Exeunt.

◀ *Whom did Othello kill in Aleppo? Whom does he kill now?*

Respond to the Selection

Who do you think was more responsible for this tragedy, Iago or Othello? Explain.

Investigate, Inquire, and Imagine

Recall: GATHERING FACTS

1a. Whom do Iago and Roderigo attack at the beginning of act V, scene i? What is the outcome of the attack? Whom does Iago attempt to blame for what happened?

2a. What piece of evidence does Othello cite in his claim that Desdemona is a "perjured woman"? How does he kill Desdemona?

3a. Explain how Othello and the others learn the truth about Iago.

Interpret: FINDING MEANING

→ 1b. What reasons did Iago have for wanting both Roderigo and Cassio dead?

→ 2b. Why does Othello ask Desdemona if she has said her prayers?

→ 3b. Why does Othello look down at Iago's feet, once he has learned the truth about him?

Analyze: TAKING THINGS APART

4a. Analyze Othello's final speech. How does he want to be remembered? To whom does he compare himself?

Synthesize: BRINGING THINGS TOGETHER

→ 4b. Recall Othello's words in act II, as he discovers Cassio and Montano in a drunken brawl: "Are we turn'd Turks"? (II, iii, 170). To the Venetians of the Renaissance, what did it mean to be a Turk? In what way has Othello, in his own mind, "turn'd Turk"?

Evaluate: MAKIING JUDGMENTS

5a. In act V, scene ii, Othello completes his "trial" of Desdemona and carries out the penalty of death on her. What evidence is there that Othello thinks he is committing a just act? Why does he call himself an "honorable murderer"? Could such an act ever be justified? Does justice triumph at the end of this play? Why, or why not?

Extend: CONNECTING IDEAS

➤ 5b. Is the death penalty ever just, in your opinion? Explain.

Understanding Literature

SOLILOQUY. A **soliloquy** is a speech given by a character alone onstage, in which the character reveals his or her thoughts and feelings to the audience. What misgivings does Othello reveal in his soliloquy at the beginning of act V, scene ii? What is the "cause" he speaks of? How is Desdemona's life unlike the flame of a candle? What mood do Othello's words create?

MOTIF. A **motif** is any element that recurs in one or more works of literature or art. One recurring motif in *Othello* is the imagery of hell, demons, and monsters. What examples can you find of this motif in act V? How is this motif echoed in the names of the two doomed lovers themselves? In the Christian morality plays of the Middle Ages, the protagonist was often tempted to his damnation by an evil villain called Vice. How does this compare with the plot of *Othello*?

CATASTROPHE AND DÉNOUEMENT. The **catastrophe**, in tragedy, is the event that resolves, or ends, the central conflict and marks the ultimate tragic fall of the central character. Often this event is the character's death. The **dénouement** is any material that follows and ties up loose ends. Who witnesses the catastrophe in *Othello*? What information is given as part of the dénouement?

TRAGEDY AND TRAGIC FLAW. A **tragedy** is a drama that tells about the downfall of a person of high status. Tragedy tends to be serious. It celebrates the courage and dignity of a tragic hero in the face of inevitable doom. Sometimes that doom is made inevitable by a **tragic flaw** in the hero, a personal weakness that leads to his or her downfall. In what ways does *Othello, the Moor of Venice* fit the definition of a tragedy? What is Othello's tragic flaw?

Plot Analysis of
Othello, the Moor of Venice

A **plot** is a series of events related to a **central conflict,** or struggle. The following plot diagram illustrates the main plot of *Othello*.

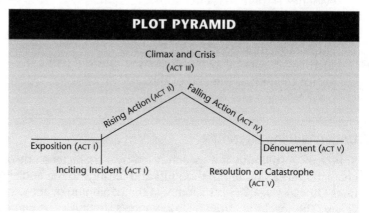

PLOT PYRAMID

Climax and Crisis
(ACT III)

Rising Action (ACT II)

Falling Action (ACT IV)

Exposition (ACT I)

Dénouement (ACT V)

Inciting Incident (ACT I)

Resolution or Catastrophe
(ACT V)

The parts of a plot are as follows:

The **exposition** is the part of a plot that provides background information about the characters, setting, or conflict.

The **inciting incident** is the event that sets into motion the central conflict, or struggle.

The **rising action,** or complication, develops the conflict to a high point of intensity.

The **crisis,** or turning point, presents a decisive occurrence that determines the future course of events in the play. This event may or may not be the same as the **climax.**

The **falling action** is all the events that come as the result of the crisis.

The **resolution** is the point at which the central conflict is ended, or resolved. In a tragedy, this event is called the **catastrophe** because it marks the ultimate fall of the central character.

The **dénouement** is any material that follows the resolution and that ties up loose ends.

The plot of *Othello* follows the same general pattern found in most five-act plays of Renaissance times. **Act I** contains the exposition and inciting incident. In **act II**, the central conflict is developed through the rising action, or complication. The crisis or climax comes in **act III**, and the falling action in **act IV**. **Act V** consists of the resolution (or catastrophe) and the dénouement. Following is a brief summary of the plot of *Othello*.

Exposition and Inciting Incident (Act I)

The inciting incident is the elopement of Othello and Desdemona, which actually occurs prior to the events in scene i. This event touches off all the conflict to follow. In act I, we meet Iago and learn of his relationship with Roderigo and his feelings toward Othello. We also meet Othello and Desdemona and hear them speak before the Senate in defense of their love, in response to the charge by Desdemona's father that the Moor has taken his daughter by unlawful means. Once Brabantio's charges have been dismissed, the Duke announces that Othello must be sent immediately to Cyprus in order to ward off an attack by the enemy Turks. He gives Othello permission to bring along his bride. At the end of the act, Iago explains in a soliloquy how he plans to get his revenge on Othello: he will "abuse Othello's ear / That [Cassio] is too familiar with his wife."

Rising Action (Act II)

At the beginning of act II, several weeks have passed and the conflict with the Turks has ended, the Turkish fleet having been destroyed by a storm at sea. The characters all land safely on the island of Cyprus and a party is planned for that evening. During the night's revels, Iago enacts the first part of his plan by getting Cassio drunk. As the pair had arranged earlier, Roderigo picks a fight with the drunken Cassio, and a fight ensues. Othello intervenes, and finding Cassio at fault, dismisses him from his position as lieutenant. Iago encourages Cassio to appeal to Desdemona for help in winning back Othello's favor.

Crisis and Climax (Act III)

The rising action continues in act III, as Cassio visits Desdemona and she promises to plead his case to Othello. Iago and Othello spot Cassio leaving, and Iago suggests to Othello that Cassio looks guilty. He continues to make insinuating remarks about Cassio and Desdemona, suggesting that the two have been intimate. When Othello presses him for proof, Iago tells him that he has seen Desdemona's handkerchief in Cassio's hand. This detail pushes Othello to the breaking point and brings about the crisis of the play— a point we can also consider to be the climax. Othello is completely convinced and vows his revenge: "Now do I see 'tis true. Look here, Iago; / All my fond love thus do I blow to heaven. / 'Tis gone. / Arise, black vengeance, from thy hollow cell!" (III, iii, 444–447). He asks Iago to kill Cassio for him, and promotes Iago to lieutenant. Now that the crisis or climax has been reached, the action begins to fall to its inevitable conclusion. In act III, scene iv, Othello questions Desdemona about the handkerchief, which, unbeknownst to the two of them, was stolen by Emilia and given to Iago, who has placed it in Cassio's chamber. A bewildered Desdemona tries to change the subject by bringing up Cassio's case. As she pleads that he be reinstated, Othello becomes even more enraged by what he sees as proof of her love for Cassio.

Falling Action (Act IV)

Iago continues with his lies, telling Othello that Cassio admitted to having an affair with Desdemona. He arranges for Othello to hide while he questions Cassio about Desdemona. While Othello looks on, Iago asks Cassio about Bianca, a subject which provokes Cassio's laughter. Meanwhile Bianca comes by at that moment with Desdemona's handkerchief, which Cassio gave her to copy. This serves as the "ocular proof" Othello had wanted—he is now completely convinced that his wife has been unfaithful, and is going mad with grief and the desire for vengeance. Emissaries arrive from Venice at the end of act IV, scene i with the news that Othello is recalled to Venice, leaving Cassio as governor of Cyprus. When Desdemona declares that she is happy about this, Othello strikes her, shocking everyone. In act IV, scene ii, Othello questions Emilia about Desdemona's fidelity, but refuses to believe her that Desdemona is chaste. Later in that scene, Iago and

Roderigo plot Cassio's murder. In scene iii, Desdemona waits for Othello in their bedchamber, and as Emilia helps her prepare for bed, the women talk about infidelity. Desdemona declares that she would never cheat on Othello for "all the world." This knowledge, in the eyes of the audience, makes her impending doom all the more tragic.

Resolution and Dénouement (Act V)

The falling action continues throughout act V. In scene i, Roderigo and Iago fail in their attempt to murder Cassio. Roderigo and Cassio are both wounded, and Iago kills Roderigo to cover up for his role in the attack. In scene ii, Othello enters the bedchamber to kill Desdemona. When she realizes what he is about to do, she begs for mercy, but he smothers her. Emilia comes in and discovers the murder, whereupon Othello tells her Desdemona was unfaithful and that Iago knew the whole story. A stunned Emilia repeats, "My husband!" She calls for help, and Montano, Gratiano, Iago, and the others enter. In front of everyone, Emilia accuses her husband of bringing on the murder of Desdemona, and an enraged Iago stabs her. Now that Iago's role in the tragedy is clear, Othello stabs him (but does not kill him), then stabs himself. Othello's death is the catastrophe, the event that resolves the central conflict and makes the tragedy complete. The dénouement comes in Lodovico's lines at the end of the play, through which we learn that Gratiano will inherit all of Othello's possessions, and that Cassio will supervise the punishment and torture of the villain Iago.

from *Gli Hecatommithi* (1565)
by Giovanbattista Giraldi Cinthio, translated by J. E. Taylor

ABOUT THE RELATED READING

During the Renaissance, all of Europe was reading the *novelle,* or short stories, of Italy. These dramatic, action-filled tales provided Elizabethan playwrights with a gold mine of source material. Matteo Bandello's "Tragical Historie of Rhomeo and Giulietta" provided Shakespeare with the plot of his famous play *Romeo and Juliet.* The plot of *Othello* came from the following tale, written by Italian novelist and poet **Giovanbattista Giraldi Cinthio** (1504–1573) and published in 1565 in a collection of one hundred tales called *Gli Hecatommithi.* As you will see, Shakespeare changed some of the details, but the basic plot is the same.

There once lived in Venice a Moor, who was very valiant and of a handsome person; and having given proofs in war of great skill and <u>prudence</u>, he was highly esteemed by the Signoria[1] of the Republic, who in rewarding deeds of valor advanced the interests of the State.

It happened that a virtuous lady of marvelous beauty, named Disdemona, fell in love with the Moor, moved thereto by his valor; and he, vanquished by the beauty and the noble character of Disdemona, returned her love; and their affection was so mutual that, although the parents of the lady strove all they could to induce her to take another husband, she consented to marry the Moor; and they lived in such harmony and peace in Venice that no word ever passed between them that was not affectionate and kind.

Now it happened at this time that the Signoria of Venice made a change in the troops whom they used to maintain in Cyprus, and they appointed the Moor commander of the soldiers whom they dispatched thither. Joyful as was the Moor at the honor proffered him—such dignity being only

▶ Why must the Moor go to Cyprus?

---

1. **Signoria.** The government of Venice, made up of the Duke, or *doge,* and a council of noblemen.

---

words for everyday use

pru • dence (prü´ dən[t]s) *n.,* caution as to danger or risk; shrewdness and good judgment in the management of affairs or resources. *The zookeepers exercised <u>prudence</u> when dealing with the tigers, knowing that wild animals can be unpredictable.*

conferred on men of noble rank and well-tried faith, and who had displayed bravery in arms—yet his pleasure was lessened when he reflected on the length and dangers of the voyage, fearing that Disdemona would be pained at his absence. But Disdemona, who had no other happiness in the world than the Moor, and who rejoiced to witness the testimony of his valor her husband had received from so powerful and noble a Republic, was all impatient that he should embark with his troops, and longed to accompany him to so honorable a post. And all the more it vexed her to see the Moor so troubled; and not knowing what could be the reason, one day, when they were at dinner, she said to him, "How is it, O Moor, that when so honorable a post has been conferred on you by the Signoria, you are thus melancholy?"

The Moor answered Disdemona, "My pleasure at the honor I have received is disturbed by the love I bear you; for I see that of necessity one of two things must happen— either that I take you with me, to encounter the perils of the sea, or, to save you from this danger, I must leave you here in Venice. The first could not be otherwise than serious to me, for all the toil you would have to bear, and every danger that might befall you, would cause me extreme anxiety and pain. Yet, were I to leave you behind me, I should be hateful to myself, since in parting from you I should part from my own life."

◀ What reasons does the Moor give for being melancholy?

Disdemona, on hearing this, replied: "My husband, what thoughts are these that wander through your mind? Why let such things disturb you? I will accompany you whithersoe'er[2] you go, were it to pass through fire, as now to cross the water in a safe and well-provided ship: if indeed there are toils and perils to encounter, I will share them with you. And in truth I should think you loved me little, were you to leave me here in Venice, denying me to bear you company, or could believe that I would liefer bide[3] in safety here than share the dangers that await you. Prepare then for the voyage with all the readiness which the dignity of the post you hold deserves."

◀ What solution does Disdemona offer?

The Moor, in the fullness of his joy, threw his arms around his wife's neck, and with an affectionate and tender kiss exclaimed, "God keep you long in such love, dear wife!" Then speedily donning his armor, and having prepared everything for his expedition, he embarked on board the galley with his wife and all his troops, and, setting sail, they pursued their voyage, and with a perfectly tranquil sea arrived safely at Cyprus.

---

2. **whithersoe'er.** Whithersoever: wherever
3. **liefer bide.** Rather live

Now amongst the soldiery there was an Ensign,[4] a man of handsome figure, but of the most <u>depraved</u> nature in the world. This man was in great favor with the Moor, who had not the slightest idea of his wickedness; for, despite the malice lurking in his heart, he cloaked with proud and valorous speech and with a <u>specious</u> presence the villainy of his soul with such art that he was to all outward show another Hector or Achilles.[5] This man had likewise taken with him his wife to Cyprus, a young, and fair, and virtuous lady; and being of Italian birth she was much loved by Disdemona, who spent the greater part of every day with her.

In the same Company there was a certain Captain of a troop, to whom the Moor was much affectioned. And Disdemona, for this cause, knowing how much her husband valued him, showed him proofs of the greatest kindness, which was all very grateful to the Moor. Now the wicked Ensign, regardless of the faith that he had pledged his wife, no less than of the friendship, fidelity and obligation which he owed the Moor, fell passionately in love with Disdemona, and bent all his thoughts to achieve his conquest; yet he dared not to declare his passion openly, fearing that, should the Moor perceive it, he would at once kill him. He therefore sought in various ways, and with secret <u>guile</u>, to betray his passion to the lady. But she, whose every wish was centered in the Moor, had no thought for this Ensign more than any other man, and all the means he tried to gain her love had no more effect than if he had not tried them. But the Ensign imagined that the cause of his ill success was that Disdemona loved the Captain of the troop; and he pondered how to remove him from her sight. The love which he had borne the lady now changed into the bitterest hate, and, having failed in his purposes, he devoted all his thoughts to plot the death of the Captain of the troop and to divert the affection of the Moor from Disdemona. After revolving in his mind various schemes, all alike wicked, he at length

▶ What motivates the Ensign to practice "an artful fraud upon the Moor"?

---

4. **Ensign.** A low-ranking officer; one who displayed the ensign, or flag, in battle. Shakespeare uses the term *ancient.*

5. **Hector or Achilles.** Heroes of the Trojan War. Their story is told in Homer's *Iliad.*

words for everyday use

de • praved (di prāvd´) *adj.,* marked by corruption or evil; perverted. *The criminal was completely <u>depraved</u>—no amount of rehabilitation could make him fit to rejoin society.*

spe • cious (spē´ shəs) *adj.,* having a false look of truth or genuineness. *I was warned that the gems being sold at the market were <u>specious</u>.*

guile (gīl´ [ə]l) *n.,* cunning deception. *It doesn't take much <u>guile</u> to trick naïve people.*

resolved to accuse her of unfaithfulness to her husband, and to represent the Captain as her paramour. But knowing the singular love the Moor bore to Disdemona, and the friendship which he had for the Captain, he was well aware that, unless he practiced an artful fraud upon the Moor, it were impossible to make him give ear to either accusation: wherefore he resolved to wait until time and circumstance should open a path for him to engage in his foul project.

Not long afterwards it happened that the Captain, having drawn his sword upon a soldier of the guard, and struck him, the Moor deprived him of his rank; whereat Disdemona was deeply grieved, and endeavored again and again to reconcile her husband to the man. This the Moor told to the wicked Ensign, and how his wife importuned him so much about the Captain that he feared he should be forced at last to receive him back to service. Upon this hint the Ensign resolved to act, and began to work his web of intrigue. "Perchance," said he, "the lady Disdemona may have good reason to look kindly upon him."

"And wherefore?" said the Moor.

"Nay, I would not step 'twixt man and wife," replied the Ensign; "but let your eyes be witness to themselves."

In vain the Moor went on to question the officer—he would proceed no further; nevertheless, his words left a sharp, stinging thorn in the Moor's heart, who could think of nothing else, trying to guess their meaning and lost in melancholy. And one day, when his wife had been endeavoring to pacify his anger toward the Captain, and praying him not to be unmindful of ancient services and friendship for one small fault, especially since peace had been made between the Captain and the soldier he had struck, the Moor was angered, and exclaimed, "Great cause have you, Disdemona, to care so anxiously about this man! Is he a brother, or your kinsman, that he should be so near your heart?"

The lady, with all gentleness and humility, replied, "Be not angered, my dear lord; I have no other cause to bid me speak than sorrow that I see you lose so dear a friend as, by your own words, this Captain has been to you; nor has he done so grave a fault that you should bear him so much enmity. Nay, but you Moors are of so hot a nature that every little trifle moves you to anger and revenge."

◄ *What stereotypical image does Disdemona have of Moors?*

Still more enraged at these words, the Moor replied, "I could bring proofs—by heaven it mocks belief! but for the wrongs I have endured revenge must satisfy my wrath."

Disdemona, in astonishment and fright, seeing her husband's anger kindled against her, so contrary to his wont,[6] said humbly and with timidness, "None save a good intent has led me thus to speak with you, my lord; but to give cause no longer for offense, I'll never speak a word more on the subject."

The Moor, observing the earnestness with which his wife again pleaded for the Captain, began to guess the meaning of the Ensign's words; and in deep melancholy he went to seek that villain and induce him to speak more openly of what he knew. Then the Ensign, who was bent upon injuring the unhappy[7] lady, after feigning at first great reluctance to say aught[8] that might displease the Moor, at length pretended to yield to his entreaties, and said, "I can't deny it pains me to the soul to be thus forced to say what needs must be more hard to hear than any other grief; but since you will it so, and that the regard I owe your honor compels me to confess the truth, I will no longer refuse to satisfy your questions and my duty. Know, then, that for no other reason is your lady vexed to see the Captain in disfavor than the pleasure that she has in his company whenever he comes to your house, and all the more since she has taken an <u>aversion</u> to your blackness."

These words went straight to the Moor's heart; but in order to hear more (now that he believed true all that the Ensign had told him) he replied, with a fierce glance, "By heavens, I scarce can hold this hand from plucking out that tongue of thine, so bold, which dares to speak such slander of my wife!"

"Captain," replied the Ensign, "I looked for such reward for these my faithful offices—none else; but since my duty, and the jealous care I bear your honor, have carried me thus far, I do repeat, so stands the truth, as you have heard it from these lips; and if the lady Disdemona hath, with a false show of love for you, blinded your eyes to what you should

▶ What does the Ensign say is Disdemona's reason for speaking in favor of the Captain? What does he say Disdemona has "taken an aversion to"?

---

6. **wont.** Habitual way of behaving
7. **unhappy.** Unlucky
8. **aught.** Anything

---

words for everyday use
aver • sion (ə vər´ zhən) n., strong dislike or repugnance. *Ever since I got food poisoning from it, I've had an <u>aversion</u> to tuna.*

have seen, this is no argument but that I speak the truth. Nay, this same Captain told it me himself, like one whose happiness is incomplete until he can declare it to another; and, but that I feared your anger, I should have given him, when he told it me, his merited reward, and slain him. But since informing you of what concerns you more than any other man brings me so undeserved a <u>recompense</u>, would I had held my peace, since silence might have spared me your displeasure."

Then the Moor, burning with indignation and anguish, said, "Make thou these eyes self-witnesses of what thou tell'st or on thy life I'll make thee wish thou hadst been born without a tongue."

"An easy task it would have been," replied the villain, "when he was used to visit at your house; but now that you have banished him, not for just cause, but for mere frivolous <u>pretext</u>, it will be hard to prove the truth. Still, I do not forgo the hope to make you witness of that which you will not credit from my lips."

Thus they parted. The wretched Moor, struck to the heart as by a barbed dart, returned to his home, and awaited the day when the Ensign should disclose to him the truth which was to make him miserable to the end of his days. But the evil-minded Ensign was, on his part, not less troubled by the chastity which he knew the lady Disdemona observed <u>inviolate</u>; and it seemed to him impossible to discover a means of making the Moor believe what he had falsely told him; and, turning the matter over in his thoughts in various ways, the villain resolved on a new deed of guilt.

Disdemona often used to go, as I have already said, to visit the Ensign's wife, and remained with her a good part of the day. Now, the Ensign observed that she carried about with her a handkerchief, which he knew the Moor had given her, finely embroidered in the Moorish fashion, and which was precious to Disdemona, nor less so to the Moor. Then he conceived the plan of taking this kerchief from her secretly, and thus laying the snare for her final

◄ How does the Ensign get Disdemona's handkerchief?

| words for everyday use | **re • com • pense** (re´ kəm pen[t]s) *n.*, compensation; payment. *The boy was given twenty dollars as <u>recompense</u> for his labor.*

pre • text (prē´ tekst) *n.*, reason or motive assumed or pretended as a cover for the real reason or motive. *Brian said he had errands to run, but I knew that was just a <u>pretext</u> for getting out of the house.* | **in • vi • o • late** (in vī´ ə lət) *adj.*, pure; that is, not violated or profaned. *In 1929, the Migratory Bird Conservation Act was passed, which stated that refuges were to be managed as "<u>inviolate</u> sanctuaries" for migratory birds, where no hunting was allowed.* |

ruin. The Ensign had a little daughter, a child three years of age, who was much loved by Disdemona; and one day, when the unhappy lady had gone to pay a visit at the house of this vile man, he took the little child up in his arms, and carried her to Disdemona, who took her and pressed her to her bosom; whilst at the same instant this traitor, who had extreme dexterity of hand, drew the kerchief from her sash so cunningly that she did not notice him, and overjoyed he took his leave of her.

Disdemona, ignorant of what had happened, returned home, and, busied with other thoughts, forgot the handkerchief. But a few days afterwards, looking for it and not finding it, she was in alarm, lest the Moor should ask her for it, as he oft was wont to do. Meanwhile the wicked Ensign, seizing a fit opportunity, went to the Captain of the troop, and with crafty malice left the handkerchief at the head of his bed without his discovering the trick; until the following morning, when, on his getting out of bed, the handkerchief fell upon the floor, and he set his foot upon it. And not being able to imagine how it had come into his house, knowing that it belonged to Disdemona, he resolved to give it to her; and waiting until the Moor had gone from home, he went to the back door and knocked. It seemed as if fate conspired with the Ensign to work the death of the unhappy Disdemona. Just at that time the Moor returned home, and hearing a knocking at the back door, he went to the window, and in a rage exclaimed, "Who knocks there?" The Captain, hearing the Moor's voice, and fearing lest he should come downstairs and attack him, took to flight without answering a word. The Moor went down, and opening the door hastened into the street and looked about, but in vain. Then, returning into the house in great anger, he demanded of his wife who it was that had knocked at the door. Disdemona replied, as was true, that she did not know; but the Moor said, "It seemed to me the Captain."

"I know not," answered Disdemona, "whether it was he or another person."

The Moor restrained his fury, great as it was, wishing to do nothing before consulting the Ensign, to whom he hastened instantly, and told him all that had passed, praying him to gather from the Captain all he could respecting the affair. The Ensign, overjoyed at the occurrence, promised the Moor to do as he requested; and one day he took occasion to speak with the Captain when the Moor was so placed that he could see and hear them as they conversed. And whilst talking to him of every other subject than of

▶ What does the Ensign do with the handkerchief? What does the Captain do with it?

Disdemona, he kept laughing all the time aloud, and feigning astonishment, he made various movements with his head and hands, as if listening to some tale of marvel. As soon as the Moor saw the Captain depart, he went up to the Ensign to hear what he had said to him. And the Ensign, after long entreaty, at length said, "He has hidden from me nothing, and has told me that he has been used to visit your wife whenever you went from home, and that on the last occasion she gave him this handkerchief which you presented to her when you married her."

The Moor thanked the Ensign, and it seemed now clear to him that, should he find Disdemona not to have the handkerchief, it was all true that the Ensign had told to him. One day, therefore, after dinner, in conversation with his wife on various subjects, he asked her for the kerchief. The unhappy lady, who had been in great fear of this, grew red as fire at this demand; and to hide the scarlet of her cheeks, which was closely noted by the Moor, she ran to a chest and pretended to seek the handkerchief, and after hunting for it a long time, she said, "I know not how it is— I cannot find it—can you, perchance, have taken it?"

"If I had taken it," said the Moor, "why should I ask it of you? But you will look better another time."

On leaving the room, the Moor fell to meditating how he should put his wife to death, and likewise the Captain of the troop, so that their deaths should not be laid to his charge. And as he ruminated over this day and night, he could not prevent his wife's observing that he was not the same toward her as he had been wont; and she said to him again and again, "What is the matter? What troubles you? How comes it that you, who were the most light-hearted man in the world, are now so melancholy?"

The Moor feigned various reasons in reply to his wife's questioning, but she was not satisfied, and, although conscious that she had given the Moor no cause, by act or deed, to be so troubled, yet she feared that he might have grown wearied of her; and she would say the Ensign's wife, "I know not what to say of the Moor; he used to be all love toward me; but within these few days he has become another man; and much I fear that I shall prove a warning to young girls not to marry against the wishes of their parents, and that the Italian ladies may learn from me not to wed a man whom nature and habitude of life estrange from us.[9] But as

◀ *What lesson does Disdemona fear her tale may provide to young Italian girls?*

9. **whom nature . . . estrange from us.** Whose nature and customs make him so different from us. This line echoes Disdemona's earlier statement that all Moors are "hot of nature."

I know the Moor is on such terms of friendship with your husband, and communicates to him all of his affairs, I pray you, if you have heard from him aught that you may tell me of, fail not to befriend me." And as she said this, she wept bitterly.

▶ How much does the Ensign's wife know of the plot to kill Disdemona? Why doesn't she tell Disdemona what she knows?

The Ensign's wife, who knew the whole truth (her husband wishing to make use of her to compass[10] the death of Disdemona), but could never consent to such a project, dared not, from fear of her husband, disclose a single circumstance: all she said was, "Beware lest you give any cause of suspicion to your husband, and show to him by every means your fidelity and love."

"Indeed I do so," replied Disdemona, "but it is all of no avail."

Meanwhile the Moor sought in every way to convince himself of what he fain[11] would have found untrue; and he prayed the Ensign to contrive that he might see the handkerchief in the possession of the Captain. This was a difficult matter to the wicked Ensign, nevertheless he promised to use every means to satisfy the Moor of the truth of what he said.

▶ Where does the Moor see his wife's handkerchief?

Now the Captain had a wife at home, who worked the most marvelous embroidery upon lawn;[12] and seeing the handkerchief, which belonged to the Moor's wife, she resolved, before it was returned to her, to work one like it. As she was engaged in this task, the Ensign observed her standing at a window, where she could be seen by all the passers-by in the street, and he pointed her out to the Moor, who was now perfectly convinced of his wife's guilt. Then he arranged with the Ensign to slay Disdemona and the Captain of the troop, treating them as it seemed they both deserved. And the Moor prayed the Ensign that he would kill the Captain, promising eternal gratitude to him. But the Ensign at first refused to undertake so dangerous a task, the Captain being a man of equal skill and courage; until at length, after much entreating and being richly paid, the Moor prevailed on him to promise to attempt the deed.

Having formed this resolution, the Ensign, going out one dark night, sword in hand, met the Captain on his way to visit a courtesan, and struck him a blow on his right thigh, which cut off his leg and felled him to the earth. Then the Ensign was on the point of putting an end to his life, when the Captain, who was a courageous man and

---

10. **compass.** Bring about, achieve
11. **fain.** Gladly
12. **lawn.** A fine sheer linen or cotton fabric

used to the sight of blood and death, drew his sword, and, wounded as he was, kept on his defense, exclaiming with a loud voice, "I'm murdered!" Thereupon the Ensign, hearing the people come running up, with some of the soldiers who were lodged thereabouts, took to his heels to escape being caught; then turning about again, he joined the crowd, pretending to have been attracted by the noise. And when he saw the Captain's leg cut off, he judged that if not already dead, the blow must at all events end his life; and whilst in his heart he was rejoiced at this, yet he feigned to compassionate[13] the Captain as he had been his brother.

The next morning the tidings of this affair spread through the whole city, and reached the ears of Disdemona; whereat she, who was kindhearted and little dreamed that any ill would betide her, evinced the greatest grief at the calamity. This served but to confirm the Moor's suspicions, and he went to seek for the Ensign, and said to him, "Do you know, that fool my wife is in such grief at the Captain's accident that she is well nigh gone mad?"

"And what could you expect, seeing he is her very soul?" replied the Ensign.

"Ay, soul forsooth!" exclaimed the Moor; "I'll draw the soul from out her body; call me no man if that I fail to shut the world upon this wretch."

Then they consulted of one means and another—poison and daggers—to kill poor Disdemona, but could resolve on nothing. At length the Ensign said, "A plan comes to my mind, which will give you satisfaction and raise cause for no suspicion. It is this: the house in which you live is very old, and the ceiling of your chamber has many cracks; I propose we take a stocking, filled with sand, and beat Disdemona with it till she dies; thus will her body bear no signs of violence. When she is dead, we can pull down a portion of the ceiling, and thus make it seem as if a rafter falling on her head had killed the lady. Suspicion can not rest on you, since all men will impute her death to accident."

◀ What plan do the Ensign and the Moor have for killing Disdemona?

This cruel counsel pleased the Moor, and he only waited for a fitting time to execute the plot. One night, when he and Disdemona had retired to bed, the Ensign, whom the Moor had concealed in a closet which opened into the

---

13. compassionate. Pity

words for everyday use

evince (i vin[t]s´) vt., display clearly: reveal. From childhood, Donna evinced an extraordinary talent for gymnastics.

im • pute (im pyüt´) vt., lay the responsibility or blame for, often falsely or unjustly. Many imputed the loss to poor pitching, but really the team just couldn't score.

chamber, raised a noise in the closet, according to a concerted plan; whereat the Moor said to his wife, "Did you not hear that noise?"

"Indeed I heard it," she replied.

"Rise," said the Moor, "and see what 'tis."

The unhappy Disdemona rose from bed, and the instant she approached the closet, out rushed the Ensign, and being strong and of stout nerve, he beat her cruelly with the bag of sand across her back; upon which Disdemona fell to the ground, scarce able to draw her breath; but with the little voice she had left, she called upon the Moor for aid. But the Moor, leaping from bed, exclaimed, "Thou wickedest of women, thus has thy falseness found its just reward—the recompense to wives who, counterfeiting love, place horns upon their husbands' brows."[14]

The wretched lady, hearing these words, and feeling that she was near her end (for the Ensign had given her another blow), appealed to the justice of Heaven, since justice here had failed her, in proof of her fidelity and truth; and as she was thus calling Heaven to witness, the wicked Ensign inflicted a third blow, under which she sank lifeless to the floor.

Then the Ensign and the Moor, laying Disdemona on the bed and wounding her head, pulled down part of the ceiling of the chamber, as they had arranged; whereupon the Moor began to call aloud for help, exclaiming that the house was falling. Hearing this uproar, the neighbors all came running up, and there found Disdemona lying dead beneath a rafter—a sight which, from the good life of that poor lady, did fill all hearts with sorrow.

On the following day Disdemona was buried, followed to the grave by the universal grief of the people. But Heaven, the just regarder of all hearts, willed not that so wicked a deed should go unpunished. Ere long the Moor, whom Disdemona had loved more than her own life, began to feel such sorrow at her loss that he went wandering about as one bereft of reason, searching in every part of the house. And reflecting in his thoughts that the Ensign had been the cause that he had lost, with Disdemona, all joy in life, he conceived so deep a hatred to that wicked man, he could not bear to set eyes on

▶ What happens between the Moor and the Ensign after Disdemona's death?

---

14. **place horns . . . brows.** Make their husbands into cuckolds

words for everyday use be • reft (bi reft´) adj., deprived or robbed (usually used with of). _Bereft of all joy, Nadia became cynical and bitter._

him; and had it not been for his fear of the inviolable justice of the Signoria of Venice, he would have slain him openly. But being unable to do this with safety, he deprived him of his rank, and would not allow him to remain in his Company; whereat such an enmity arose between the two that no greater or more deadly can be imagined.

The Ensign, that wickedest of all bad men, now turned his thoughts to injuring the Moor; and seeking out the Captain, whose wound was by this time healed, and who went about with a wooden leg in place of the one that had been cut off, he said to him, "'Tis time you should be avenged for your lost limb; and if you will come with me to Venice, I'll tell you who the malefactor is, whom I dare not mention to you here for many reasons; and I will bring you proofs."

The Captain of the troop, whose anger returned fiercely but without knowing why, thanked the Ensign, and went with him to Venice. On arriving there, the Ensign told him that it was the Moor who had cut off his leg, on account of the suspicion he had formed of Disdemona's conduct with him; and for that reason he had slain her, and then spread the report that the ceiling had fallen and killed her. Upon hearing which, the Captain accused the Moor to the Signoria, both of having cut off his leg and killed his wife, and called the Ensign to witness the truth of what he said. The Ensign declared both charges to be true, for that the Moor had disclosed to him the whole plot, and had tried to persuade him to perpetrate both crimes; and that, having afterwards killed his wife out of jealousy he had conceived, he had narrated to him the manner in which he had perpetrated her death.

The Signori[15] of Venice, when they heard of the cruelty inflicted by a barbarian upon a lady of their city, commanded that the Moor's arms should be pinioned in Cyprus, and he be brought to Venice, where, with many tortures, they sought to draw from him the truth. But the Moor, bearing with unyielding courage all the torment, denied the whole charge so resolutely that no confession could be drawn from him. But although by his constancy and firmness he

---

15. **Signori.** Noblemen (plural of *Signor,* Italian for *sir*)

words for everyday use

mal • e • fac • tor (maˊ lə fakˊ tər) *n.,* one who does bad things to another person or commits an offense against the law. *The police caught the malefactor in the act of robbing the store.*

pin • ion (pinˊ yən) *vt.,* restrain or shackle, especially by the arms. *The two bullies pinioned their victim against the wall so that he could not fight back.*

► *What happens to the Moor and the Ensign in the end?*

escaped death, he was, after being confined for several days in prison, condemned to perpetual banishment, in which he was eventually slain by the kinsfolk of Disdemona, as he merited. The Ensign returned to his own country, and, following up his wonted villainy, he accused one of his companions of having sought to persuade him to kill an enemy of his, who was a man of noble rank; whereupon this person was arrested and put to the torture; but when he denied the truth of what his accuser had declared, the Ensign himself was likewise tortured to make him prove the truth of his accusation; and he was tortured so that his body ruptured, upon which he was removed from prison and taken home, where he died a miserable death. Thus did Heaven avenge the innocence of Disdemona, and all these events were narrated by the Ensign's wife, who was <u>privy</u> to the whole, after his death, as I have told them here.

Critical Thinking

1. In Cinthio's tale, the Moor and Disdemona have been married for some time before going to Cyprus. In Shakespeare, the couple are newlyweds. What difference, if any, does this make to the story?

2. Cinthio's story seems to unfold over several months, but Shakespeare compressed the action into several days. Why do you suppose Shakespeare made this change to the time scheme? What effect does it have? Which time scheme do you prefer, and why?

3. Compare the two villains, the Ensign and Iago. How do their motives differ? Some critics claim that Iago, not Othello, is the true protagonist of Shakespeare's play. What does Shakespeare do to flesh out the villain character and make him more central to the story?

4. What stereotypes about African people are repeated in this tale? Do you think that Cinthio intended the moral of the story to be that "Italian ladies should not marry Moors"?

---

words for everyday use **privy** (pri´ vē) *adj.,* know about something; as a secret. *The president's advisors were <u>privy</u> to much top-secret information.*

from *The History* and *Description of Africa* (1526)
by Leo Africanus, translated by John Pory

ABOUT THE RELATED READING

Leo Africanus, also known as John Leo, was born Al-Hasan Ibn Muhammad in Granada, Spain between 1489 and 1495. He was raised on the Barbary Coast in northern Africa, where Morocco is today. As an adult, he traveled to other areas of Africa, including the Sudan, Mali, and Bornu (modern-day Nigeria). Captured by pirates around the year 1518, he was taken to Rome to be a slave of Pope Leo X. There he converted to Christianity and took the name of Giovanni (John) Leo. The Pope soon recognized Leo's intelligence and set him free; however, Leo stayed in Italy where he taught Arabic and published an Arabic grammar book and medical dictionary. It is believed that he returned to North Africa and died a Muslim around 1552.

Leo's *History and Description of Africa,* from which this reading was taken, was originally written in Arabic, then translated into Italian in 1526. The book soon became popular among Europeans and was for many years the only known source on the Sudan. Shakespeare probably read the English translation by John Pory, which was published in 1600, and used Leo's description of the inhabitants of Barbary to draw the character of Othello. In fact, he may have based Othello on Leo himself—a wise and respected north African who had undergone many adventures, then converted to Christianity and lived among the Italians.

This reading describes, in the author's words, some of the "virtues" and "vices" of the African peoples. As you read, decide whether any of these describe Othello.

from *The History and Description of Africa*

The commendable actions and virtues of the Africans.

▶ Which Africans does Leo discuss first?

The Arabians which inhabit in Barbary[1] or upon the coast of the Mediterranean Sea are greatly addicted[2] unto the study of good arts and sciences, and those things which concern their law and religion[3] are esteemed by them in the first place. Moreover they have been heretofore[4] most studious of the Mathematiques, of Philosophy, and of Astrology: but these arts (as it is aforesaid) were, four hundred years ago, utterly destroyed and taken away by the chief professors of their law. The inhabitants of the cities do most religiously observe and reverence those things which appertain unto their religion; yea, they honor those doctors and priests of whom they learn their law as if they were petie-gods.[5] Their Churches they frequent very diligently, to the end they may repeat certain prescript[6] and formal prayers; most superstitiously persuading themselves that the same day wherein they make their prayers it is not lawful for them to wash certain of their members,[7] when as at other times they will wash their whole bodies. Whereof we will (by God's help) discourse more at large in the second Book of this present treatise, when we shall fall into the mentioning of *Mahumet*[8] and his religion.

Moreover those which inhabit Barbary are of great cunning & dexterity for building & for mathematical inven-

---

1. **Barbary.** The Barbary Coast, or Barbary, was the term Europeans used to refer to the coastal regions of modern-day Morocco, Algeria, Tunisia, and Libya. Leo divided African into four regions: Barbary, Numidia, Libya, and "the land of the Negroes." Of Barbary, his native land, Leo wrote: "This is the most noble and worthy region of all Africa, the inhabitants whereof are of a white or tawny color, being a civil people, and prescribe wholesome laws and constitutions unto themselves."
2. **addicted.** In this text, the word means "devoted," "prone [to]," or "tending [toward]."
3. **their law and religion.** That is, Islamic law and religion. The Barbarians were a Muslim people.
4. **heretofore.** At one time; previously
5. **petie-gods.** Minor gods
6. **prescript.** Prescribed by law; laid down as a rule
7. **members.** Body parts
8. *Mahumet.* Also spelled *Mohammed* or *Muhammad;* the Arab prophet who founded the religion of Islam. He lived from about 570–632 AD.

tions, which a man may easily <u>conjecture</u> by their artificial works.[9] Most honest people they are, and <u>destitute</u> of all fraud and guile; not only embracing all simplicity and truth, but also practicing the same throughout the whole course of their lives—<u>albeit</u> certain Latin authors,[10] which have written of the same regions, are far otherwise of opinion. Likewise they are most strong and valiant people, especially those which dwell upon the mountains. They keep their <u>covenant</u> most faithfully; insomuch that they had rather die than break promise. No nation in the world is so subject unto jealousy; for they will rather lose their lives than put up any disgrace in the behalf of their women. So desirous they are of riches and honor that therein no other people can go beyond them. They travel in a manner over the whole world to exercise traffic.[11] For they are continually to be seen in Egypt, in Ethiopia, in Arabia, Persia, India, and Turkey: and whithersoever they go, they are most honorably esteemed of: for none of them will possess any art,[12] unless he hath attained unto great exactness and perfection therein. They have always been much delighted with all kind of civility and modest behavior: and it is accounted <u>heinous</u> among them for any man to utter in company any bawdy or unseemly word. They have always in mind this sentence of a grave author: "Give place to thy superior." If any youth, in presence of his father, his uncle, or any other of his kindred, doth sing or talk aught of love matters, he is deemed to be worthy of grievous punishment. Whatsoever lad or youth there lighteth by chance into any company which discourseth of love, no sooner heareth nor understandeth what their talk tendeth unto, but immediately he withdraweth himself from among them. These are the things which we thought most worthy of relation as concerning

◀ *What does Leo say is true of these people, despite what "certain Latin authors" have claimed?*

◀ *What does Leo say these people are subject unto, more than any other nation in the world?*

---

9. **artificial works.** Man-made constructions, such as dams and canals
10. **certain Latin authors.** Probably a reference to Pliny the Elder, a Roman historian whose *Naturalis Historia* was widely known and a principal source of European knowledge about Africa
11. **traffic.** Trade
12. **art.** Skill

words for everyday use

con • jec • ture (kən jek' chər) *vt.*, conclude based on evidence; infer. *Looking at the x-rays, the doctor <u>conjectured</u> that the patient's joint pain was caused by a bone spur.*

des • ti • tute (des' tə tüt') *adj.*, devoid of; lacking. *The country was <u>destitute</u> of natural resources and had to import almost everything from abroad.*

al • be • it (ȯl bē´ ət) *conj.*, even though; although. *I had to leave, <u>albeit</u> I didn't want to.*

co • ve • nant (kuv' nənt, ku' və nənt) *n.*, an agreement or contract. *Marriage is one of the oldest <u>covenants</u>.*

hei • nous (hā' nəs) *adj.*, shockingly evil. *The entire community was shocked and outraged by the <u>heinous</u> crime.*

the civility, humanity, and upright dealing of the Barbarians: let us now proceed unto the residue.[13]

Those Arabians which dwell in tents, that is to say, which bring up cattle, are of a more liberal and civil disposition: to wit, they are in their kind as devout, valiant, patient, courteous, hospital,[14] and as honest in life and conversation as any other people. They be most faithful observers of their word and promise; insomuch that the people, which before we said to dwell in the mountains, are greatly stirred up with <u>emulation</u> of their virtues. Howbeit[15] the said mountainers, both for learning, for virtue, and for religion, are thought much inferior to the Numidians,[16] albeit they[17] have little or no knowledge at all in natural philosophy. They are reported likewise to be most skillful warriors, to be valiant, and exceeding lovers and practicers of all humanity.[18] Also, the Moors and Arabians inhabiting Libya[19] are somewhat civil of behavior, being plain dealers, void of <u>dissimulation</u>, favorable to strangers, and lovers of simplicity. Those which we before named white, or tawny Moors, are steadfast in friendship, as likewise they indifferently and favorably esteem of other nations, and wholly endeavor themselves in this one thing; namely, that they may lead a most pleasant and <u>jocund</u> life. Moreover, they maintain most learned professors of liberal arts, and such

▶ What does Leo say is the one aim of the "tawny Moors"?

---

13. **residue.** Remaining peoples; that is, the peoples from regions other than Barbary.
14. **hospital.** Hospitable
15. **Howbeit.** Although
16. **Numidians.** People dwelling in Numidia, an ancient African kingdom and Roman province on the northern coast of Africa. Today, this area makes up the northeastern part of Algeria.
17. **they.** That is, the Numidians
18. **exceeding lovers and practicers of all humanity.** They [the Arabians that dwell in tents] love and interact with all kinds of people. Here, *practicer* means "one who deals with, treats, or interacts with [people]."
19. **Libya.** This word referred to a larger area of Africa than that encompassed by the country of Libya today. According to Leo, it began at the Atlantic Ocean in the west and the Nile River in the east. North of Libya were Numidia and Barbary, and south of it was "the land of the Negroes," mostly unknown to Europeans at the time.

words for everyday use

em • u • la • tion (em′ yə lā′ shən) n., imitation; ambition to equal or excel. *Clarissa often did things in <u>emulation</u> of her older sister, whom she greatly admired and envied.*

dis • sim • u • la • tion (di sim′ yə lā′ shən) n., the act of putting on a false appearance. *Marvin smiled and acted happy to see me, but his <u>dissimulation</u> did not fool me, since I knew full well he hated me.*

jo • cund (jä′ kənd; jō′ kənd) adj., merry; marked by high spirits and mirthfulness. *The <u>jocund</u> atmosphere of the party cheered everyone up.*

men are most devout in their religion. Neither is there any people in all Africa that lead a more happy and honorable life.

What vices the foresaid Africans are subject unto.

Never was there any people or nation so perfectly endued with virtue, but that they had their contrary faults and blemishes: now therefore let us consider whether the vices of the Africans do surpass their virtues & good parts. Those which we named the inhabitants of the cities of Barbary are somewhat needy and covetous, being also very proud and high-minded, and wonderfully addicted unto wrath; insomuch that (according to the proverb) they will deeply engrave in marble any injury be it never so small, & will in no wise blot it out of their remembrance. So rustical they are & void of good manners, that scarcely can any stranger obtain their familiarity and friendship. Their wits are but mean, and they are so credulous that they will believe matters impossible, which are told them. So ignorant are they of natural philosophy, that they imagine all the effects and operations of nature to be extraordinary and divine. They observe no certain order of living nor of laws. Abounding exceedingly with choler,[20] they speak always with an angry and loud voice. Neither shall you walk in the day-time in any of their streets, but you shall see commonly two or three of them together by the ears.[21] By nature they are a vile and base people, being no better accounted of by their governors than if they were dogs. [. . .] No people under heaven are more addicted unto covetise[22] than this nation: neither is there (I think) to be found among them one of an hundred, who for courtesy, humanity, or devotion's sake will vouchsafe[23] any entertainment upon a

◀ What does Leo think of the Barbarians' wits?

---

20. **choler.** Anger. Choler, or yellow bile, was believed to be an actual substance secreted by the liver which caused irritability and ire. It was one of the four *humors,* or fluids, which were believed to influence a person's temperament; the others were blood, phlegm, and melancholy (black bile).
21. **together by the ears.** Fighting; scuffling
22. **covetise.** Covetousness: a tendency to covet, or strongly desire, the possessions of others
23. **vouchsafe.** Grant or give, as a favor

words for everyday use

en • due (in dü′) *vt.,* provide; endow. *The people were endued with good fortune.*

cred • u • lous (kre′ jə ləs) *adj.,* ready to believe anything, even with slight or

uncertain evidence. *Children are often credulous and will believe anything they are told.*

stranger. Mindful they have always been of injuries, but most forgetful of benefits. Their minds are perpetually possessed with vexation and strife, so that they will seldom or never show themselves <u>tractable</u> to any man; the cause whereof is supposed to be for that they are so greedily addicted unto their filthy lucre,[24] that they never could attain unto any kind of civility or good behavior. [. . .]

All the Numidians, being most ignorant of natural, domestical, & commonwealth-matters,[25] are principally addicted unto treason, treachery, murder, theft, and robbery. This nation, because it is most slavish, will right gladly accept of any service among the Barbarians, be it never so vile or contemptible. For some will take upon them to be dung-farmers, others to be scullions,[26] some others to be ostlers,[27] and such like servile occupations.

Likewise the inhabitants of Libya live a brutish kind of life; who neglecting all kinds of good arts and sciences, do wholly apply their minds unto theft and violence. Never as yet had they any religion, any laws, or any good form of living; but always had, and ever will have, a most miserable and distressed life. There cannot any treachery or villainy be invented so damnable which for lucre's sake they dare not attempt. They spend all their days either in most lewd[28] practices, or in hunting, or else in warfare: neither wear they any shoes nor garments.

The Negroes[29] likewise lead a beastly kind of life, being utterly destitute of the use of reason, of dexterity of wit, and of all arts. Yea, they so behave themselves as if they had continually lived in a forest among wild beasts. They have great swarms of harlots among them; whereupon a man may easily conjecture their manner of living; except their conversation perhaps be somewhat more tolerable who dwell in the principal towns and cities: for it is like that they are somewhat more addicted to civility.

▶ What vices do the Numidians possess, according to Leo?

▶ How does Leo characterize Libyans and Negroes? What stereotypes does he reinforce with his description?

---

24. **lucre.** Money. The phrase "filthy lucre" is a cliché.
25. **domestical, & commonwealth-matters.** Matters having to do with local or national politics or political organization
26. **scullions.** Kitchen servants employed to do menial tasks
27. **ostlers.** Servants employed in a stable to take care of horses
28. **lewd.** Immoral, especially in a sexual way
29. **Negroes.** Black Africans, as distinct from those with Arab blood such as the author himself

words for everyday use

tract • a • ble (trak' tə bəl) *adj.*, easy to deal with or manage; docile. *The teacher was happy to find her students an easygoing and tractable group.*

Critical Thinking

1. What is the meaning today of the word *barbarian,* and how does this meaning compare with the picture of Barbarians given by Leo in this reading?

2. How does Leo distinguish between the Barbarians (his native people) and the other Africans he discusses? What evidence do you see of racial and cultural prejudice in his writing?

3. What are the principal virtues and failings of the Barbarians, in Leo's words? Could any of these be said to describe Othello? Explain, using evidence from the play to support your answer.

"*Othello:* A Bloody Farce" (1693)
by Thomas Rymer

ABOUT THE RELATED READING

English literary critic **Thomas Rymer** (c.1643–1713) was extremely influential in the 18th century, although his work was ridiculed later for being too narrow-minded. Rymer believed that all drama should adhere to classical principles and that it should be morally instructive. Following the ideas of classical theorists, he also insisted that for a drama to be believable, characters should behave in a way that was typical of their class and station in life. In the following excerpt, from his book *A Short View of Tragedy* (1693), Rymer explains why, in his view, *Othello* is simply "a Bloody Farce" with little or no value to the theatergoer.

From all the Tragedies acted on our English Stage, *Othello* is said to bear the Bell away.[1] The *Subject* is more of a piece, and there is indeed something like—there is, as it were, some phantom of—a *Fable*.[2] The *Fable* is always accounted the *Soul* of Tragedy, and it is the *Fable* which is properly the *Poets* part. [. . .]

The Fable.

Othello, a Blackamoor Captain, by talking of his Prowess and Feats of War, makes Desdemona a Senator's Daughter to be in love with him; and to be married to him, without her Parents knowledge; And having preferred Cassio, to be his Lieutenant (a place which his Ensign Jago[3] sued for), Jago in revenge, works the Moor into a Jealousy that Cassio Cuckolds him: which he effects by stealing and conveying a certain handkerchief, which had, at the Wedding, been by the Moor presented to his Bride. Hereupon, Othello and Jago plot the Deaths of Desdemona and Cassio, Othello Murders her, and soon after is convinced of her Innocence. And as he is about to be carried to Prison, in order to be punish'd for the Murder, He kills himself.

---

1. **bear the Bell away.** That is, win the top prize
2. *Fable.* Plot; with a pun on the meaning "a story with a moral."
3. **Jago.** Iago. In Renaissance times, the letters *i* and *j* were often used interchangeably, as were the letters *u* and *v*. You will notice other spelling differences in Rymer's piece.

What ever rubs or difficulty may stick on the Bark, the Moral, sure, of this Fable is very instructive: *First,* This may be a caution to all Maidens of Quality how, without their Parents consent, they run away with Blackamoors. [. . .] *Secondly,* This may be a warning to all good Wives, that they look well to their Linnen. *Thirdly,* This may be a lesson to Husbands, that before their Jealousie be Tragical, the proofs may be Mathematical.[4]

◀ What morals does Rymer say one can draw from the plot of Othello?

Cinthio affirms that *She was not overcome by a Womanish Appetite, but by the Vertue of the Moor.* It must be a good-natur'd Reader that takes Cinthio's word in this case, tho' in a Novel. Shakespear, who is accountable both to the Eyes, and to the Ears, And to convince the very heart of an Audience, shews that Desdemona was won, by hearing Othello talk:

OTHELLO: [. . .] *I spake of most disastrous chances, Of Moving accidents by flood and field* [. . .] [I, iii, 134–45]

This was the Charm, this was the philtre,[5] the love-powder that took the Daughter of this Noble Venetian. This was sufficient to make the Black-amoor White, and reconcile all, tho' there had been a Cloven-foot into the bargain.

Shakespear in this Play calls 'em the supersubtle Venetians. Yet examine throughout the Tragedy there is nothing in the noble Desdemona, that is not below any Countrey Chamber-maid with us.

◀ What does Rymer think of the character of Desdemona?

And the account he gives of their Noblemen and Senate, can only be calculated for the latitude of Gotham.[6]

The Character of that State is to employ strangers in their Wars; But shall a Poet thence fancy that they will set a Negro to be their General; or trust a Moor to defend them against the Turk? With us a Black-amoor might rise to be a Trumpeter; but Shakespear would not have him less than a Lieutenant-General. With us a Moor might marry some little drab,[7] or Small-coal Wench: Shake-spear, would provide him the Daughter and Heir of some great Lord, or Privy-Councellor, and all the Town should reckon it a very suitable match: [. . .]

◀ What does Rymer find unbelievable about Othello's rank and status in the play?

---

4. **Mathematical.** Logical
5. **philtre.** Love potion
6. **Gotham.** Town in England with a reputation for being the home of the stupid or insane
7. **drab.** Whore

Nothing is more odious in Nature than an improbable lye;[8] and, certainly, never was any Play fraught like this of *Othello* with improbabilities.

The Characters or Manners, which are the second part in a Tragedy, are not less unnatural and improper, than the Fable was improbable and absurd.

Othello is made a Venetian General. We see nothing done by him, nor related concerning him, that <u>comports</u> with the condition of a General, or, indeed, of a Man, unless the killing himself, to avoid a death the Law was about to inflict upon him. When his Jealousy had wrought him up to a resolution of's taking revenge for the suppos'd injury, he sets Jago to the fighting part, to kill Cassio, and chuses himself to murder the silly Woman his Wife, that was like to make no resistance.

His Love and his Jealousie are no part of a Souldiers Character, unless for Comedy.

▶ Why does Rymer think that Iago is an inconsistent character?

But what is most intolerable is Jago. He is no Black-amoor Souldier, so we may be sure he should be like other Souldiers of our acquaintance; yet never in Tragedy, nor in Comedy, nor in Nature was a Souldier with his Character; take it in the Authors own words:

EMILIA: . . . *some Eternal Villain,*
Some busie, and insinuating Rogue,
Some cogging, couzening Slave, to get some Office.
[IV, ii, 131–3]

Horace Describes a Souldier otherwise: *Impiger, iracundus, inexorabilis, acer.*[9]

Shakespear knew his Character of Jago was inconsistent. In this very Play he pronounces,

If thou dost deliver more or less than Truth,
. . . Thou are no Souldier. [II, iii, 211–12]

---

8. **lye.** Lie
9. ***Impiger . . . acer.*** Latin for "Active, irascible, unyielding, fierce." From Roman writer Horace's *Art of Poetry*. According to Horace (65–8 BC), characters in plays should display certain personality traits, according to what would be typical of their station in life. Rymer argues that the character of Iago is not believable because it doesn't fit the typical character of a soldier.

---

words for everyday use   com • port (kəm pȯrt'; kəm pōrt') *vi.*, to be fitting; to be in accord with. *The president was criticized for making decisions that did not <u>comport</u> with national policy.*

This he knew, but to entertain the Audience with something new and surprising, against common sense, and Nature, he would pass upon us a close,[10] dissembling, false, insinuating rascal, instead of an open-hearted, frank, plain-dealing Souldier, a character constantly worn by them for some thousands of years in the World.

Nor is our Poet more discreet in his Desdemona, He had chosen a Souldier for his Knave: And a Venetian Lady is to be the Fool. This Senators Daughter runs away to (a Carriers Inn) the Sagittary, with a Black-amoor: is no sooner wedded to him, but the very night she Beds him, is importuning and teizing[11] him for a young smock-fac'd[12] Lieutenant, Cassio. And tho' she perceives the Moor Jealous of Cassio, yet will she not forbear, but still rings *Cassio, Cassio* in both his Ears.

Roderigo is the Cully[13] of Jago, brought in to be murdered by Jago, that Jago's hands might be the more in Blood, and be yet the more abominable Villain: who without that was too wicked on all Conscience; And had more to answer for, than any Tragedy, or Furies could inflict upon him. So there can be nothing in the characters, either for the profit, or to delight an Audience.

The third thing to be considered is the Thoughts. But from such Characters, we need not expect many that are either true, or fine, or noble. [. . .]

Step then amongst the Scenes to observe the Conduct in this Tragedy. [. . .] Michael Cassio came not from Venice in the Ship with Desdemona, nor till this Morning could be suspected of an opportunity with her. And [in Act III, scene iii] 'tis now but Dinner time; yet the Moor complains of his Forehead. He might have set a Guard on Cassio, or have lockt up Desdemona, or have observ'd their carriage[14] a day or two longer. He is on other occasions phlegmatick enough: this is very hasty.

---

10. **close.** Secretive
11. **teizing.** Teasing, that is, pursuing or urging him on
12. **smock-fac'd.** Smooth-faced; girlish
13. **Cully.** Dupe
14. **carriage.** Behavior

words for everyday use

dis • sem • bling (di səm' bliŋ) *adj.*, describing someone who dissembles, or puts on a false appearance in order to deceive. *The dissembling wolf put on a sheep's skin so he could get at the sheep without the shepherd noticing him.*

phleg • ma • tic (fleg ma' tik) *adj.*, slow to move or act; not easily excited; sluggish. *The phlegmatic dog slumbered all day, rarely rousing himself to bark at passers-by.*

But after Dinner we have a wonderful flight:[15]

OTHEL. *What sense had I of her stol'n hours of lust?*
I saw't not, thought it not, it harm' d not me:
I slept the next night well, was free and merry;
I found not Cassio's kisses on her lips [. . .]
[III, iii, 342–5]

A little after this, says he,

OTH. *Give me a living reason that she's disloyal.*
JAGO. *I lay with Cassio lately,*
. . . In sleep I heard him say: sweet Desdemona,
Let us be wary, let us hide our loves: [. . .]
[III, iii, 413–30]

▶ *According to Rymer, what does Othello seem to have forgotten?*

By the <u>Rapture</u> of Othello, one might think that he raves, is not of sound Memory, forgets that he has not yet been two nights in the Matrimonial Bed with his Desdemona. But we find Jago, who should have a better memory, forging his lies after the very same Model. The very night of their Marriage at Venice, the Moor, and also Cassio, were sent away to Cyprus. In the Second Act, Othello and his Bride go the first time to Bed; the Third Act opens the next morning. The parties have been in view to this moment. We saw the opportunity which was given for Cassio to speak his bosom to her; once, indeed, might go a great way with a Venetian. But once, will not do the Poets business; The Audience must suppose a great many bouts,[16] to make the plot operate. They must deny their senses, to reconcile it to common sense: or make it any way consistent, and hang together. [. . .]

So much ado, so much stress, so much passion and repetition about an Handkerchief? Why was not this call'd the Tragedy of the Handkerchief? [. . .] Had it been Desdemona's <u>Garter</u>, the <u>Sagacious</u> Moor might have smelt a Rat: but the

---

15. **flight.** Flight of passion
16. **great many bouts.** That is, many meetings between Cassio and Desdemona

---

words for everyday use

rap • ture (rap' chər) *n.*, state of being carried away by overwhelming emotion. *The prince gazed in rapture at the princess, completely overwhelmed by her beauty.*

sag • a • cious (sə gā' shəs) *adj.*, wise. *The sagacious old man dispensed much sage advice.*

Handkerchief is so remote a trifle, no Booby, on this side Mauritania, cou'd make any consequence from it. [. . .]

Desdemona dropt the Handkerchief, and missed it that very day after her Marriage; it might have been rumpl'd up with her Wedding sheets: And this Night that she lay in her wedding sheets, the Fairey Napkin (whilst Othello was stifling her) might have started up to disarm his fury, and stop his ungracious mouth. Then might she (in a Traunce for fear) have lain as dead. Then might he, believing her dead, touched with remorse, have honestly cut his own Throat, by the good leave, and with the applause of all the Spectators. Who might thereupon have gone home with a quiet mind, admiring the beauty of Providence;[17] fairly and truly represented on the Theatre.

◀ What does Rymer say would have been a fitting ending to the play?

But from this Scene to the end of the Play we meet with nothing but blood and butchery [. . .] What can remain with the Audience to carry home with them from this sort of Poetry, for their use and <u>edification</u>? how can it work, unless (instead of settling the mind, and purging our passions[18]) to delude our senses, disorder our thoughts, addle our brain, pervert our affections, hair our imaginations, corrupt our appetite, and fill our head with vanity, confusion, Tintamarre,[19] and Jingle-jangle, beyond what all the Parish Clarks of London, with their old Testament farces, and interludes, in Richard the seconds time cou'd ever pretend to? Our only hopes, for the good of their Souls, can be, that these people go to the Playhouse, as they do to Church, to sit still, look on one another, make no reflection, nor mind the Play, more than they would a Sermon.

There is in this Play, some burlesk,[20] some humour, and ramble of Comical Wit, some shew, and some Mimickry[21] to divert the spectators: but the tragical part is, plainly none other, than a Bloody <u>Farce</u>, without salt or savour.

---

17. **Providence.** God as guide of human destiny
18. **settling the mind . . . passions.** According to the classical theorists, a proper tragedy was supposed to do these things
19. **Tintamarre.** A confused noise: clamor, racket, or hubbub
20. **burlesk.** Burlesque; that is, a theatrical entertainment with broad and earthy humor
21. **Mimickry.** Impersonation; acting

words for everyday use

ed • i • fi • ca • tion (e' də fə kā' shən) n., process of being enlightened, educated, or uplifted, especially with moral or religious knowledge. *The school offered many excellent programs for the <u>edification</u> of its students.*

farce (färs') n., a comedy characterized by broad satire and improbable situations; ridiculous or empty show. *The Mel Brooks movie was an entertaining <u>farce</u>.*

Critical Thinking

1. What does Rymer find to be improbable in the plot of *Othello?* What does he think of the characters? How would you respond to each of his criticisms?

2. What point does Rymer make about the time scheme in the play? Do you agree or disagree? Why?

3. Do you agree with Rymer's belief that a drama should be edifying, or educational, to its audience? Why, or why not? Do you think *Othello* is edifying? Explain.

4. Imagine that you are a contemporary of Rymer and wish to respond to his review. Write a response to his review in the form of a letter to the editor.

Notes on *Othello* (c.1836–39)
by Samuel Taylor Coleridge

ABOUT THE RELATED READING

Samuel Taylor Coleridge (1772–1834) is best known for his lyrical poems, which are classics of English Romantic literature; however, he was also a formidable critic and philosopher. The following commentary on *Othello* is taken from Coleridge's notes and lectures on Shakespeare, which were collected and published after his death. The first two excerpts were published in *Literary Remains* between 1836 and 1839. In the first excerpt, he discusses the character of Iago, showing his awe at the "motiveless malignity" in Shakespeare's notorious villain. In the second excerpt, he explains why he believes that Othello should *not* be viewed as a "blackamoor or negro"—not a black man, but a brown one. In the third excerpt (taken from a talk he delivered in December 1822 and published in the book *Table Talk* in 1835), Coleridge repeats that Othello should be seen, again, not as a negro, but rather a "high and chivalrous Moorish chief." Coleridge's racist view was still in evidence one hundred years later when, in 1930, American audiences were outraged by the idea of black actor Paul Robeson playing the Moor onstage.

On the character of Iago:

Virtue? a fig! 'Tis in ourselves that we are thus, or thus . . .

This speech[1] comprises the passionless character of Iago. It is all will in intellect; and therefore he is here a bold <u>partisan</u> of a truth, but yet of a truth converted into a falsehood by the absence of all the necessary modifications caused by the frail nature of man. And then comes the last sentiment,—

---

1. **This speech.** You may read the entire speech in Act I, scene iii, lines 322–336.

---

words for everyday use

par • ti • san (pär′ tə zən; pär′ tə sən) *n.*, a passionate supporter of something (as a cause or a political party). *The Douglas family are enthusiastic <u>partisans</u> of the Republican party and often volunteer their time to help with local campaigns.*

. . . our raging motions, our carnal stings, our unbitted lusts; whereof I take this, that you call love, to be a sect or scion . . .

▶ What does Iago repeat that makes him, in Coleridge's eyes, even more wicked?

Here is the true Iagoism of, alas! how many! Note Iago's pride of mastery in the repetition of "Go, make money!" to his anticipated dupe, even stronger than his love of lucre: and when Roderigo is completely won—

I am chang'd. I'll go sell all my land.

when the effect has been fully produced, the repetition of triumph—

Go to: farewell; put money enough in your purse!

The remainder—Iago's soliloquy[2]—the motive-hunting of a motiveless <u>malignity</u>—how awful it is! Yea, whilst he is still allowed to bear the divine image, it is too fiendish for his own steady view,[3]—for the lonely gaze of a being next to devil, and only not quite devil,—and yet a character which Shakspeare has attempted and executed, without disgust and without scandal![4]

On Othello's race:

RODERIGO. *What a full fortune does the "thick-lips" owe,*
   If he can carry't thus.

Roderigo turns off to Othello; and here comes one, if not the only, seeming justification of our blackamoor or negro Othello. Even if we supposed this an uninterrupted tradition of the theatre, and that Shakspeare himself, from

---

2. **Iago's soliloquy.** That is, act I, scene iii, lines 383–404.

3. **whilst he . . . his own steady view.** While Iago is still attempting to appear "divine," or saintly, in the eyes of the other characters, he is unwilling to own up to the truth about himself. The truth—that he has no motives at all and is simply evil—is "too fiendish" for him to admit, even to himself.

4. **without disgust and without scandal.** That is, Shakespeare does not make a fuss over Iago or make any apologies for him—he simply presents him as he is.

---

words for everyday use   ma • lig • ni • ty (mə lig′ nə tē) *n.*, malignancy: the quality or state of being malignant, that is, evil or harmful. *The <u>malignity</u> of the villain was contrasted with the kindness and goodness of the hero.*

want of scenes,[5] and the experience that nothing could be made too marked for the senses of his audience, had practically sanctioned it,—would this prove aught concerning his own intention as a poet for all ages? Can we imagine him so utterly ignorant as to make a barbarous negro plead royal birth,—at a time, too, when negros were not known except as slaves?—As for Iago's language to Brabantio, it implies merely that Othello was a Moor, that is, black.[6] Though I think the rivalry of Roderigo sufficient to account for his wilful confusion of Moor and Negro,—yet, even if compelled to give this up, I should think it only adapted for the acting of the day, and should complain of an enormity built on a single word, in direct contradiction to Iago's "Barbary horse."[7] Besides, if we could in good earnest believe Shakspeare ignorant of the distinction, still why should we adopt one disagreeable possibility instead of a ten times greater and more pleasing probability? It is a common error to mistake the epithets applied by the "dramatis personae"[8] to each other, as truly descriptive of what the audience ought to see or know. No doubt Desdemona saw Othello's visage in his mind; yet, as we are constituted, and most surely as an English audience was disposed in the beginning of the seventeenth century, it would be something monstrous to conceive this beautiful Venetian girl falling in love with a veritable negro. It would argue a disproportionateness, a want of balance, in Desdemona, which Shakspeare does not appear to have in the least contemplated.

◀ What does Coleridge say would be "something monstrous to conceive"?

---

5. **want of scenes.** A desire to create a scene, or spectacle, that would shock the audience

6. **black.** Of dark skin; swarthy in appearance, but not "black" in the sense of "negro"

7. **contradiction to Iago's "Barbary horse."** Iago's reference to Othello as a "Barbary horse" implies that Othello was from Barbary, and therefore would be "a tawny Moor," not a black African.

8. **"dramatis personae."** The characters in a drama

words for everyday use

sanc • tion (saŋ[k]′ shən) vt., to approve or consent to. *In Communist China, only certain churches are sanctioned by the government; others are outlawed.*

ep • i • thet (e′ pə thət) n., a descriptive word or phrase applied to a person or thing; often used in place of the person's name. *Because she often forgot to turn in her homework, the student earned the epithet "Forgetful Sam."*

ver • i • ta • ble (ver′ ə tə bəl) adj., being in fact the thing named; actual, real. Often used as an intensifier. *Marie Curie was not only smart, she was a veritable genius.*

On the character of Othello:

Othello must not be conceived as a negro, but a high and <u>chivalrous</u> Moorish chief. Shakspere learned the spirit of that character from the Spanish poetry which was prevalent in England in his time.

Jealousy does not strike me as the point in his passion; I take it to be rather an agony that the creature, whom he had believed angelic, with whom he had garnered up his heart, and whom he could not help still loving, should be proved impure and worthless. It was the struggle *not* to love her. It was a moral indignation and regret that virtue should so fall:—"But yet the *pity* of it, Iago!—O Iago! the *pity* of it, Iago!" In addition to this, his honour was concerned: Iago would not have succeeded but by hinting that his honour was compromised. There is no ferocity in Othello; his mind is majestic and composed. He deliberately determines to die; and speaks his last speech with a view of showing his attachment to the Venetian state, though it had <u>superseded</u> him.

Schiller[9] has the material <u>sublime</u>; to produce an effect, he sets you a whole town on fire, and throws infants with their mothers into the flames, or locks up a father in an old tower. But Shakspere drops a handkerchief, and the same or greater effects follow. Lear is the most tremendous effort of Shakspere as a poet; Hamlet[10] as a philosopher or meditator and Othello is the union of the two. There is something gigantic and unformed in the former two; but in the latter, everything assumes its due place and proportion, and the whole mature powers of his mind are displayed in an admirable equilibrium.

▶ What does Coleridge was "not the point" in Othello's character? How does he describe Othello's mind?

---

9. **Schiller.** German dramatist Friedrich von Schiller (1759–1805). Here Coleridge refers to Schiller's famous play *The Robbers* (1781).
10. **Lear . . . Hamlet.** The heroes of two of Shakespeare's other great tragedies: *The Tragedy of King Lear* and *The Tragedy of Hamlet, Prince of Denmark.*

words for everyday use

chiv • al • rous (shi' vəl rəs) *adj.,* having the qualities of courtesy and grace, as outlined in the laws of chivalry, or knighthood. *Opening the door for a lady was long considered a <u>chivalrous</u> act expected of all men; nowadays it is considered equally proper for a woman to hold a door for a man.*

su • per • sede (sü' pər sēd') *vt.,* to displace or set aside, and put another in place of. *The gruff army general was forced into retirement and <u>superseded</u> by a younger and more personable officer.*

sub • lime (sə blīm´) *adj.,* lofty, grand, or exalted in thought or expression; more broadly, excellent. *The critic described the orchestra's performance as "nothing short of <u>sublime.</u>"*

Critical Thinking

1. Coleridge writes that Iago's soliloquies are the "motive-hunting of motiveless malignity." Do you agree? Does Iago have any true motive for wanting revenge on Othello?

2. How and why does Coleridge distinguish between "Moor" and "Negro"? Why does he think Shakespeare must have intended for Othello to be a Moor, and not a black African? How would you respond to his arguments?

3. Many critics have stated that it is Othello's jealous nature—the stereotypical "hot Moorish blood"—that leads to his downfall. Coleridge, on the other hand, says that "jealousy does not strike me as the point." What feelings does Coleridge see as motivating Othello, if not jealousy? Do you agree or disagree? Explain.

from *Shakespearean Tragedy* (1904)
by A. C. Bradley

ABOUT THE RELATED READING

British literary critic **A. C. Bradley** (1851–1935) was well known as a critic and scholar of Shakespeare's works. His book *Shakespearean Tragedy* (1904) is a classic which has helped to shape our modern understanding of Shakespeare. In the first two excerpts, Bradley describes the distinctive impression created by *Othello* and discusses the romantic character of its hero. In the third excerpt, he discusses the question of Othello's race, offering a compelling retort to Coleridge and other critics who found it impossible to believe such a noble and eloquent hero as Othello could have been black.

On the distinctive impression of *Othello:*

▶ *According to Bradley, what is it that makes* Othello *distinct from all of Shakespeare's tragedies?*

    What is the peculiarity of *Othello*? What is the distinctive impression that it leaves? Of all Shakespeare's tragedies, I would answer, not even excepting *King Lear, Othello* is the most painfully exciting and the most terrible. From the moment when the temptation of the hero begins, the reader's heart and mind are held in a vice, experiencing the extremes of pity and fear, sympathy and repulsion, sickening hope and dreadful expectation.

On the character of Othello:

    Othello is, in one sense of the word, by far the most romantic figure among Shakespeare's heroes; and he is so partly from the strange life of war and adventure which he has lived from childhood. He does not belong to our world, and he seems to enter it we know not whence—almost as if from wonderland. There is something mysterious in his descent from men of royal siege; in his wanderings in vast deserts and among marvellous peoples; in his tales of magic handkerchiefs and prophetic Sibyls; in the sudden vague glimpses we get of numberless battles and sieges in which he has played the hero and has borne a charmed life; even in chance references to his baptism, his being sold to slavery, his sojourn in Aleppo.

And he is not merely a romantic figure; his own nature is romantic. He has not, indeed, the meditative or <u>speculative</u> imagination of Hamlet; but in the strictest sense of the word he is more poetic than Hamlet. Indeed, if one recalls Othello's most famous speeches—those that begin "Her father loved me," "O now for ever," "Never, Iago," "Had it pleased heaven," "It is the cause," "Behold, I have a weapon," "Soft you, a word or two before you go"—and if one places side by side with these speeches an equal number by any other hero, one will not doubt that Othello is the greatest poet of them all. There is the same poetry in his casual phrases—like "These nine moon wasted," "Keep up your bright swords, for the dew will rust them," "You chaste stars," "It is a sword of Spain, the ice brook's temper," "It is the very error of the moon"—and in those brief expressions of intense feeling which ever since have been taken as the absolute expression, like

◀ How does Bradley describe Othello's nature? How does Othello compare to Hamlet, in Bradley's view?

> If it were now to die,
> 'Twere now to be most happy; for, I fear,
> My soul hath her content so absolute
> That not another comfort like to this
> Succeeds in unknown fate,

or

> If she be false, O then Heaven mocks itself.
> I'll not believe it;

or

> No, my heart is turned to stone; I strike it, and it hurts
> my hand,

or

> But yet the pity of it, Iago! O Iago, the pity of it, Iago!

or

> O thou weed,
> Who art so lovely fair and smell'st so sweet
> That the sense aches at thee, would thou hadst ne'er
>   been born.

---

words for everyday use

spec • u • la • tive (spə′ kyə lə tiv) *adj.*, involved in intellectual speculation, that is, pondering intellectual questions. *Shakespeare's Hamlet is a <u>speculative</u> character, not a man of action.*

And this imagination, we feel, has accompanied his whole life. He has watched with a poet's eye the Arabian trees dropping their med'cinable gum, and the Indian throwing away his chance-found pearl; and has gazed in a fascinated dream at the Pontic sea rushing, never to return, to the Propontic and the Hellespont; and has felt as no other man ever felt (for he speaks of it as none other ever did) the poetry of the pride, pomp, and circumstance of glorious war.

So he comes before us, dark and grand, with a light upon him from the sun where he was born; but no longer young, and now grave, self-controlled, steeled by the experience of countless perils, hardships and vicissitudes, at once simple and stately in bearing and in speech, a great man naturally modest but fully conscious of his worth, proud of his services to the State, unawed by dignitaries and unelated by honours, secure, it would seem, against all dangers from without and all rebellion from within. And he comes to have his life crowned with the final glory of love, a love as strange, adventurous and romantic as any passage of his eventful history, filling his heart with tenderness and his imagination with ecstasy. For there is no love, not that of Romeo in his youth, more steeped in imagination than Othello's.

▶ What traits in Othello lead to his downfall, according to Bradley?

The sources of danger in this character are revealed but too clearly by the story. In the first place, Othello's mind, for all its poetry, is very simple. He is not observant. His nature tends outward. He is quite free from introspection, and is not given to reflection. Emotion excites his imagination, but it confuses and dulls his intellect. On this side he is the very opposite of Hamlet, with whom, however, he shares a great openness and trustfulness of nature. In addition, he has little experience of the corrupt products of civilised life, and is ignorant of European women.

In the second place, for all his dignity and massive calm (and he has greater dignity than any other of Shakespeare's men), he is by nature full of the most vehement passion. [. . .]

---

words for everyday use

vi • cis • si • tude (və sis′ sə tüd′) n., chance occurrence or fluctuation in state or condition; a difficulty or hardship that occurs in the course of life. *Melissa weathered all the vicissitudes of life with a cheerful attitude.*

in • tro • spec • tion (in′ trə spek′ shən) n., act of looking inward. *After much introspection, Henry felt that he had a better understanding of who he was and what he wanted out of life.*

ve • he • ment (vē′ ə mənt) adj., marked by extreme intensity or force. *When asked if they would like to take a test, the class responded with a vehement "No!"*

Lastly, Othello's nature is all of one piece. His trust, where he trusts, is absolute. Hesitation is almost impossible to him. He is extremely self-reliant, and decides and acts instantaneously. If stirred to indignation, as "in Aleppo once," he answers with one lightning stroke. Love, if he loves, must be to him the heaven where either he must leave or bear no life. If such a passion as jealousy seizes him, it will swell into a well-nigh uncontrollable flood. He will press for immediate conviction or immediate relief. Convinced, he will act with the authority of a judge and the swiftness of a man in mortal pain. Undeceived, he will do like execution on himself.

This character is so noble, Othello's feelings and actions follow so inevitably from it and from the forces brought to bear on it, and his sufferings are so heart-rending, that he stirs, I believe, in most readers a passion of mingled love and pity which they feel for no other hero in Shakespeare. [. . .]

On Othello's race:

[T]here is a question, which, though of little conse-quence, is not without dramatic interest, whether Shakespeare imagined Othello as a Negro or as a Moor. Now I will not say that Shakespeare imagined him as a Negro and not as a Moor, for that might imply that he dis-tinguished Negroes and Moors precisely as we do; but what appears to me nearly certain is that he imagined Othello as a black man, and not as a light-brown one.

In the first place, we must remember that the brown or bronze to which we are now accustomed in the Othellos of our theatres is a recent <u>innovation</u>. Down to Edmund Kean's[1] time, so far as is known, Othello was always quite black. This stage-tradition goes back to the Restoration[2], and it almost settles our question. For it is impossible that the colour of the original Othello should have been forgot-ten so soon after Shakespeare's time, and most improbable that it should have been changed from brown to black.

◀ *What does Bradley say appears to him nearly certain, regarding Shakespeare's idea of Othello?*

1. **Edmund Kean's.** Kean (1789–1833) was an acclaimed English actor who portrayed Othello onstage in the early 1800s.
2. **Restoration.** The re-establishment of the British monarchy in 1660 after the rule of the Puritans from 1642–1660. Theaters were reopened in England at this time, after having been closed during the Puritan rule.

words for everyday use   in • no • va • tion (i′ nə vā′ shən) *n.*, introduction of something new. *In 1955, there was a new innovation in fasteners, known as "Velcro."*

RELATED READINGS: FROM *SHAKESPEAREAN TRAGEDY*   **253**

If we turn to the play itself, we find many references to Othello's colour and appearance. Most of these are indecisive; for the word "black" was of course used then where we should speak of a "dark" complexion now; and even the nickname "thick-lips," appealed to as proof that Othello was a Negro, might have been applied by an enemy to what we call a Moor. On the other hand, it is hard to believe that, if Othello had been light-brown, Brabantio would have taunted him with having a "sooty bosom," or that (as Mr. Furness[3] observes) he himself would have used the words,

> her name, that was as fresh
> As Dian's visage, is now begrimed and black
> As mine own face.

These arguments cannot be met by pointing out that Othello was of royal blood, is not called an Ethiopian, is called a Barbary horse, and is said to be going to Mauritania. All this would be of importance if we had reason to believe that Shakespeare shared our ideas, knowledge and terms. Otherwise it proves nothing. And we know that sixteenth-century writers called any dark North African a Moor, or a black Moor, or a blackamoor. Sir Thomas Elyot,[4] according to Hunter,[5] calls Ethiopians Moors; and the following are the first two illustrations of "Blackamoor" in the Oxford *English Dictionary*: 1547, "I am a blake More borne in Barbary"; 1548, "*Ethiopo*, a blake More, or a man of Ethiope." Thus geographical names can tell us nothing about the question how Shakespeare imagined Othello. He may have known that a Mauritanian is not a Negro nor black, but we cannot assume that he did. He may have known, again, that the Prince of Morocco, who is described in the *Merchant of Venice* as having, like Othello, the complexion of a devil,[6] was no Negro. But we cannot tell: nor is there any reason why he should not have imagined the Prince as a brown Moor and Othello as a Blackamoor.

Titus Andronicus appeared in the Folio among Shakespeare's works. It is believed by some good critics to

▶ How did sixteenth-century writers use the terms "Moor," "black Moor," and "blackamoor"?

▶ Who was Aaron? Why does Bradley mention him?

3. **Mr. Furness.** American Shakespeare scholar Horace Furness (1833–1912)

4. **Sir Thomas Elyot.** English diplomat and scholar who lived c.1490–1546

5. **Hunter.** American critic Joseph Hunter (1783–1861). Bradley here refers to Hunter's *New Illustrations of the Life, Studies, and Writings of Shakespeare* (1845), vol. ii, page 281.

6. **complexion of a devil.** That is, black. The devil was believed to be black in color, a fact which went hand-in-hand with the racial prejudice of Europeans.

be his: hardly anyone doubts that he had a hand in it: it is certain that he knew it, for reminiscences of it are scattered through his plays. Now no one who reads *Titus Andronicus* with an open mind can doubt that Aaron[7] was, in our sense, black; and he appears to have been a Negro. To mention nothing else, he is twice called "coal-black"; his colour is compared with that of a raven and a swan's legs; his child is coal-black and thick-lipped; he himself has a "fleece of woolly hair." Yet he is "Aaron the Moor," just as Othello is "Othello the Moor." In the *Battle of Alcazar*,[8] Muly the Moor is called "the negro"; and Shakespeare himself in a single line uses "negro" and "Moor" of the same person (*Merchant of Venice*, III, v, 42).

The horror of most American critics (Mr. Furness is a bright exception) at the idea of a black Othello is very amusing, and their arguments are highly instructive. But they were anticipated, I regret to say, by Coleridge, and we will hear him. "No doubt Desdemona saw Othello's visage in his mind; yet, as we are constituted, and most surely as an English audience was disposed in the beginning of the seventeenth century, it would be something monstrous to conceive this beautiful Venetian girl falling in love with a veritable Negro. It would argue a disproportionateness, a want of balance, in Desdemona, which Shakespeare does not appear to have in the least contemplated." Could any argument be more self-destructive? It actually did appear to Brabantio "something monstrous to conceive" his daughter falling in love with Othello—so monstrous that he could account for her love only by drugs and foul charms. And the suggestion that such love would argue "disproportionateness" is precisely the suggestion that Iago *did* make in Desdemona's case:

> *Foh! one may smell in such a will most rank,*
> *Foul **disproportion**, thoughts unnatural*

In fact he spoke of the marriage exactly as a filthy-minded cynic now might speak of the marriage of an English lady to a Negro like Toussaint.[9] Thus the argument of Coleridge and others points straight to the conclusion against which they argue.

---

7. **Aaron.** In *Titus Andronicus*, Aaron the Moor is a villain.

8. **Battle of Alcazar.** A play attributed to English dramatist George Peele (1558–1598).

9. **Toussaint.** Toussaint L'Ouverture (1743–1803), a former slave and leader of the Haitian slave revolt of 1791

▶ According to Bradley, how do Coleridge and some American writers regard Desdemona's love?

But this is not all. The question whether to Shakespeare Othello was black or brown is not a mere question of isolated fact or historical curiosity; it concerns the character of Desdemona. Coleridge, and still more the American writers, regard her love, in effect, as Brabantio regarded it, and not as Shakespeare conceived it. They are simply blurring this glorious conception[10] when they try to lessen the distance between her and Othello, and to smooth away the obstacle which his "visage" offered to her romantic passion for a hero. Desdemona, the "eternal womanly"[11] in its most lovely and adorable form, simple and innocent as a child, <u>ardent</u> with the courage and idealism of a saint, radiant with that heavenly purity of heart which men worship the more because nature so rarely permits it to themselves, had no theories about universal brotherhood, and no phrases about "one blood in all the nations of the earth"[12] or "barbarian, Scythian, bond and free";[13] but when her soul came in sight of the noblest soul on earth, she made nothing of the shrinking of her senses, but followed her soul until her senses took part with it, and "loved him with the love which was her doom."[14] It was not prudent. It even turned out tragically. She met in life with the reward of those who rise too far above our common level; and we continue to allot her the same reward when we consent to forgive her for loving a brown man, but find it monstrous that she should love a black one.

▶ What does Bradley say leads to Desdemona's tragic end? What does he say about the difference in audience perceptions regarding whether she loves a "brown" or "black" man?

---

10. **this glorious conception.** That is, the glorious conception Shakespeare had of Desdemona's love, as something noble and true.
11. **"eternal womanly."** The archetypal woman: one who embodies all the qualities thought to represent ideal womanhood. The phrase comes from German writer Johann von Goethe (1749–1832).
12. **"one blood . . . earth."** From the Bible, Acts 17:26
13. **"barbarian . . . free."** From the Bible, the Epistle of Paul to the Colossians, 3:11. A *Scythian* was a member of Eurasian nomadic people who were believed to be very savage and fierce.
14. **"loved him . . . doom."** A quote from the poem "Lancelot and Elaine" by Alfred, Lord Tennyson (1809–1892)

---

words for everyday use

ar • dent (är' dənt) adj., full of strong enthusiasm or intense emotion. *Lyle was an <u>ardent</u> fan of Shakespeare, and his voice glowed with enthusiasm when he spoke of the Bard.*

Critical Thinking

1. What does Bradley say is the peculiarity or uniqueness of *Othello,* as compared to Shakespeare's other great tragedies? How does *Othello* compare with the other Shakespearean tragedies you have read, if any?

2. How does Bradley describe the nature of Othello? According to Bradley, which characteristics in Othello lead to his downfall? Do you agree or disagree with Bradley's view? Is there anything you might add?

3. Summarize Bradley's argument as to Othello's race. Compare his viewpoint to that of Coleridge. In your opinion, did Shakespeare intend for us to see Othello as a black man or a white man with dark skin? Does it matter? Why, or why not?

"Against Jealousy" (pub. 1640)
by Ben Jonson

ABOUT THE RELATED READING

English dramatist and poet **Ben Jonson** (1572–1637) was a contemporary of Shakespeare. The two men likely first met in the London theater in the late 1500s, since in 1598, Shakespeare acted in Jonson's play *Every Man in His Humour*. The two men were rivals while Shakespeare was alive, but Jonson clearly admired his fellow playwright. In a poem published in the First Folio in 1632, Jonson called Shakespeare the "soul of the Age! The applause! delight! the wonder of our Stage!"

Published in 1640, **"Against Jealousy"** is a poem about jealousy, a central motif in *Othello*. As you read, consider how Jonson's depiction of jealousy compares to that portrayed in Shakespeare's play.

> Wretched and foolish Jealousy,
> How cam'st thou thus to enter me?
> I ne'er was of thy kind:
> Nor have I yet the narrow mind
> To vent that poor[1] desire,
> That others should not warm them[2] at my fire:
> I wish the sun should shine
> On all men's fruit and flowers, as well as mine.

▶ *What does Jealousy claim it is there to prove?*

> But under the disguise of love,
> Thou say'st, thou only cam'st to prove
> What my affections were.
> Think'st thou that love is help'd by fear?
> Go, get thee quickly forth,
> Love's sickness, and his[3] noted want of worth.[4]
> Seek doubting men[5] to please;
> I ne'er will owe my health to a disease.

---

1. **poor.** Worthless; despicable
2. **them.** Themselves
3. **his.** Love's
4. **noted want of worth.** Well-known defect
5. **doubting men.** That is, men who are not sure whether they are in love or not, and who therefore need proof in the form of jealous feelings

Critical Thinking

1. In this poem, what words and phrases are used to describe jealousy? Would the characters of *Othello* agree with this attitude toward jealousy? Think in particular of the words Desdemona, Emilia, and Iago used when describing jealousy in the play.

2. Do you think that jealousy can ever be a sign of a healthy love relationship, or is it a "disease," as described here? Explain.

Creative Writing Activities

Creative Writing Activity A: Alternate Ending

What would *Othello* be like with a happy ending? Try it! Write a new act V for the play, with a Hollywood-style happy ending. Make sure to keep the same style as Shakespeare, using iambic pentamenter for all the characters' lines.

Creative Writing Activity B: An Updated *Othello*

Choose one of the scenes or acts from *Othello* and rewrite it using contemporary language and references. You may collaborate with other students to adapt the entire play in this manner. You may choose to write the part or lines in prose, or keep with the verse format.

Creative Writing Activity C: Journal Entry

Write a journal entry from the point of view of one of the characters in *Othello*. For example, you might have Roderigo describe his feelings about Desdemona and relate his fears that Iago is leading him on. Or, you might write the entry Desdemona would have written after the events in act III, scene iv, describing her bewilderment at the change in Othello's behavior.

Creative Writing Activity D: Newspaper

Newspapers as we know them did not exist in the 1500s, when the events of this play took place. Nonetheless, imagine that you are on the staff of a newspaper in sixteenth-century Venice. Work with other students to prepare a series of news articles telling about the events related in the play, including the appointment of Cassio as Othello's lieutenant, the news of Desdemona's elopment, the Turkish attack on Cyprus, the event that led to Cassio's dismissal, the attack on Cassio's life, and the murder of Desdemona.

Creative Writing Activity E: Talk Show

Imagine the characters of *Othello* were to appear on a Jerry Springer-style talk show to air their differences. Assume that the appearance is taking place sometime before the tragic events of act V. What information might be revealed on the show? What conflicts might break out on stage? Write the script of the show and act it out for the class.

Critical Writing Activities

The following are suggested topics for short critical essays on *Othello, the Moor of Venice.* An essay written on any of these topics should begin with an introductory paragraph that states the **thesis**, or main idea, of the essay. The introductory paragraph should be followed by several paragraphs that support the thesis using evidence from the play. This evidence may be presented in the form of quotations or summaries of events or dialogue. The essay should conclude with a paragraph that summarizes the points made in the body of the essay and that restates the thesis in different words.

Critical Writing Activity A: Women in *Othello*

In *Othello,* Shakespeare gives a representation of three types of women: the privileged noblewoman, the tough middle-class servant, and the low-class prostitute. Examine his depictions of each of these women. Was Shakespeare sexist? That is, do you think he would agree with Iago that women are useless creatures who "rise to play, and go to bed to work"? Was he classist? For example, would he agree with Cassio that it would be ridiculous to marry a common prostitute like Bianca? Does he mean for us to view the high-class Desdemona as a more pure and better person than Emilia? Brainstorm on these questions, and then come up with a thesis statement about Shakespeare's depiction of women. In your essay, use quotes and examples from the play to support your thesis.

Critical Writing Activity B: Othello as Tragic Hero

Is Othello a true tragic hero? Is he the central character of the play? If Othello is a tragic hero, what is his tragic flaw? Some critics have said it is his jealousy; others have said it is his gullibility, in that he is too quick to believe Iago's insinuations. Other critics have claimed that Othello is not a true tragic hero, because he is brought down not by a tragic flaw but by the machinations of the villain Iago. Still others have claimed that the true hero of the play is not Othello, but Iago. Write an essay in which you defend your position on the matter. Discuss how well *Othello* fits the definition of a tragedy, and how well Othello fits the definition of a tragic hero.

Critical Writing Activity C: The Villainy of Iago

Write an essay in which you discuss the character of Iago. Here are some possible positions you might take in your essay:

- Iago is a classic two-faced villain, with no motives for his crimes other than to "plume up his will." His soliloquies are, as Coleridge put it, merely the "motive-hunting of motiveless malignity."

- Iago is not a believable character: he is too evil, like a caricature of a villain. Shakespeare should have made him more human, more realistic.

- Iago is not as terrible a villain as he is commonly thought, and certainly no evil genius. He never meant for his plan to go as far as it did—he never meant for Desdemona or Cassio or Othello to die. He just wanted to get revenge on Othello, who he believed slept with his wife, but his plan spun out of his control.

- Although it is commonly believed that the Moor's jealousy leads to the tragic events in *Othello*, it is actually Iago's jealousy that causes all the trouble.

Critical Writing Activity D: The Character of Desdemona

Write a critical essay examining the character of Desdemona. Before you start, brainstorm about questions such as the following: Why did Desdemona marry Othello, when she could have chosen from all the "wealthy curled darlings" of Venice? What does that choice say about her? Why does she continue to declare her love for Othello even as his actions become more abusive and irrational? In your essay, consider how Desdemona's character is developed not only through her own words and actions but also through what other characters say about her—notably Brabantio, Cassio, and Emilia.

Critical Writing Activity E: Race in *Othello*

Write an essay examining the role of race in *Othello*. In your essay, you might deal with such questions as the following: Is Othello's race an important factor in the play? Does racism contribute to Othello's tragic downfall? If so, how? If not, why not? Why did critics like Samuel Taylor Coleridge insist that Othello "should not be viewed as a negro"?

Critical Writing Activity F: Analysis

Choose one of the following speeches and analyze it in detail. Begin by explaining where the speech appears in the play and its connection to the plot. Then go through the speech line by line, explaining what it says. Finally, summarize the primary message of the speech.

"We cannot all be masters . . ." (I, i, 43–65)
"And what's he then that says I play the villain . . ." (II, iii, 337–363)
"Haply, for I am black . . ." (III, iii, 263–277)
"But I do think it is their husbands' faults . . ." (IV, iii, 87–104)
"It is the cause . . ." (V, ii, 1–15)
"Then must you speak / Of one that loved not wisely but too well . . ." (V, ii, 342–355)

Projects

Project A: Set Design

Choose one scene from *Othello* and design a set for it. Begin by making sketches. Then create a finished illustration of the set or construct a model of the set out of balsa wood, foam rubber, or other materials. You might wish to design a set using a computer draw/paint or computer-aided drafting (CAD) program.

Project B: Costuming

Design a costume for one of the characters in the play, such as Othello, Desdemona, Iago, or Bianca. Create an illustration of the costume and explain, in writing, why you have designed the costume as you have. In creating your design, you may want to research hair and clothing styles that were popular in Venice in the sixteenth century. Some information is available on the Internet.

Project C: The "Willow" Song

Desdemona's "willow" song from act IV plays an important role in the play, as it foreshadows her sad fate. If you are musically inclined, you may want to try playing and/or singing the ballad. The words and music for the song can be found in Tom Kines' book *Songs From Shakespeare's Plays* (1964, Oak Publications). If you have trouble locating this book, you might make up your own tune. Perform your version for the class.

Project D: *Othello: A Novel*

Now that you are familiar with *Othello* in its original form, you may want to read a different version of the story. The book *Othello: A Novel* (1998) by Julius Lester is a novelization of the play, with some adjustments to the historical context and some surprising differences in characterization. Read the book and prepare a review to share with your classmates. In the review, be sure to discuss the changes Lester made to the story.

Project E: Paul Robeson's *Othello*

In 1930, Paul Robeson became the first black actor to play Othello on the stage, alongside white actor Peggy Ashcroft as Desdemona. The mixed-race production, staged in London, caused a flurry of controversy. Conduct a research project with the aim of learning more about this incident, as well as facts about Paul Robeson's life and career as an actor. If possible, locate news articles and reviews that were published at the time, and share copies of these with the class. What did critics have to say about Robeson's performance? Why was the production so controversial?

Project F: Reviewing a Performance of *Othello*

View a stage performance or a film version of *Othello* and write a review of it. Several excellent films are available. Consult with your teacher before selecting one to review. If you are interested in music, you might want to view a performance of the opera *Otello,* written by Italian composer Giuseppe Verdi. One version, starring Placido Domingo, is widely available on videocasette.

Project G: Twenty Questions

Have a classmate assume the role of some character from the play. Ask yes or no questions of that character until you figure out which character it is.

Project H: Jealousy

Explore the theme of jealousy in literature and other media, such as song, film, and television. Create a book or visual display about jealousy. Include vivid images of jealousy, such as Shakespeare's green-eyed monster, and quotations about it. You might want to start by thinking about your own thoughts or experiences with jealousy.

Glossary of Words for Everyday Use

PRONUNCIATION KEY

VOWEL SOUNDS

a	hat	ō	go	ʉ	burn
ā	play	ȯ	paw, born	ə	extra
ä	star	u̇	book, put		under
e	then	ü	blue, stew		civil
ē	me	oi	boy		honor
i	sit	ou	wow		bogus
ī	my	u	up		

CONSONANT SOUNDS

b	but	l	lip	t	sit
ch	watch	m	money	th	with
d	do	n	on	th	the
f	fudge	ŋ	song, sink	v	valley
g	go	p	pop	w	work
h	hot	r	rod	y	yell
j	jump	s	see	z	pleasure
k	brick	sh	she		

ab • hor (əb hȯ[ə]rʹ) *vt.,* hate strongly; loathe.

a • lac • ri • ty (ə lakʹ rət ē) *n.,* promptness; cheerful readiness.

al • be • it (ȯl bēʹ ət) *conj.,* even though; although.

alms (ä[l]mzʹ) *n.,* something (as money or food) given as charity.

a • mend (ə mendʹ) *vt.,* fix or change for the better.

am • o • rous (amʹ ə rəs) *adj.,* indicative of love.

ap • pre • hend (apʹ ri həndʹ) *vt.,* arrest; seize.

ar • dent (ärʹ dənt) *adj.,* full of strong enthusiasm or intense emotion.

aver • sion (ə vərʹ zhən) *n.,* strong dislike or repugnance.

bal • my (bämʹ ē, bälmʹ ē) *adj.,* soothing.

bau • ble (bȯʹ bəl, bäbʹ əl) *n.,* trinket; something insignificant.

be • guile (bə gīlʹ) *vt.,* lead astray by means of tricks or deception.

be • reft (bi reftʹ) *adj.,* deprived or robbed (usually used with *of*).

best • ial (besʹ chəl, beshʹ chəl) *adj.,* of or relating to beasts.

boon (bünʹ) *n.,* favor; blessing.

breach (brēchʹ) *n.,* break in relations.

cape (kāp´) *n.*, land formation that juts out into the water as a point or a peninsula.

cas • ti • ga • tion (kas´ tə gā´ shən) *n.*, punishment.

chide (chīd´) *vt.*, scold or voice disapproval.

chiv • al • rous (shi´ vəl rəs) *adj.*, having the qualities of courtesy and grace, as outlined in the laws of chivalry, or knighthood.

cho • ler (kä´ lər) *n.*, anger, irateness.

cit • a • del (sit´ ə del, sit´ əd əl) *n.*, fortress that commands a city; or, a fortified part of a city.

com • mence • ment (kəm men[t]s´ mənt) *n.*, beginning.

com • port (kəm pȯrt´; kəm pōrt´) *vi.*, to be fitting; to be in accord with.

con • jec • ture (kən jek´ chər) *vt.*, conclude based on evidence; infer.

con • jur • a • tion (kän´ jü rā´ shən) *n.*, magic spell or trick.

con • se • crate (kän´ sək rāt´) *vt.*, dedicate, as to a sacred purpose.

con • strue (kən strü´) *vt.*, understand or explain the intention of a word or action, usually in a particular way given a set of circumstances.

co • ve • nant (kuv´ nənt, ku´ və nənt) *n.*, an agreement or contract.

cred • u • lous (kre´ jə ləs) *adj.*, ready to believe anything, even with slight or uncertain evidence.

de • lude (di lüd´) *vt.*, mislead; trick.

de • praved (di prāvd´) *adj.*, marked by corruption or evil; perverted.

des • cry (diz skrī´) *vt.*, catch sight of.

des • ti • tute (des´ tə tüt′) *adj.*, devoid of; lacking.

dire (dī[ə]r´) *adj.*, dreadful.

dis • cern (dis ərn´, diz ərn´) *vt.*, detect with the eyes.

dis • cord (dis´ kȯ[ə]rd) *n.*, lack of agreement or harmony.

dis • course (dis´ kō[ə]rs´) *n.*, conversation; verbal expression or exchange of ideas.

dis • sem • ble (dis em´ bəl) *vt.*, hide under a false appearance.

dis • sem • bling (di səm´ bliŋ) *adj.*, describing someone who dissembles, or puts on a false appearance in order to deceive.

dis • sim • u • la • tion (di sim´ yə lā´ shən) *n.*, the act of putting on a false appearance.

di • vine (də vīn´) *vt.*, discover intuitively; infer.

dote (dōt´) *vi.*, be lavish or excessive in one's attention.

ed • i • fi • ca • tion (e´ də fə kā´ shən) *n.*, process of being enlightened, educated, or uplifted, especially with moral or religious knowledge.

ed • i • fy (ed´ ə fī´) *vi.,* inform or enlighten.

egre • gious • ly (i grē´ jəs lē) *adv.,* in a way that is obviously or conspicuously bad: glaringly.

em • i • nent (em´ ə nənt) *adj.,* prominent; standing out.

em • u • la • tion (em´ yə lā´ shən) *n.,* imitation; ambition to equal or excel.

en • due (in dü´) *vt.,* provide; endow.

en • gen • der (in jen´ dər) *vt.,* bring into being.

en • mi • ty (en´ mə tē) *n.,* openly expressed hostility.

ep • i • thet (e´ pə thət) *n.,* a descriptive word or phrase applied to a person or thing; often used in place of the person's name.

evince (i vin[t]s´) *vt.,* display clearly: reveal.

ex • pos • tu • late (ik späs´ chə lāt´) *vi.,* express objection in the form of earnest reasoning.

fa • ci • li • ty (fə sil´ ət ē) *n.,* ease.

farce (färs´) *n.,* a comedy characterized by broad satire and improbable situations; ridiculous or empty show.

filch (filch´) *vt.,* steal.

for • bear (fō[ə]r ba[ə]r´) *vt.,* refrain from.

for • swear (fȯr swa[ə]r´, fōr swa[ə]r´) *vt.,* reject or renounce.

frail • ty (frā[ə]l´ tē) *n.,* weakness.

gait (gāt´) *n.,* manner of walking.

gra • vi • ty (grav´ ət ē) *n.,* seriousness.

griev • ous (grē´ vəs) *adj.,* serious; characterized by severe pain, suffering, or sorrow.

guile (gī´ [ə]l) *n.,* cunning deception.

gull (gəl´) *n.,* person who is easily deceived or cheated.

hei • nous (hā´ nəs) *adj.,* shockingly evil.

im • ped • i • ment (im ped´ ə mənt) *n.,* obstacle; something that impedes.

im • por • tune (im´ pər tyün´, im pȯr´ chən) *vt.,* beg or urge with annoying persistence.

im • pu • ta • tion (im´ pyə tā´ shən) *n.,* accusation; insinuation.

im • pute (im pyüt´) *vt.,* lay the responsibility or blame for, often falsely or unjustly.

in • cense (in sen[t]s´) *vt.,* cause to become angry.

in • dict (in dīt´) *vt.,* criticize; accuse; charge with a crime.

in • fir • mi • ty (in fər´ mət ē) *n.,* personal failing; defect.

in • iq • ui • ty (in ik´ wə tē) *n.*, wickedness.

in • no • va • tion (i´ nə vā´ shən) *n.*, introduction of something new.

in • or • di • nate (in ȯrd´ [ə]n ət) *adj.*, exceeding reasonable limits; excessive.

in • sin • u • ating (in sin´ yə wā´ tiŋ) *adj.*, ingratiating: winning favor and confidence by imperceptible degrees.

in • ter • im (int´ ə rəm) *n.*, intervening time; time in between.

in • tro • spec • tion (in´ trə spek´ shən) *n.*, act of looking inward.

in • vi • o • late (in vī´ ə lət) *adj.*, pure; that is, not violated or profaned.

jo • cund (jä´ kənd; jō´ kənd) *adj.*, merry; marked by high spirits and mirthfulness.

lan • guish (laŋ´ gwish) *vi.*, live in a state of depression, to pine away or, to suffer neglect.

las • civ • i • ous (lə siv´ ē əs) *adj.*, lustful; obscene.

loll (läl´) *vt.*, hang loosely or laxly; lounge.

maim (mām´) *vt.*, mutilate or disfigure.

mal • e • fac • tor (ma´ lə fak´ tər) *n.*, one who does bad things to another person or commits an offense against the law.

mal • ice (mal´ əs) *n.*, wickedness.

ma • lig • ni • ty (mə lig´ nə tē) *n.*, malignancy: the quality or state of being malignant, that is, evil or harmful.

man • date (man´ dāt´) *n.*, formal order.

man • i • fest (man´ ə fest) *vt.*, show.

met • tle (met´ əl) *n.*, strength of spirit; courage.

minion (min´ yən) *n.*, servile follower or underling.

mu • ti • ny (myüt´ ə nē) *n.*, revolt against authority, esp. of a naval crew.

neg • li • gence (neg´ li jən[t]s) *n.*, carelessness or neglect.

nup • tial (nəp´ shəl, nəp´ shə wəl) *n.*, marriage; wedding [usu. used in plural].

ob • se • qui • ous (əb sē´ kwē əs) *adj.*, showing an exaggerated desire to help or serve; fawning.

odi • ous (ō´ dē əs) *adj.*, hateful.

pa • late (pal´ ət) *n.*, taste or liking (often refined).

par • a • dox (par´ ə däks´) *n.*, seemingly contradictory statement or idea.

par • ti • san (pär´ tə zən; pär´ tə sən) *n.*, a passionate supporter of something (as a cause or a political party).

pelt (pelt´) v., strike with blows or with thrown objects; beat or dash repeatedly against.

pen • i • tent (pen´ ə tənt) adj., feeling sorry about offenses; repentant.

per • di • tion (pər dish´ ən) n., damnation; hell.

per • jur • y (pərj´ ə rē) n., violation of an oath; often, referring to a person lying on the stand in court.

per • ni • cious (pər nish´ əs) adj., destructive; deadly.

pes • ti • lence (pes´ tə len[t]s) n., anything destructive or deadly.

pes • ti • lent (pes´ tə lənt) adj., causing displeasure or annoyance; extremely disagreeable.

phleg • ma • tic (fleg ma´ tik) adj., slow to move or act; not easily excited; sluggish.

pil • gri • mage (pil´ grə mij) n., long journey, often made for religious purposes.

pin • ion (pin´ yən) vt., restrain or shackle, especially by the arms.

por • tent (pȯ[ə]r´ tənt) n., sign of things to come: omen.

prat • tle (prat´ əl) n., idle chatter; chattering noise.

pre • text (prē´ tekst) n., reason or motive assumed or pretended as a cover for the real reason or motive.

privy (pri´ vē) adj., know about something; as a secret.

pro • cure (prə kyu̇[ə]r´, prō kyu̇[ə]r´) vt., obtain; get possession of.

pro • fane (pro fān´) adj., vulgar.

pro • mul • gate (präm´ əl gāt´, prō´ məl gāt´) vt., declare openly or make known; also, to spread (knowledge or ideas).

pro • voke (prə vōk´) vt., incite to anger.

pro • vok • ing (prə vō´ kiŋ) adj., causing anger or outrage.

pru • dence (prü´ dən[t]s) n., caution as to danger or risk; shrewdness and good judgment in the management of affairs or resources.

quay (kē´) n., structure built as a landing place along water.

rail (rā[ə]l´) vt., utter harsh or abusive language.

rap • ture (rap´ chər) n., state of being carried away by overwhelming emotion.

re • buke (ri byük´) n., expression of strong disapproval.

re • com • pense (re´ kəm pen[t]s) n., compensation; payment.

re • proach (ri prōch´) n., disgrace or discredit; expression of disapproval.

re • quite (ri kwīt´) vt., repay or return; avenge.

res • ti • tu • tion (res´ tə t[y]ü´ shən) *n.*, making up for an injury or restoring something to its rightful owner.

ruf • fi • an (rəf´ ē ən) *n.*, bully.

ru • mi • nate (rü´ mə nāt´) *vi.*, go over in the mind; ponder, reflect.

sag • a • cious (sə gā´ shəs) *adj.*, wise.

sanc • ti • mo • ny (saŋ[k]´ tə mō´ nē) *n.*, affected or hypocritical holiness.

sanc • tion (saŋ[k]´ shən) *vt.*, to approve or consent to.

sans (sanz´) *adj.*, without.

sa • ti • ety (sə tī´ ət ē) *n.*, state of being satisfied fully or to excess.

so • lic • it (sə lis´ ət) *vt.*, approach with a request or plea.

spe • cious (spē´ shəs) *adj.*, having a false look of truth or genuineness.

spec • u • la • tive (spə´ kyə lə tiv) *adj.*, involved in intellectual speculation, that is, pondering intellectual questions.

strife (strīf´) *n.*, conflict or struggle; often bitter and violent.

sub • due (səb dü´) *vt.*, bring under control; conquer.

sub • lime (sə blīm´) *adj.*, lofty, grand, or exalted in thought or expression; more broadly, excellent.

suf • fice (sə fīs´) *vi., vt.*, to meet or satisfy a need; to be enough or be enough for.

suit (süt´) *n.*, act or instance of seeking by entreaty: an appeal.

suit • or (sü´ tər) *n.*, one who courts a woman or seeks to marry her; also, anyone who petitions or entreats.

su • per • sede (sü´ pər sēd´) *vt.*, to displace or set aside, and put another in place of.

taint (tānt´) *vt.*, spoil; contaminate.

to • ken (tō´ kən) *n.*, something done or given as a sign of obligation or affection.

tract • a • ble (trak´ tə bəl) *adj.*, easy to deal with or manage; docile.

tra • duce (trə düs´, trə dyüs´) *vt.*, destroy the reputation of someone or cause shame by misrepresenting or telling falsehoods.

tran • quil (traŋ´ kwəl) *adj.*, peaceful.

tri • fle (trī´ fəl) *n.*, something of little significance or value; *vi.*, treat something or someone as unimportant.

tyr • an • ny (tir´ ə nē) *n.*, state of being a tyrant, a ruler who exercises absolute power brutally and oppressively.

ve • he • ment (vē´ ə mənt) *adj.*, intensely emotional; deeply felt or strongly expressed; marked by extreme intensity or force.

ver • i • ta • ble (ver´ ət ə bəl) *adj.,* true; being truly or very much so; being in fact the thing named; actual, real. Often used as an intensifier.

vex • a • tion (vek sā´ shən) *n.,* state of being vexed, or irritated.

vice (vīs´) *n.,* moral fault or failing.

vi • cis • si • tude (və si´ sə tüd´) *n.,* chance occurrence or fluctuation in state or condition; a difficulty or hardship that occurs in the course of life.

vile (vi[ə]l´) *adj.,* morally or physically despicable.

vi • per (vī´ pər) *n.,* vicious or treacherous person.

vis • age (viz´ əj) *n.,* appearance; face.

vi • tal (vī´ təl) *adj.,* having to do with life; characteristic of life.

vol • u • ble (väl´ yə bəl) *adj.,* marked by ease and fluency in speech; glib.

Glossary of Literary Terms

ASIDE. An **aside** is a statement made by a character in a play, intended to be heard by the audience, but not by other characters on the stage. In *Othello,* Iago's many asides allow the audience to learn about his plot, which is kept secret from the other characters onstage.

CATASTROPHE. The **catastrophe**, in tragedy, is the event that resolves, or ends, the central conflict and marks the ultimate tragic fall of the central character. Often this event is the character's death. Also known as the *resolution.* See *plot.*

CENTRAL CONFLICT. A **central conflict** is the primary struggle dealt with in the plot of a story or drama. See *plot.*

CHARACTER. A **character** is a person (or sometimes an animal) who figures in the action of a literary work. A *protagonist,* or *main character,* is the central figure in a literary work. An *antagonist* is a character who is pitted against a protagonist. *Major characters* are those who play significant roles in a work. *Minor characters* are those who play lesser roles. A *one-dimensional character, flat character,* or *caricature* is one who exhibits a single dominant quality, or character trait. A *three-dimensional, full,* or *rounded* character is one who exhibits the complexity of traits associated with actual human beings. A *static character* is one who does not change during the course of the action; a *dynamic character* is one who does change. A *stock character* is a character found again and again in different literary works. An example of a stock character is the mad scientist of nineteenth- and twentieth-century fiction.

CHARACTERIZATION. **Characterization** is the use of literary techniques to create a character. In creating a character, a playwright may use the following techniques: showing what characters themselves say, do, and think; showing what other characters say about him or her; and showing, through stage directions or other references, what physical features, dress, and personality the characters display.

CLIMAX. The **climax** of a play is the high point of interest or suspense in the plot. See *plot.*

COMIC RELIEF. Writers sometimes insert into a serious work of fiction or drama a humorous scene that is said to provide **comic relief** because it relieves the seriousness or emotional intensity felt by the audience. The character of the Clown in *Othello* is introduced to provide comic relief.

CRISIS. The **crisis**, or **turning point**, is the point in the plot where something decisive happens to determine the future course of events and the eventual working out of the conflict. This turning point can change things for the better or for the worse. In a tragedy, things are changed for the worse. Note that often, the crisis also marks the climax, or climactic moment, in the plot. In a five-act play such as *Othello*, the crisis usually occurs in act III. See *plot*.

DÉNOUEMENT. The **dénouement** is any material that follows the catastrophe or resolution and ties up loose ends. See *plot*.

DRAMATIC IRONY. Irony is a difference between appearance and reality. **Dramatic irony** occurs when something is known to the reader or audience but not to the characters. Shakespeare employs dramatic irony to great effect in *Othello*. Iago's evil scheming is revealed to the audience through his soliloquies and asides, but the other characters in the play remain ignorant, believing that Iago is honest when quite the opposite is true.

EXPOSITION. See *plot*.

FALLING ACTION. The **falling action** of a plot is all of the events that happen as a result of the crisis. In a five-act play such as *Othello*, the falling action occurs throughout acts IV and V. See *plot*.

FOIL. A **foil** is a character whose attributes, or characteristics, contrast with and therefore throw into relief the attributes of another character. Emilia acts as a foil for Desdemona in *Othello*.

FORESHADOWING. **Foreshadowing** is the act of presenting materials that hint at events to occur later in the story.

INCITING INCIDENT. The **inciting incident** is the event that introduces the central conflict of a story or drama. In a five-act play, the inciting incident is typically introduced in act I. However, the inciting incident of *Othello*—that is, Othello's marriage—actually occurs just prior to the beginning of act I. See *plot*.

MOOD. **Mood,** or **atmosphere,** is the emotion created in the reader by part or all of a literary work. A writer creates mood through judicious use of concrete details. A somber, tragic mood is created in Othello's soliloquy at the beginning of act V, scene i.

MOTIF. A **motif** is any element or image that recurs in one or more works of literature or art. One recurring motif in *Othello* is the imagery of hell, demons, and monsters.

ONE-DIMENSIONAL CHARACTER. A **one-dimensional character, flat character,** or **caricature** is one who exhibits a single dominant quality, or character trait. The character of Iago is sometimes criticized as being too one-dimensional, and therefore not believable. You may explore this idea in the Critical Writing Activity C described on page 262. See also *character*.

PLOT. A **plot** is a series of events related to a central *conflict,* or struggle. A typical plot involves the introduction of a conflict, its development, and its eventual resolution. Terms used to describe elements of plot include the following:

- The **exposition,** or **introduction,** sets the tone or mood, introduces the characters and the setting, and provides necessary background information.
- The **inciting incident** is the event that introduces the central conflict.
- The **rising action,** or **complication,** develops the conflict to a high point of intensity.
- The **climax** is the high point of interest or suspense in the plot.
- The **crisis,** or **turning point,** often the same event as the climax, is the point in the plot where something decisive happens to determine the future course of events and the eventual working out of the conflict.

- The **falling action** is all of the events that follow the crisis, or climax.
- The **resolution** is the point at which the central conflict is ended, or resolved.
- The **catastrophe**, in tragedy, is the event that resolves, or ends, the central conflict and marks the ultimate tragic fall of the central character. Often this event is the character's death.
- The **dénouement** is any material that follows the resolution and ties up loose ends.

Plots rarely contain all these elements in precisely this order. Elements of exposition may be introduced at any time in the course of a work. A work may begin with a catastrophe and then use flashback to explain it .The exposition or dénouement or even the resolution may be missing. The inciting incident may occur before the beginning of the action actually described in the work, as in the case of *Othello,* in which the inciting incident, Othello's marriage, occurs before the beginning of act I. See page 214 for a discussion of the plot of *Othello.*

PUN. A **pun** is a play on words, one that wittily exploits a double meaning. Shakespeare used many puns in his plays.

RESOLUTION. See *plot.*

RISING ACTION. The **rising action,** or **complication,** is the part of a plot that develops the central conflict to a high point of intensity. In a five-act play such as *Othello,* the rising action begins in act I and continues until the climax or crisis in act III. See *plot.*

SOLILOQUY. A **soliloquy** is a speech given by a character alone onstage, in which the character reveals his or her thoughts and feelings to the audience.

STOCK CHARACTER. A **stock character** is one found again and again in different literary works. The character of Iago is somewhat similar to the stock character of Vice found in medieval morality plays. Vice was a villain who tempted the protagonist to commit a sin so grave that he or she would be condemned to Hell.

SYMBOL. A **symbol** is a thing that stands for or represents both itself and something else. In *Othello*, Desdemona's handkerchief is symbolic.

THEME. A **theme** is a central idea in a literary work. One of the themes of *Othello* is the destructive power of jealousy.

TRAGEDY. A **tragedy** is a drama that tells about the downfall of a person of high status. Tragedy tends to be serious. It celebrates the courage and dignity of a tragic hero in the face of inevitable doom. Sometimes that doom is made inevitable by a **tragic flaw** in the hero, a personal weakness that leads to his or her downfall.

TRAGIC FLAW. See *tragedy.*

TURNING POINT. See *crisis* and *plot.*